THE PSYCHOLOGY OF READING

Insights from Chinese

ERIK D. REICHLE
Macquarie University

LILI YU
Macquarie University

Shaftesbury Road, Cambridge CB2 8EA, United Kingdom

One Liberty Plaza, 20th Floor, New York, NY 10006, USA

477 Williamstown Road, Port Melbourne, VIC 3207, Australia

314–321, 3rd Floor, Plot 3, Splendor Forum, Jasola District Centre, New Delhi – 110025, India

103 Penang Road, #05–06/07, Visioncrest Commercial, Singapore 238467

Cambridge University Press is part of Cambridge University Press & Assessment, a department of the University of Cambridge.

We share the University's mission to contribute to society through the pursuit of education, learning and research at the highest international levels of excellence.

www.cambridge.org
Information on this title: www.cambridge.org/9781009272810

DOI: 10.1017/9781009272780

© Erik D. Reichle and Lili Yu 2024

This publication is in copyright. Subject to statutory exception and to the provisions of relevant collective licensing agreements, no reproduction of any part may take place without the written permission of Cambridge University Press & Assessment.

First published 2024

A catalogue record for this publication is available from the British Library

A Cataloging-in-Publication data record for this book is available from the Library of Congress

ISBN 978-1-009-27281-0 Hardback
ISBN 978-1-009-27277-3 Paperback

Cambridge University Press & Assessment has no responsibility for the persistence or accuracy of URLs for external or third-party internet websites referred to in this publication and does not guarantee that any content on such websites is, or will remain, accurate or appropriate.

This book is dedicated to our family and especially our parents,
for their endless love and support.

谨以此书献给我们的父母和家人们，
谢谢他们无尽的爱和支持。

Contents

List of Figures		*page* ix
List of Tables		xi
Acknowledgments		xii

1	**The Psychology of Reading**		1
	1.1	Communication, Language, and Reading	3
	1.2	Methods to Study Reading	6
	1.3	Models of Reading	11
	1.4	Chapter Previews	19
2	**The Chinese Language and Writing System**		21
	2.1	The Chinese Language	21
	2.2	The History of the Chinese Writing System	28
	2.3	The Modern Chinese Writing System	35
	2.4	Conclusion	44
3	**Character and Word Identification**		46
	3.1	Behavioral Experiments	47
	3.2	Theories and Models	71
	3.3	Conclusion	88
4	**Skilled Reading**		90
	4.1	Eye-Tracking Experiments	92
	4.2	Theories and Models	109
	4.3	Conclusion	127
5	**Reading Skill Development, Dyslexia, and Cognitive Neuroscience**		129
	5.1	Reading Skill Development	129
	5.2	Dyslexia	142
	5.3	Cognitive Neuroscience	154
	5.4	Conclusion	166

viii *Contents*

6	**Future Directions**	168
	6.1 English vs. Chinese: A Summary	168
	6.2 Our Predictions	173
	6.3 Conclusion	187

References 189
Index 221

Figures

1.1	Schematic diagram of McClelland and Rumelhart's (1981) interactive-activation model of word identification	*page* 13
1.2	Schematic diagram of Reichle et al.'s (2012) E-Z Reader model of eye-movement control in reading	16
2.1	A map of China showing the main dialects and where they are spoken	22
2.2	An example illustrating the four tones used to differentiate the meanings of the spoken syllable /ma/ in Mandarin	24
2.3	A few examples of the earliest form of Chinese writing	29
2.4	A few examples showing how early pictographs changed into their modern character equivalents during the evolution of the Chinese writing system	31
2.5	A few examples illustrating the similarities and differences between traditional and simplified Chinese characters	33
2.6	An example sentence written in modern Chinese using simplified characters	35
2.7	An example illustrating the eight basic types of strokes and the order in which character strokes are normally written	39
2.8	Example phonograms of phonetic radical variation	41
3.1	Taft et al.'s (1999) Chinese word-identification model	73
3.2	Perfetti et al.'s (2005) lexical-constituency model	76
3.3	The patterns of orthographic, phonological, and semantic priming that have been simulated by Perfetti et al.'s (2005) lexical-constituency model	78
3.4	X. Li et al.'s (2009) word segmentation and identification model	81
3.5	J. F. Yang et al.'s (2009) "triangle" model of Chinese character naming	85
4.1	Examples of the gaze-contingent paradigms that are used in eye-tracking research	93

x *List of Figures*

4.2 The default-targeting (M. Yan et al., 2010) (A) statistical artifact (X. Li et al., 2011) (B) and dynamic-adjustment (Y. P. Liu, Yu, Fu, et al., 2019) (C) accounts of saccadic targeting in Chinese reading 112

4.3 X. Li and Pollatsek's (2020) Chinese reading model (CRM) 115

4.4 Y. P. Liu et al.'s (2023) Chinese E-Z Reader (CEZR) model 121

4.5 A schematic diagram illustrating the character-segmentation heuristic used by Y. P. Liu et al.'s (2023) Chinese E-Z Reader (CEZR) model 122

4.6 Fan and Reilly's (2022) variant of the Glenmore model adapted to the reading of Chinese 125

5.1 Xing et al.'s (2002, 2004) connectionist model of Chinese character pronunciation 140

5.2 The attractor network models used by J. F. Yang et al. (2013) in their simulations of English word and Chinese character naming and how performance in these tasks might be impaired by phonological vs. surface dyslexia 150

5.3 Images showing the left (*L*) and right (*R*) cerebral hemispheres of the human brain and the major cortical regions and anatomical pathways that are involved in the identification of printed words 155

5.4 The "split fovea" connectionist model of Chinese character pronunciation proposed by Hsiao and Shillcock (2004, 2005) 164

Tables

3.1	Important findings related to the learning and identification of alphabetic words
	page 48
3.2	Important findings related to the learning and identification of Chinese characters and words
	58
6.1	Key findings related to the orthographic processing of English vs. Chinese words
	169
6.2	Key findings related to the phonological processing of English vs. Chinese words
	170
6.3	Key findings related to the semantic processing of English vs. Chinese words
	171
6.4	Key findings related to the skilled reading of English vs. Chinese
	172

Acknowledgments

Our initial motivation for writing this book was our belief that reading scientists have neglected much of the research that has been done on the reading of Chinese. We therefore hope that this book brings more recognition of this important topic and credit to the scientists who are undertaking this research. We have been lucky to have collaborated with a number of those scientists and are friends with several of them. Our ability to write this book has benefited greatly from those collaborations and friendships and so we want to thank those people for involving us in their research and providing the opportunity to learn more about the reading of Chinese.

The first author would also like to thank his kung fu brothers and sisters at Choy Lee Fut in Sydney. Our hours of training together each week have provided me with a fun and healthy way to disengage from my academic work and the task of writing this book, and for that I am very grateful.

Both authors would also like to thank two people at Cambridge University Press who were instrumental in helping us write this book. The first is Stephen Acerra, Commissioning Editor for Psychology and Neuroscience. Your unwavering support and patience have made the process of writing this book as painless as it could be, and for that reason we owe you our sincere gratitude. The second is Rowan Groat, Senior Editorial Assistant. Your support and guidance were also invaluable in shaping the initial draft of our book into its final form.

And in relation to the editorial process, we are also extremely grateful to Marcus Taft and Ronan Reilly for their constructive feedback on the first draft of our book. Their suggestions and insightful comments significantly improved the quality of our work.

Finally, two important disclaimers are necessary. The first is that the order of authorship was decided by a coin flip because both authors contributed equally to the writing of this book. The second is that any errors in the content of this book are unintentional and entirely our responsibility; we offer our apologies in advance for any such mistakes.

CHAPTER I

The Psychology of Reading

On first appearances, the task of reading sentences like this one is seemingly so simple that it requires no explanation: The reader – in this instance, you – simply looks at the words on the page, identifying them in turn, and then (somehow) combining their meanings to understand the contents of each new sentence. But this subjective experience is misleading. The science of reading has shown that reading is one of – if not *the* – most difficult activities in which we routinely engage but for which we have no biological predisposition. Reading thus stands in contrast to spoken language, which is another difficult activity that we routinely engage in but for which we are genetically predisposed. It is an activity that arguably requires a significant portion of the brain and the cognitive systems that it supports to execute, including the systems that support vision and attention (to identify the printed words), long-term memory (the repository of our world knowledge), language (to construct the meanings of sentences), and even motor control (to move the eyes from one word to the next). The main goal of the *psychology of reading*, therefore, is to develop an account of how we, as readers, can coordinate these activities to convert the sequences of ink marks on a printed page into the potentially infinite number of ideas that can be conveyed through writing.

Although the "psychology of reading" might sound strange to the uninitiated (given that many people view psychology as the study and treatment of mental health problems), it refers to a subdiscipline of a particular branch of psychology called *cognitive psychology*. As its name might suggest, cognitive psychology is the study of the basic perceptual and mental processes (i.e., cognition) that make us who we are (for an introductory text, see Eysenck & Keane, 2015). A short list of these processes include vision, attention, memory, language, reasoning, problem solving, consciousness, and any of the many tasks that we humans engage in, including reading and many others (e.g., driving automobiles, solving syllogisms, playing chess, etc.).

Because of the sheer complexity of what needs to be explained by the psychology of reading, researchers in the field have developed a variety of ingenious methods to study the behaviors of reading, the mental processes and representations that are produced by or are the product of those behaviors, and the neural systems that support those mental processes and behaviors. These research methods are the building blocks of subsequent chapters in this book, and as such, they will be discussed in some detail below. However, an equally important tool for reading researchers are the theories that guide the experimental research. Because the psychology of reading is an advanced science, the field has benefited from the development of several formal *models*, or theories that have been implemented using mathematical equations and computer programs, that both describe and simulate the various processes that are involved in reading (e.g., the identification of printed words), often with remarkable accuracy (for an introduction and review of these models, see Reichle, 2021). Because these reading models play a central role in motivating new empirical research, this chapter will also provide a brief introduction to two prominent examples and briefly discuss how models are compared and evaluated.

Before we review the methods and models of reading research, however, it is first necessary to have a clear understanding about what reading is, and how it is related to both spoken language and other forms of communication. The next section of this chapter does exactly that. But before we launch into this discussion, we also want to say briefly what this book is about, and where subsequent chapters will take us. As the title of this book suggests, it is about the psychology of reading, and more specifically, what has recently been learned about the psychology of reading from experiments on and models of the reading of one language and writing system – Chinese.

At this point, a perfectly natural question to ask might be: Why Chinese? The short answer to this question is that most research that has been done to understand the psychology of reading has focused on how people who speak European languages go about reading alphabetic texts (e.g., English, Spanish, Russian, etc.). Although this research has been highly informative and has taught us a considerable amount about reading (e.g., see the monographs by Crowder & Wagner, 1992; Dehaene, 2009; Perfetti, 2005; Rayner & Pollatsek, 1989; Rayner et al., 2012; Reichle, 2021; Seidenberg, 2017; Taft, 1991; Wolf, 2008; see also the edited volumes by Coltheart, 1987; Klein & McMullen, 2001; Pollatsek & Treiman, 2015; Snowling & Hulme, 2005), this endeavor has until recently largely avoided the possible implications of languages and writing systems that differ markedly from the ones that have been studied – languages and writing systems like those required to read Chinese. This oversight is perhaps a bit like an ornithologist who concludes that all birds can fly because he or she has never encountered a penguin, emu, or ostrich. This oversight has at least in some instances resulted in theoretical assumptions about the psychology of reading that are likely to be incomplete or even incorrect. Subsequent chapters in this book will explore some of these (potentially) faulty assumptions, but for now, we will continue with our exposition of reading, language, and communication.

1.1 Communication, Language, and Reading

Although anyone reading this book will be intimately familiar with both reading and language, it is important to distinguish between the two to avoid unwarranted assumptions. To begin with, spoken language is a natural endowment of the human species – a capacity to communicate that develops in all neurologically normal children, irrespective of their culture, and with only minimal explicit instruction (Deacon, 1997; Pinker, 2015). All spoken languages also share several necessary and sufficient features that are not shared by other forms of animal communication.

The first of these features is that language is *generative* (Chomsky, 1959). By this, we simply mean that, even if one only knows a finite number of words, it is still possible to express an infinite number of ideas. This unlimited power of expression is possible because *grammar*, or the rules that permit individual words to be combined into the larger units of meaning corresponding to phrases and sentences, allow for the expression of an unlimited number of novel ideas – ideas that vary along the continuum from being simple to tremendously complex, or that differ from other ideas in often subtle ways. And if one ignores the many non-linguistic restrictions on language comprehension (e.g., one's attention span or the degradation in understanding caused by background noise), then these sentences can in principle be of unlimited length. (A good example of this is Mike McCormack's single-sentence, 232-page novel, *Solar Bones*, 2016, which won the 2018 International Dublin Literary Award.)

A second feature of human language that also contributes to its generativity is the fact that words are *symbolic* in nature, allowing an infinite number of objects and concepts to be referenced by arbitrary combinations of sounds (i.e., *phonemes*) and visual forms (i.e., *graphemes*) within a given language. This point is immediately obvious if one compares the words for a given concept, for example "cat," across languages; in English, the word is written "cat" and pronounced /kæt/, whereas in Italian it is written as "gatto" and pronounced as /ˈgatːo/, while in Chinese it is written as "猫" and pronounced as /maoɪ/.[1] These three examples illustrate how the mappings between the thing or concept being referred to, on the one hand, and the symbols that are used to represent the thing or concept, on the other, are completely arbitrary, having been established through historical accident and convention within a group of language speakers. Importantly, the symbolic nature of language adds to its generativity in that new words can and constantly are being coined. For example, consider one word that, although it is in worldwide circulation now, was largely unheard of until 2020: "Covid-19."

The generative and symbolic nature of human language also affords its third and final feature – that the speakers of language can refer to things or situations outside of the immediate present. This allows one to speak, for example, of something that happened in the past, or that might be anticipated to happen in the future, or in the context of fantasy and science fictions stories, situations or things that are not possible in the real world. In short, languages allow their speakers to traverse time, escaping the bounds of whatever is happening in the immediate present.

These three features of human language – the fact that it is generative, symbolic, and allows one to reference the past and future – stand in stark contrast to animal communication. For example, consider the warning signals that are issued by vervet monkeys in response to different predator threats (Seyfarth et al., 1980). Although these monkeys use different calls to warn their compatriots of eagles, snakes, and leopards, these calls cannot be combined to convey more complex or novel warnings (e.g., something equivalent to "Ignore the eagle in the distance because a leopard is approaching!"). Nor can the monkeys issue warning about novel threats (e.g., "Avoid the humans!"). And finally, the calls are only issued in response to immediate danger, and cannot, for example, be issued in advance (e.g., "Beware of the leopard that will return later."). Thus, although vervet monkeys use their warning calls to communicate important information to other vervet monkeys, this communication is extremely rigid, being fixed to a small number of messages that are directly related to the immediate present. As far as we know, these same

---

[1] The International Phonetic Alphabet (see Akmajian et al., 2010) will be used here and in subsequent chapters to represent all examples of phonological forms or pronunciations of words. And as will be discussed in more detail in Chapter 2, the Chinese spoken languages are tonal, with each written character having an associated tone or pitch that can be represented by a number. In the example given, the 1 represents a flat tone (i.e., one that does not change).

limitations seem to apply to all other forms of animal communication, making human language truly unique in the animal kingdom.

With this background on what language is and is not, it is now possible to contrast spoken language, on one hand, with written language (and reading), on the other.[2] As mentioned previously, the capacity to use spoken language is part of our genetic endowment. As such, the capacity to speak has been subject to evolutionary pressure and likely emerged over millions of years (Deacon, 1997). And during the past few millennia, spoken languages have continued to evolve among populations of speakers within different geographical regions, resulting in the roughly 6,500 languages that are spoken in the world today. The evolution of these languages can often be traced using comparative methods, allowing, for example, for a comprehensive understanding of how modern English and German diverged from a single common language to become two distinct languages.

In contrast to spoken language, the capacity to read and write are relatively recent cultural inventions in that the best available evidence suggests have only been around for approximately 5,500 years (Robinson, 1995). Like many other significant cultural inventions (e.g., legal and political systems), the insights that led to the capacity to read and write likely occurred independently across different cultures separated by vast geographic distances. Robinson provides summary evidence, for example, that economic transactions were likely being recorded on clay tablets by 3,500 BCE, with these simple notations changing to cuneiform within a few hundred years. And independently of that, other very different forms of writing seem to have developed at other locations around the world. Key milestones in the development include the emergence of hieroglyphs in ancient Egypt by 3,000 BCE, the emergence of various scripts in and around the Indus valley and Aegean sea (e.g., Linear A and B) by 2,500–1,500 BCE, the use of ideograms (the early precursors to characters) in China by 1,200 BCE, the development of the Phoenician alphabet by 1,000 BCE, the subsequent adoption and modification (e.g., addition of letters representing vowels) of the Phoenician alphabet by the Greeks around 730 BCE, and evidence of Mesoamerican scripts and hieroglyphs by 600 BCE.

Despite their tremendous variety, what all these early writing systems share with modern writing systems is their capacity to represent the sounds

---

[2] This discussion will ignore various forms of sign language that are used by the deaf. It is worth noting, however, that these languages are true languages, and that as such, what was said about spoken languages is equally applicable to sign languages. And in the same vein, although our discussion of reading will ignore the reading of braille, it is also a true writing system.

and meanings of spoken language, fixing the information in media that allows for a permanent record of not only financial transactions, but also of history and culture, as well as religious texts, poetry, and literature. The significance of this new technology cannot be overstated. As the astronomer Carl Sagan (1980) rightly noted, this capacity is "perhaps the greatest of human inventions, binding together people who never knew each other," allowing one to be "inside of the mind of another person, maybe somebody dead for thousands of years."

The challenge, therefore, is to develop methods for understanding this most amazing of cognitive tasks. Fortunately, this has been possible; the experimental methods and technologies of modern cognitive psychology and neuroscience have allowed reading researchers to make informed inferences about mental processes that support reading by measuring their neural correlates (e.g., patterns of brain activity) and the overt behavior required to perform various types of reading-related tasks (e.g., pronouncing words aloud).[3] Section 1.2 will provide a brief introduction to the main methods and technologies that are available to do this and that have been productively used to advance the science of reading. However, please note that this introduction is not intended to be comprehensive in scope, but instead only provides the minimal background that might be required to understand the remaining chapters of this book. Readers with backgrounds in either cognitive psychology or neuroscience may therefore opt to skip ahead to those chapters.

1.2 Methods to Study Reading

The psychology of reading has a long history of scientifically rigorous experimental investigation (e.g., Huey's, seminal *The Psychology and Pedagogy of Reading*, 1908, is perhaps the earliest comprehensive account). It is therefore not surprising that many of the experimental methods that have been used to study reading also have a long history. This section will review those methods, as well as new technologies that have only recently made it possible for researchers to study the internal behaviors of a reader's mind or brain – the patterns of cortical activity that can be measured using the brain's electrophysiology and metabolism.

---

[3] We will avoid the thorny philosophical issue of specifying precisely how the mind differs – if it even does – from the brain, but will instead simply acknowledge that it is useful to think about the mind as being a more abstract description of how the brain operates. This approach is analogous to how one might think about a computer program as being an abstract description of how a computer operates (e.g., see Coltheart, 2012).

1.2 Methods to Study Reading

The earliest methods used to study reading involve simple behavioral tasks that, despite their simplicity, were used with ingenuity to good effect. For example, someone unfamiliar with how reading research is conducted might suggest the simple task of having participants read extended passages of text for some amount of time and then answering questions to gauge their understanding of the text's contents. This task can be used to determine the maximal reading speed or what a reader is likely to remember about a given text, but unfortunately says very little about the moment-to-moment inner workings of the mind, or how the processing of words and sentences allows a reader to construct the mental representations that are necessary to answer comprehension questions. Such insights require more sophisticated methods, typically involving tasks coupled with experimental designs that allow researchers to focus on one specific process of interest.

For example, because the key component of reading is the identification of printed words, or *lexical access*, many of the earliest techniques for studying reading were designed to shed light on this process. For example, one technique called the *perceptual-identification task* involves displaying a word under well-controlled viewing conditions using a device called a *tachistoscope*. This device contains a camera shutter that allows a word (usually printed on a card) to be displayed for a precise amount of time under specific lighting conditions. By asking participants to name or otherwise identify words that are displayed using a tachistoscope, it is possible to determine the minimum amount of time that is needed to identify a word, as well as the types of information that might be extracted when participants make errors. For example, one early and theoretically important finding from such experiments that has also withstood the scrutiny of time is the *word-superiority effect*. This effect is the seemingly paradoxical finding that a letter displayed in the context of a word can be identified more rapidly and accurately than a letter displayed in isolation (Reicher, 1969; Wheeler, 1970). For example, the letter "k" can be identified more efficiently if it is displayed in the context of "work" than if "k" is displayed in isolation. This suggests that the perception of letters is somehow facilitated or supported by the processing of the word in which they occur, and explanations of the effect typically refer to the "top-down" influence of word representations in memory influencing the visual perception of letters, with letters that are displayed in words benefiting from this additional support (e.g., see McClelland & Rumelhart, 1981; Rumelhart & McClelland, 1982).

Over the last few decades, the behavioral tasks that are used to study word identification have been refined into a small set of standardly used tasks. Although each of these tasks is useful, it is fair to say that all of these

8 The Psychology of Reading

tasks also have their limitations. For example, the first of these tasks is *naming*, wherein participants simply pronounce words that are displayed on a computer monitor as rapidly and accurately as possible, with a microphone being used to detect the onset time of the naming response (Balota et al., 2007; Schilling et al., 1998). Although this task is (at least somewhat) natural and can under some conditions guarantee that participants have accessed a word's pronunciation from memory (see, e.g., Rossmeissl & Theios, 1982), it is also clear that words can be sounded out and thus performance in this task can have little to do with lexical access. (The easiest demonstration of this is the fact that you can pronounce non-words like "fark" that, by virtue of being non-words, are not represented in the lexicon.) Another limitation of the naming task is that words beginning with certain phonemes (e.g., voiced consonants, which are more likely to trigger the voice key) are more likely to be named more rapidly and/or accurately than words beginning with other phonemes (Rastle & Davis, 2002).

A second standardly used task is *lexical decision*, wherein participants view a series of words and non-words displayed one at a time on a computer monitor, with the task of indicating as rapidly and accurately as possible via button presses whether each letter string is a word or non-word (Balota et al., 2007; Schilling et al., 1998). Because both "word" and "non-word" responses are registered using button presses, this task avoids much of the messiness of naming. But because the task requires binary decisions, the task is subject to strategies that reflect a variety of variables, including the relative proportion of words versus non-words being used in the experiment (West & Stanovich, 1982), and the degree to which the non-words resemble words (e.g., it is easier to decide that the consonant string "rxwmq" is a non-word than it is to decide that the pseudo-homophone "brane" is a non-word; Van Orden et al., 1990). For those reasons, the lexical-decision task has been criticized on the grounds that it often measures more than just lexical access (e.g., Balota & Chumbley, 1984).

Given the limitations of the naming and lexical-decision tasks, one might ask why researchers do not simply ask participants to somehow indicate the meaning of a word, as a way of guaranteeing that lexical access has occurred. One task that has been developed to do exactly that is *semantic verification*, wherein participants indicate (usually via button presses) whether or not each word in a series has some particular semantic attribute (e.g., Lewellen et al., 1993). Participants might be asked, for example, to indicate whether each of a series of words refers to something animate. For example, the sequence "cat," "hammer," and "sink" would be expected to elicit "yes," "no," and "no" responses, respectively.

1.2 *Methods to Study Reading*

Although the semantic-verification task avoids most of the pitfalls of naming and lexical decision, it also requires binary decisions that can bias responses and thus has also been criticized for being unnatural (e.g., see Van Orden, 1987).

One final task that avoids the criticism of being unnatural uses the measurement of eye movements during natural reading – an approach that is most often referred to as *eye tracking* (Rayner, 1979; for reviews, see Rayner, 1998, 2009). This technique obviously requires an *eye tracker*, or device that measures the position of a reader's eyes as they read text that is displayed on a computer monitor. The most widely used eye trackers today, for example, typically measure the position of a reader's dominant eye once every millisecond as they read sentences or passages of text, allowing the experimenter to reconstruct a variety of different measures that reflect (on average, across a sample of participants) how long and often each word is looked at during reading. Using these word-based measures, it is then possible to make informed inferences about what is happening in the mind of a reader because there is a tight coupling between the eye and mind during reading (Reingold et al., 2012). Moreover, because the task is natural (i.e., doesn't require binary decisions or other secondary task demands) and is both non-intrusive and highly sensitive (i.e., fixation durations and locations can be measured very accurately), the only real drawback of this approach is its inherent complexity. In other words, to interpret a pattern of eye movements as they move through a sentence, one must make informed inferences about how visual processing, attention, word identification, and sentence comprehension drive the moment-to-moment movement of the eyes – the inner workings of the mind that are of interest to reading researchers.

Although each of the behavioral methods differ in important ways, and although each has its merits and limitations, all have proven useful, and many of the key findings have been documented using more than one of the methods, with this convergence further validating the methods. These key findings will be discussed in subsequent chapters of this book, but for now, it is important to note that arguably most of what has been learned about the psychology of reading has been learned using the behavioral methods. However, it is also important to note that technology has rapidly expanded the arsenal of methods that reading researchers now have at their disposal. These new technologies allow researchers to make informed inferences about the mental processes that support reading by examining their neural correlates, the activity of the cortical systems that support cognition.

The oldest of these more recent methods entails the recording of the electrical currents generated by large ensembles of neurons that are engaged in the coordinated activity that occurs during reading. For example, as a participant names a sequence of words in the naming task, an *electoencephalogram* (*EEG*), or recording of the electrical activity of the participant's brain, is first recorded and then averaged across the individual responses to produce *event-related potentials*, or *ERPs* (for a review, see Handy, 2005). The ERPs that are collected from two different conditions (e.g., words read with vs. without normal parafoveal preview) can then be compared to make inferences about what happens during word identification (Antúnex et al., 2021). Because these recordings are analog and recorded continuously over time, ERPs have a fine temporal resolution, allowing researchers to examine how the brain's electrical activity changes over small intervals of time (e.g., milliseconds). The main drawback of this approach, however, is that the neural generators that give rise to the ERPs are difficult to localize. In other words, although the electrical activity is often recorded from a high number of electrodes (e.g., sixty-four) that are widely distributed across a participant's scalp, and although sophisticated mathematical techniques can be used to make inferences about the foci of the neural generators (Jatoi et al., 2014), the spatial resolution of these localization techniques is poor, often only allowing coarse inferences about the location of a neural generator (e.g., left vs. right cerebral hemisphere).

Fortunately, a few more recent brain-imaging methods have been developed to sidestep the problems of ERPs. The oldest of these methods, *positron emission tomography* (*PET*) and *functional magnetic resonance imaging* (*fMRI*), measure cortical activity indirectly, by measuring changes in blood flow that occur with increases in neural activity. With PET, these blood-flow changes are measured using radioactive tracers (for an introduction to this method, see Raichle, 1983). With fMRI, participants are placed in a strong magnetic field, so that the hydrogen atoms in the blood can be aligned with the magnetic field. With each off pulse of the magnetic field, the hydrogen atoms relax (i.e., spin randomly) and emit radio waves that are then detected by antennae situated around the participant's head (see Logothetis, 2003). Although both methods allow much better spatial resolution than ERPs, the resolution of fMRI is superior (typically a few cubic millimeters) and fMRI is less invasive because it does not require the injection of radioactive tracers. Where the two methods fare less well, however, is temporal resolution: PET measures brain activity within a given cortical region across several tens of seconds, whereas fMRI measures brain activity across several seconds.

The final method to be reviewed here, *magnetoencephography (MEG)*, is related to EEG in that it uses highly sensitive sensors to measure the magnetic induction that is generated by the post-synaptic potentials of neurons, with this measure of induction then being used to generate a composite image of the brain's electrical activity (see Baillet, 2017). This method is much less invasive than PET, with a spatial resolution comparable to fMRI but with a temporal resolution comparable to EEG. With all these strengths, one might ask why MEG is not used instead of the other brain-imaging methods? Apart from a few practical limitations (e.g., operating costs), one of the main limitations of MEG is that it is better suited to measuring the magnetic induction generated by neurons located near the surface of the brain rather than those generated by deep brain structures. A second limitation is that relative to both PET and fMRI, the nature of the signals being measured are complex and thus more poorly understood. For those reasons, although MEG is an extremely useful methodology, it is probably more useful to view MEG as complementary to (rather than superior to) the other brain-imaging methods.

With that brief introduction to the methods used in reading science, it is important to emphasize that *none* of the methods that have been mentioned in this section – behavioral or neurophysiological – are without limitations, and that *all* the methods have proven useful, especially when two or more methods converge to provide mutual support for some finding or conclusion. Our approach throughout the remainder of this book will therefore be to sample from these methods in a manner that allows us to cover key findings related to the psychology of reading, utilizing the insights afforded by each method.

1.3   Models of Reading

As indicated previously, a key marker of progress in understanding the psychology of reading is the fact that there have been several formally implemented theories or *models* of the core processes that occur in the minds of readers. Reichle (2021) provides a comprehensive review of many of these models, which for the purposes of facilitating their exposition, are grouped according to what the models attempt to simulate and explain:

1.   the identification of printed words;
2.   the syntactic and semantic processing that is required to combine words into representations of phrases and sentences;

12 The Psychology of Reading

3. the processing that is required to construct representations of more extended discourses (i.e., the meaning of two or more sentences);

4. how each of the aforementioned processes are coordinated with attention and the oculomotor system to determine when and where the eyes move during reading (i.e., eye-movement control in reading).

Because models of Chinese reading are discussed at length in upcoming chapters of this book, it is important to have a basic understanding of what computer models are, and why they are useful. For those reasons, two such models will be reviewed briefly here. Although these two models describe processes that are involved in the reading of English, the models are important for later discussions because the theoretical assumptions of the models have been borrowed in developing models of the reading of Chinese.

The first model to be reviewed here is the *interactive-activation* model that was first proposed by McClelland and Rumelhart (1981; Rumelhart & McClelland, 1982).[4] This model, which is depicted in Figure 1.1, provides an example of an artificial neural network, and as such, consists of an interconnected network of *nodes*. These nodes are arranged in a hierarchy to represent the features or line segments of individual letters (in the bottom layer), letters (in the middle layer), and words (in the top layer). As shown, these nodes are interlinked by configurations of *excitatory* (arrows) and *inhibitory* (filled circles) connections that propagate activation among these nodes. Although this propagation of activity can be loosely conceptualized as corresponding to the propagation of neural activity among cortical areas that represent different types of lexical information (features, letters, and words), the interactive-activation model can also be viewed as an abstract description of the representations and algorithms that are engaged during word identification. Finally, it is the pattern of interconnections that is important for how the model functions. This pattern of interconnections is also what allows the model to explain the word-superiority effect (Reicher, 1969; Wheeler, 1970) discussed earlier.

As Figure 1.1 shows, the presence of a word causes the nodes corresponding to letter features (i.e., line segments corresponding to segments of the highly stylized font that is, for convenience, used to represent each letter) to become active. These letter features have specific locations, so that only

---

[4] For a detailed description of the model including the equations that determine how excitatory and inhibitory activation is propagated among the different types of representational nodes, see either the original articles (McClelland & Rumelhart, 1981; Rumelhart & McClelland, 1982) or Reichle (2021: 101–7).

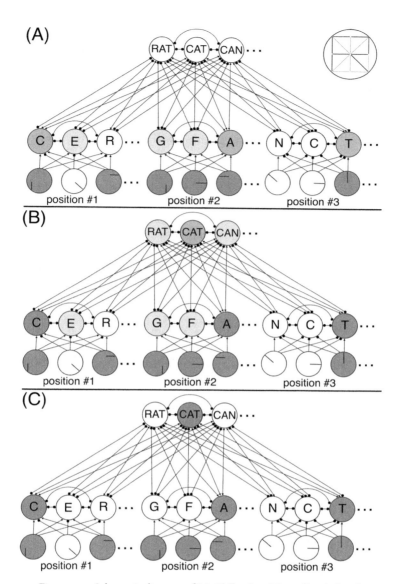

Figure 1.1 Schematic diagram of McClelland and Rumelhart's (1981) interactive-activation model of word identification

The nodes representing letter features, letters, and words are indicated, as are the excitatory (arrows) and inhibitory (circles) connections among nodes. Panels A–C show how the activation of nodes increase and decrease in their relative levels of activation (with darker gray representing more activation) in response to the word "cat" at three arbitrary points in time. The inset in the upper right of Panel A shows the full set of twenty features used in the feature nodes, with the dark gray indicating those features that would be active to represent the presence of a letter "R."

Note: For the sake of clarity, this figure depicts only a small portion of the model.

one set of features, for example, can potentially become active in a word's first letter position, a second set in the word's second letter position, and so on. The letter feature activation then propagates to nodes representing individual letters. For example, upon being presented with the word "cat," the features corresponding to the horizontal and vertical line segments of the letter "c" in the first letter position will become active, which then send their activation to a node representing the letter "c" in the first letter position, but also to similar looking letters (e.g., "e") in the same position.

Across time, a set of letter nodes will become active, which then propagate their activation to words nodes containing those letters. As Figure 1.1 shows, the word "cat" will activate the nodes corresponding to its letters in the first through third letter positions, and as the activity of those nodes continues to ramp up, they will begin propagating their activation to word nodes containing at least some of those letters. As shown, the node for "cat" will become active, but so too (but to a lesser degree) will the nodes for words like "can" and "rat" because these words share some number of letters with "cat."

Finally, notice that, as the word nodes increase in their activation, the most active node will eventually come to suppress the others in a "winner take all" manner via the set of mutually inhibitory connections among the word nodes. This mutual inhibition is necessary to ensure that one and only one node will be identified at any given point in time. And while this is happening, notice that the words nodes also propagate their activation back to the letter nodes to which they are connected, allowing a well-activated word node to support the activation of its constituent letters in a mutually reinforcing manner. This "top down" propagation of activation is what allows the interactive-activation model to explain the word-superiority effect: Whereas a letter presented in isolation will only receive significant activation from its letter-feature nodes, a letter that is displayed in the context of a word will receive activation from both letter-feature nodes and the word node with which it is connected.

The interactive-activation model can explain several empirical findings besides the word-superiority effect. For example, because the word nodes have a "resting" or baseline level of activation that reflects how often the words that they represent have been encountered in printed text, common words require less time to activate than rare words, thereby providing an account of the *word-frequency effect*, or the finding that common words are typically identified more rapidly than less common words (Reingold et al., 2012; Schilling et al., 1998). It is also worth noting that these and other successes, along with the model's conceptual simplicity, have resulted in

1.3 Models of Reading

it being highly influential in the development of other models of English (and as we shall see later, Chinese) reading. For example, the interactive-activation model is a core component of several other models of word identification (e.g., Coltheart et al., 2001; Davis, 2010; Grainger & Jacobs, 1996; Norris, 1994; Perry et al., 2007; Zorzi et al., 1998) and models of eye-movement control in reading (e.g., Reilly & Radach, 2003, 2006; Snell et al., 2018). Additionally, the more general notion of activation being propagated among a set of highly interactive nodes has been incorporated into models of sentence processing (e.g., Spivey & Tanenhaus, 1998) and discourse representation (e.g., Kintsch, 1998). Acknowledging this influence, let us now turn to a second example of a reading model.

This second example is the *E-Z Reader* model of eye-movement control during reading (Reichle et al., 1998, 2012; for a review, see Reichle, 2011). In contrast to the interactive-activation model, which provides a detailed or computationally explicit account of a single reading process, that of identifying printed words, E-Z Reader provides a high-level, more descriptive account of how several components of the mind work in a coordinated manner to determine when and where a reader's eye will move during reading. Figure 1.2 is a schematic diagram of the model.[5] As shown, it consists of an early pre-attentive stage in which visual information is propagated from across the entire visual field to the mind, but with the fine-detailed features about words being used for lexical processing and the coarser features (e.g., about the locations and lengths of words) being used for saccadic programming. Each of these two processing "streams" will be described in turn.

As Figure 1.2 shows, lexical processing is completed in two successive stages. The first, *familiarity check* stage corresponds to a rapidly available sense of familiarity (e.g., like the recognition response in dual-process theories of memory; Yonelinas, 2002) that is used as a heuristic to "know" that lexical access is imminent, thus signaling the oculomotor system to start programming a saccade to move the eyes to the next word. The second stage of lexical processing, which corresponds to *lexical access*, then continues until the meaning and pronunciation of the word are available from memory. As shown, the completion of lexical access causes the focus of attention to shift to the next word, and the initiation of whatever post-lexical processing is required to integrate the meaning of the just-identified word into the representation of the sentence that is being

---

[5] For a detailed description of the model, see Reichle (2011), Reichle et al. (2012), or Reichle (2021: 397–407).

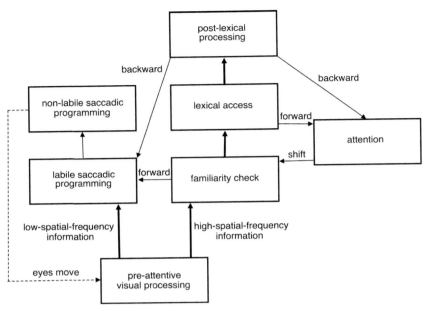

Figure 1.2 Schematic diagram of Reichle et al.'s (2012) E-Z Reader model of eye-movement control in reading
The boxes designate processes, the thick arrows indicate the propagation of information, and the thin arrows indicate the flow of control. The dashed arrow represents the actual movement of the eyes.

generated. As described so far, this part of the model instantiates the two core assumptions of E-Z Reader – that there is a dissociation between the events that trigger the movement of eyes (i.e., the familiarity check) versus attention (i.e., lexical access), and that attention is allocated in a strictly serial manner to support the processing and identification of only one word at any given time. Finally, according to the model, post-lexical processing occurs largely in the background on on-going lexical processing, only occasionally intervening if integration for some reason fails (e.g., the syntactic structure of a sentence is mis-parsed) or if integration is too slow (i.e., if word $N+1$ is identified before word N has been integrated). Either of these two situations can result in a pause or the triggering of an inter-word *regression* to move both the eyes and attention back to the source of integration difficulty.

The second processing "stream" in E-Z Reader is related to saccadic programming and execution. As Figure 1.2 shows, saccades are programmed

1.3 Models of Reading

in two successive stages: an initial *labile stage* that can be canceled if another saccade is initiated, followed by a *non-labile stage* in which the saccade cannot be canceled. This distinction allows the model to explain why words are sometimes skipped (i.e., not fixated) during reading, as follows. Imagine a situation in which both the eyes and attention are on word N. In this situation, the completion of the familiarity check on word N will cause the oculomotor system to start programming a saccade to move the eyes to word $N+1$. Now imagine that, while this labile stage of programming is being completed, lexical access of word N completes, causing attention to shift to word $N+1$ and its lexical processing to begin. If the familiarity check of word $N+1$ then completes rapidly enough, it will trigger the initiation of a second labile program to move the eyes to word $N+2$, which then cancels the original program, causing word $N+1$ to be skipped. However, if the familiarity check of word $N+1$ completes more slowly, then the labile program to move the eyes to word $N+1$ will likely complete, initiating the non-labile stage of programming and thereby resulting in an obligatory fixation on word $N+1$.

Finally, although the saccades are always directed towards the centers of upcoming words (i.e., towards their *optimal-viewing position*; O'Regan, 1992) because this viewing location affords their efficient processing, there are two sources of saccadic error. The first is random and causes fixations to be normally distributed around their intended targets, but with the amount of deviation also increasing with the length of the intended saccade. The second type of error is systematic and causes saccades that are shorter/longer than some "preferred" length to over/undershoot their intended targets. Because both sources of error often result in fixations being in suboptimal viewing locations, the model also assumes that efference copies of the intended saccade can be used to quickly determine the size of the discrepancy, and to then rapidly initiate a corrective saccade to move the eyes closer to the originally intended target (i.e., the center of the word being processed). Together, these assumptions allow the model to explain why fixation landing-site distributions tend to be normal and centered near the middle of words (McConkie et al., 1988), and why fixations near either end of a word tend to be short in duration and more likely to be followed by a refixation on the word (Vitu et al., 2001).

More generally, the E-Z Reader model as described above has been used to simulate and understand many findings related to eye movements in reading (Reichle et al., 1998) and other reading-like experiments (Reichle et al., 2012; Veldre et al., 2023; for a review, see Reichle, 2011). And like the interactive-activation model (McClelland & Rumelhart, 1981) discussed earlier, E-Z Reader has been influential, motivating a considerable amount of new empirical research (e.g., Inhoff et al., 2005; Pollatsek et al., 2006) and the development of several competitor models (e.g., Engbert et al., 2005; McDonald et al., 2005; Reilly & Radach, 2003, 2006; Schad & Engbert, 2012; Snell et al., 2018). More recently, the model has been "fleshed out" by embedding more computationally explicit models of word identification, sentence processing, and discourse representation within its framework to produce a computationally explicit account of reading in its entirety, *Über-Reader* (Reichle, 2021).

Finally, the two models that have been reviewed here, the interactive-activation model and E-Z Reader, are important for present purposes because they provide examples of the types of formal theories that have been developed to advance our understanding of the psychology of reading.[6] This advancement occurs in two ways. First and foremost, the models provide useful summary descriptions of the main processes that are involved in reading, allowing researchers to think more concretely about what happens during reading, and to make predictions about what might happen in experimental situations. Such predictions are immensely useful for advancing the science of reading because they allow researchers to formulate precise tests that can be used to disconfirm one or more assumptions of a model, thereby allowing the model to be rejected in favor of other models, or for the faulty assumptions to be modified. (For discussion of how and why formal models are useful in psychology, see Hintzman, 1991.)

In the context of the remainder of this book, models like the two that have been described have a second important use. Because most reading models have been developed to explain the reading of languages that use alphabetic scripts, like English and German, the theoretical assumptions of those models may not be appropriate for understanding the reading of languages that use non-alphabetic writing systems, like Chinese. As we will argue later, these possible discrepancies are extremely interesting because they suggest one of two basic conclusions. The first is that the theoretical assumptions in question may simply be wrong, and that they must be replaced by assumptions that are general enough to explain the

---

[6] Although both models have been formally implemented as computer programs, it is important to acknowledge that "formally implemented" is often a matter of degree, and that most models are implemented using some combination of mathematical equations, computer programs, and diagrams. That being said, less formally implemented models or verbal theories can also be important conceptual tools for both thinking and making predictions about the outcomes of experiments in new research domains, and for precisely that reason, a few examples of such theories are described in Chapters 3 and 4.

reading of, for example, English and Chinese. The second possible conclusion is that different assumptions may be required to explain the reading of English versus Chinese – that one set of assumptions may be necessary to understand the reading of one of the two languages, but either those assumptions are unnecessary or other assumptions are required to explain the reading of the other language.

Finally, given this brief discussion of why models are useful, one might ask about the process of adjudicating between two or more models. Or more generally, how are two or more models compared and evaluated? Although a complete answer to these questions can be extremely complicated (e.g., see Farrell & Lewandowsky, 2018), a short answer suffices for the purposes of this book. This short answer is that, with all else being equal, models that explain many empirical findings using a small number of theoretical assumptions are preferred to models that require many assumptions to explain just a few findings. Additional considerations that might be used in comparing and evaluating models might include: Do the models use assumptions that are consistent with what is known about either cognition or neuroscience more generally? And do the models generate predictions that are in some way novel or unexpected? After all, models are useful to the extent that they advance our understanding of some issue, and in relation to the psychology of reading, a useful model is one that provides a new insight into what might be happening in the mind of a reader as they convert the marks on a printed page into the rich and varied representations that are afforded by the capacity to read. Models of reading are useful because they can provide a window into how this capacity is possible.

1.4 Chapter Previews

This chapter has provided the basic information that might be required of someone without a strong background in cognitive psychology, linguistics, education, or one of their aligned disciplines to understand the remainder of this book. The next chapter will provide some additional background that may be especially useful for readers who lack an understanding of the Chinese languages and writing system, and the characteristics of the latter that are unique and that provide points of contrast for the research that has, to date, largely focused on the reading of alphabetic writing systems and European languages.

Chapters 3, 4, and 5 then comprise the core of the book, and as such, are organized similarly. For example, Chapter 3 will focus on lexical processing and word identification, beginning with a brief review of what has been learned about these topics from the study of the reading of alphabetic writing systems (mostly English) using the experimental methods reviewed earlier in this chapter. The bulk of Chapter 3 will then focus on what has been learned about the processing and identification of characters and words in Chinese reading from experiments using the same methods. Chapter 3 will also review the models that have been developed to explain what is known about the identification of characters and words during Chinese reading.

Chapters 4 and 5 then continue using this same organizational approach, but with the former chapter focusing on skilled reading, and the latter focusing on the development of reading skill, its impairment (i.e., dyslexia), and what has been learned from cognitive neuroscience about the reading of Chinese. Because much of our own research has used eye tracking to study reading, much of the research on skilled reading that will be discussed in Chapter 4 is based on experiments that have also used this methodology. And although neuroscience methods of the type described earlier in this chapter have been used to study both the identification of isolated words and skilled reading, this research has been collectively relegated to Chapter 5 for the purpose of maintaining coherence. As each of these chapters will demonstrate, although there are consistencies in what has been learned about these topics across languages and writing systems as different as those used in the reading of English versus Chinese, there are also important differences – differences that are usually not afforded the recognition that they warrant, especially given the theoretical and practical implications that they likely have for our general understanding of reading.

Finally, Chapter 6 closes with a more explicit comparison of what has been learned about the reading of Chinese versus English (and other alphabetic writing systems), with particular emphasis on highlighting those points of contrast that might have important ramifications for the psychology of reading. This analysis will then be used to motivate a small set of outstanding questions – questions that, if answered, we believe might advance our basic understanding of what happens in the human mind when it is engaged in reading. These questions will then motivate our predictions about future research, and a few of the more basic challenges that remain to be addressed by future reading researchers. Our goal in doing all of this, however, is modest – if we are successful, we hope to provide a few "signposts" that might be useful to reading researchers who are interested in advancing the science of reading by studying what really is one of the most intriguing writing systems that was ever developed and that is still widely used today – that of written Chinese.

CHAPTER 2

The Chinese Language and Writing System

This chapter is intended to provide a high-level description of the Chinese language and writing system. The description will not be comprehensive but will instead only be sufficient to understand how the similarities and differences between Chinese and other languages and writing systems that have been used to study reading, most notably English, have and might continue to be leveraged to provide theoretically interesting points of contrast. During the past few decades, these points of contrast have resulted in a growing appreciation that the science of reading might be advanced by studying the reading of languages that have markedly different writing systems, like Chinese. Our present description of the Chinese language and writing system will therefore focus mainly on the writing system and aspects of it that make it make it so unique and worthy of study. For a comprehensive treatment of the spoken Chinese language and its history, please consult Norman's (1988) definitive volume on the topic, which provides a wealth of information about the origins of the language, its relation to other languages, and its key linguistic attributes. With this important disclaimer, let us now begin our description of the Chinese language and writing system.

2.1 The Chinese Language

As observed by W. Wang (1973: 60), "the Chinese language has the largest number of speakers in the world and the greatest time depth of its literature," with the latter "spanning a period of 35 centuries" (51). Currently, Chinese is spoken as a first language by approximately 1.3 billion people. It is a misnomer to call it a "language," however, because it is a family of languages consisting of seven to thirteen major mutually unintelligible linguistic groups or dialects that in turn consist of hundreds of regional variants (Norman, 1988). For a variety of historical, political, and geographic reasons, the sizes of these language groups

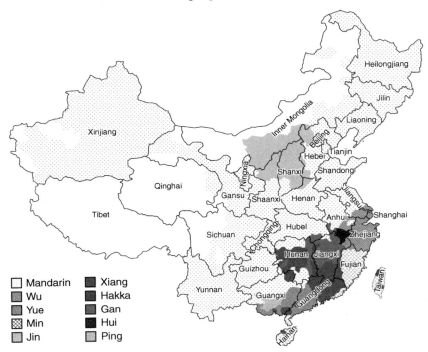

Figure 2.1 A map of China showing the main dialects and where they are spoken

vary quite considerably, with larger, more homogeneous enclaves across the northern plains of China and smaller, more heterogeneous pockets of speakers located in the mountainous regions of southern China (see Figure 2.1). These linguistic groups form a dialectic "continuum," with the degree of intelligibility often declining in a graded manner with increasing geographical distance, but with the rate of decline also punctuated by, for example, mountain ranges or large rivers that have historically separated two or more regions.

The most commonly spoken of these languages is *Mandarin*, which is based on the Beijing dialect and currently has roughly 800 million speakers.[1] Mandarin was adopted as the official language of the Republic of China in the 1930s. It is also the official language of Taiwan, is one of a handful of official languages of both Singapore and the United Nations, and is spoken by the millions of Chinese diaspora who have emigrated around the globe.

---

[1] https://en.wikipedia.org/wiki/Chinese_language (February 22, 2022).

A few other of the most widely used dialects include *Yue* or *Cantonese*, which is spoken by about 68 million people, *Wu* or *Shanghainese*, which is spoken by about 74 million people, and *Min*, which is spoken by about 75 million people. Again, it is important to emphasize that most of these dialects are distinct languages, with a speaker of Mandarin, for example, being as unintelligible to a speaker of Cantonese as a speaker of English would be to a speaker of German (Norman, 1988: 2).

The Chinese languages are also more distantly related to the *Tibeto-Burman* language group which, as its name suggests, includes both Tibetan and Burmese. This larger group can be contrasted with the main language groups that surround China, including the *Altaic* group (i.e., Turkic, Mongolian, Tungusic, and possibly Korean and Japanese) to the north, and to the south, the various *Tai* languages spoken in Vietnam, Laos, Thailand, and Burma. The languages within each of these main groups bear a "family resemblance" to each other, with the Chinese languages sharing an overlapping constellation of features that, collectively, distinguish them from the languages of the other groups. One of these features is that Chinese is monosyllabic, with each syllable corresponding to a single morpheme or unit of meaning. Thus, in contrast to English, where single-syllable words can contain multiple morphemes (e.g., *cats* = *cat* + *s* to denote plurality; *ran* = *run* + inflection to denote past-tense form) and multisyllabic words can correspond to a single morpheme (e.g., *elephant*, *hammer*, *continent*), most syllables in Chinese correspond to only one unit of meaning. (There are a few exceptions to this rule, but they are rare; e.g., the Chinese disyllabic word meaning "spider.") However, as is true in English, most Chinese words consist of two or more morphemes and are polysyllabic.

Each spoken syllable has a specific phonological structure that, at a minimum, includes the vowel, but that can also have an optional onset consisting of a consonant or a consonant and a medial glide, as well as an optional coda consonant. In English, for example, the word "steel" has an onset consisting of the consonant cluster "st" (/st/) and a body consisting of the vowels "ee" (/iː/) and the coda consonant "l" (/l/). However, in contrast to English, consonant clusters are not permitted in either the onset or coda within the syllables that make up Chinese words. And one final property of the Chinese syllable happens to be the one that is perhaps most obvious to speakers of European languages – the fact that spoken Chinese, in contrast to languages like English and German but also many other Asian languages like Korean and Japanese, sounds "melodic" to the ear because each syllable is spoken with an associated change in its

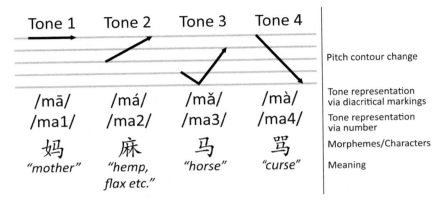

Figure 2.2 An example illustrating the four tones used to differentiate the meanings of the spoken syllable /ma/ in Mandarin
The arrows show each tone's change in the pitch contour as might be measured using an oscilloscope.

pitch contour, or *tone*. In the case of Mandarin, for example, each syllable has one of four different possible tones: (1) *level*; (2) *rising*; (3) *falling and then rising*; or (4) *falling*. (Some descriptions of Mandarin include a fifth, neutral tone that can be contrasted with the other four.) These tones are used to differentiate between the meanings that might be associated with a given syllable. For example, as Figure 2.2 illustrates, the syllable pronounced /ma/ can have one of four distinct meanings that can be differentiated by the tone that is used in its pronunciation; whereas the level tone /ma1/ means "mother," the falling-then-rising tone /ma3/ means "horse."[2] The tones thus function as phonemes in that they provide the minimal contrasts that are used to discriminate between two morphemes/words, in the same manner that the contrast between the phonemes /k/ and /b/ are used to respectively discriminate between the words "cat" and "bat" in English. And although Mandarin is spoken with four tones, there are northern dialects that are spoken using as few as three, and some southern dialects using six or more.

---

[2] There are different conventions for representing the tones associated with Chinese syllables written using the Roman alphabet (e.g., via diacritical markings above the vowels; W. Wang, 1973). The convention that will be adopted in this book entails appending numbers to the ends of syllables to indicate their tones, with 1 to 4 respectively indicating the level, rising, falling-then-rising, and falling tones. (The fifth, neutral tone is not marked with a number.) Relatedly, the pronunciations of syllables and words will be indicated by the use of forward slashes.

2.1 The Chinese Language

Because the individual syllables correspond to morphemes, they often correspond to single syllable words. However, most words are polysyllabic, with most being bi-syllabic but a non-negligible proportion consisting of three or four syllables. As is true of English, Chinese morphemes can be divided into those that convey independent meaning, or *contentives*, and those that modify the contentives in some systematic manner, or *functives*. The former can be classified as nouns, verbs, or adjectives and are used to construct words in those classes, whereas the latter are used to convey the grammatical relationships among those words. Because the syntactic structures of phrases and sentences are conveyed using prepositions, particles, and word order, with the default for the latter being subject-verb-object, Chinese is generally considered to be an analytic or isolating language (Norman, 1988). One implication of this is that the use of both derivational and inflectional morphology are comparatively rare.

Thus, in contrast to English, where an inflection requires internal changes to the base word (e.g., *ate = eat* + inflection to denote completed action), in Chinese, a small number of suffixes (e.g., /le/, /zhe/, etc.) can be used immediately after the verb to indicate aspect (e.g., perfective, or continuing). For example, /chi1/ is the basic verb meaning "eat," but by adding /le/ to the verb, the phrase /chi1 le/ now suggests that the act of eating has been completed. (Note that the aspect differs from tense in that the completed action could refer to a past or future event.) Similarly, /chi1 zhe/ indicates that the act of eating is currently in progress. As another example, the plural suffix /men/ can be added to an animate pronoun or noun to mark numerical change and thereby denote a collective (e.g., /wo3/ "I" + /men/ = /wo3 men/, meaning "we" or "us"; /xue2 sheng1/ "student" + /men/ = /xue2 sheng1 men/, meaning "students").

It is also worth noting that the obligatory use of inflected forms is limited to indicating plural pronouns (e.g., /wo3 men/ "we" or "us") and it is not obligatory in other contexts. For instance, the plural measurement /zhe4 xie1/ "these" can be combined with singular nouns (e.g., added to /xue2 sheng1/ "student" to give /zhe4 xie1 xue2 sheng1/, meaning "these students"). Similarly, durative actions can also be expressed using an adverb /zheng4 zai4/ meaning "in the process of" before the verb to indicate that the action is in progress without using inflectional suffix /zhe/. Some linguists therefore consider the use of inflectional suffixes a grammatic or syntactic process rather than a morphological one (e.g., Norman, 1988; cf. Packard, 2015). One likely implication of this is that the concept of "word" in Chinese is not clear to many of its readers – or even some linguists!

26 The Chinese Language and Writing System

There are also some derivational affixes that can be attached to a base word to form new words or phrases that have a different syntactic category or meaning. At least as compared to inflected words, these derived words appear to be more common in Chinese. To give a few examples, the prefix /fu4/ denotes "again" and can be used to generate words like /fu4 he2/ ("reunite"), /fu4 cha2/ ("re-examine"), and /fu4 yuan2/ ("recover"). Likewise, the prefix /wu2/ negates a base word, allowing for the generation of such words as /wu2 xu1/ ("no need"), /wu2 xian4/ ("unlimited"), and /wu2 chang2/ ("without pay"). As one final example, the suffix /hua4/ corresponding to "-ify" or "-ize" can likewise be used to generate /jian3 hua4/ meaning "simplify," /yang3 hua4/ meaning "oxidize," and /gong1 ye4 hua4/ meaning "industrialize."

Despite the use of inflectional and derivational affixes and suffixes in Chinese, most Chinese disyllabic or multisyllabic words are formed through compounding. Additionally, certain aspects of Chinese word formation and their grammatical features are quite different from anything that is found in English.

One example is that, in Chinese, the articles and numerals that modify nouns cannot directly precede those nouns. The articles and numerals must instead be separated from their corresponding nouns by *classifiers* that are used in reference to units of measure. Thus, while a speaker of English might perfectly well say "the cat" or "three books," the equivalent phrases in Chinese (i.e., /na4 mao1/ and /san1 shu1/, respectively) would be agrammatical. The Chinese speaker would instead by obliged to say /na4 zhi1 mao1/, or "the piece cat," and /san1 ben3 shu1/, or "three piece books," where the word "piece" is a loose English translation that has little semantic content but that serves as a placeholder for the two classifiers, /zhi1/ and /ben3/.

A second example involves the use of syllable reduplication, wherein a noun can be repeated to convey the added meaning of "every." For example, repeating the word /ren2/, which by itself means "person," will produce "every person" (i.e., /ren2 ren2/). Similarly, repeating the word for "day," /tian1/, gives "every day" (i.e., /tian1 tian1/). Applying this reduplication principle to verbs will change the word to its transitory meaning. For example, repeating the word /kan4/, which by itself means "to look," will produce "to take a look" (i.e., /kan4 kan4/), while repeating the word that means "to walk," /zou3/, will produce "to take a walk" (i.e., / zou3 zou3/). And to give one final example, an adjective can be converted into an adverb via reduplication and the addition of the /de/ suffix; for example, the adjective /kuai4/ meaning "quick" can be converted into the adverb /kuai4 kaui4 de/ meaning "quickly."

2.1 The Chinese Language

A third example is related to the formation of new words by conjoining two morphemes that have the opposite meaning. For example, the antonyms /mai3/ ("buy") and /mai4/ ("sell") can be joined to form /mai3 mai4/, meaning "business." Similarly, conjoining /chang2/ ("long") and /duan3/ ("short") gives /chang2 duan3/, or "length." However, the meaning of the conjoined words is not always transparently related to their parts; for example, /fan3/, which means "turned over," can be combined with /zheng4/, meaning "right side up," to produce /fan3 zheng4/, which means "in any case."

As indicated previously, these features of the Chinese language differentiate it from English as well as the other Asiatic language groups that were mentioned earlier. For example, although the use of mono-morphemic, tonal syllables is a feature shared by the Chinese languages and many of the languages spoken to the south of China (e.g., Miao, Thai, Vietnamese, or Yao), it differentiates Chinese from northern languages that use polymorphemic, atonal syllables (e.g., Japanese, Korean, Manchu, Mongolian). And conversely, Chinese languages share features with their northern linguistic neighbors (e.g., each syllable onset can only contain one consonant, adjectives must precede the nouns that they modify, etc.) that are at odds with their southern linguistic neighbors. These similarities and differences provide clues about the evolution of the Chinese language family and its linguistic neighbors. Although this evolution has undoubtedly been bidirectional (e.g., as evidenced by that fact that new words, especially those describing technology, have been introduced into Chinese after first being appropriated into Japanese), it is no exaggeration to say that the influence of Chinese culture has been profound. In fact, the influence of the Chinese language on other regional languages has been likened to that of ancient Greek and Latin on the development of European languages (Norman, 1988).

Finally, as was indicated at the beginning of this chapter, our main objective in providing this overview has been quite modest – to provide the minimal background that is required for someone unfamiliar with the Chinese language and writing system to gain a better understanding and appreciation of the latter (in the remainder of this chapter). This understanding is a prerequisite for understanding the topics that will be discussed in the rest of this book – namely, what has been learned about the psychology of reading from research on the reading of one writing system, Chinese. For a more in-depth discussion of the Chinese language, we again invite the reader to consult Norman (1988) because it arguably provides the most complete and authoritative treatment of the topic (at least, in English). With that caveat, we now turn to a brief discussion of the origins of the Chinese writing system.

2.2 The History of the Chinese Writing System

The Chinese writing system has played a defining role in Chinese history and is one of the most remarkable cultural inventions in all of human history. The former claim is based on the fact that the Chinese writing system has provided a foundation for the development of Chinese culture and political unity. This is due to three factors that are perhaps unique to China. First, as has already been discussed, the Chinese "language" comprises many mutually unintelligible languages. Second, the geographic region making up China is occupied by a larger number of different ethnic groups. Third, the history of China is every bit as complex and rich as that of Europe (see Keay, 2009). These three factors together have meant that the Chinese writing system has been used as a *linguae franca* for the peoples of China, allowing for ready commerce and the sharing of knowledge, much as Latin allowed for such exchanges throughout much of the history of Europe. As Norman states in his discussion of the Chinese writing system:

> The aptness of language as a symbol of cultural and even political unity was facilitated by the use of a script that for all practical purposes was independent of any particular phonetic manifestation of the language, allowing the Chinese to look upon the Chinese language as being more uniform and unchanging than it actually was. (Norman, 1988: 1)

This continuity of the written form, in combination with the fact that it has existed for *at least* 3,500 years, thus makes Chinese unique among the languages of the world. One implication of this fact is quite remarkable: Modern readers of Chinese can often read texts that were written hundreds or even thousands of years ago! This is true even though, because the spoken language (like all spoken languages) has continued to evolve, the spoken form of ancient Chinese is as different from its modern counterpart as Latin is from modern Italian and French. Thus, although a native speaker of Chinese might be able to read and understand portions of the *Analects* as they were originally written by Confucius more than two millennia ago (during the Warring States period, approximately 475–221 BCE), the same Chinese speaker would not be able to have a spoken conversation with Confucius. This is because the spoken form of the Chinese language has continued to evolve and change over the ensuing

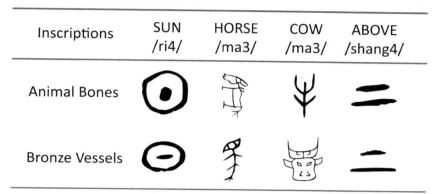

Figure 2.3 A few examples of the earliest form of Chinese writing Inscriptions that have been found on turtle shells, animal bones, and bronze vessels that were often used for oracles. These examples were extracted from www.zdic.net.

millennia. This is not to say that the writing system has not also changed because of course it has. In fact, much more is known about the evolution of the writing system due to the simple fact that physical evidence of this change has been preserved in various media.

The earliest evidence of Chinese writing comes from inscriptions on the turtle shells, animal bones, and bronze vessels that were used for divinatory purposes (e.g., predicting weather).[3] These inscriptions have been dated to the Shang dynasty (sixteenth to eleventh centuries BCE), but both their prevalence and level of sophistication suggest that they were in widespread use perhaps centuries earlier (R. Chang & Chang, 1978; Norman, 1988). A few examples of these inscriptions are illustrated in Figure 2.3. As shown, many consist of pictographs in that the referent of each inscription can be readily inferred in the absence of any knowledge of written Chinese. For example, the inscription meaning "sun" consists of a circle with a dot in the center, while the inscription for "horse" is a simple line drawing showing the animal complete with both its mane and tail. It is important to note, however, that this is not true of all the inscriptions, and that the total number of characters that have been cataloged is more than four thousand (Robinson, 1995). These two facts indicate that the inscriptions

---

[3] For discussion of the earliest forms of writing around the world and the archeological evidence dating their development, see Robinson (1995).

30   The Chinese Language and Writing System

were in fact part of a complete writing system and not just, for example, used for artistic purposes. They also suggest that the writing system may have been developed hundreds of years earlier than the current archeological evidence indicates, perhaps by as early as the Xia dynasty, which ended the sixteenth century BCE.

Although this early Chinese writing system may have been sufficient for its purposes, careful consideration of the examples in Figure 2.3 suggests at least a few limitations inherent in the approach. The first is that the use of pictographs is by its very nature primarily applicable to concrete referents that can be drawn, such as plants, animals, geographic features, and human artifacts. Although some abstract concepts can also be represented (e.g., the concept "above" is represented by two horizontal lines, with the shorter of the two being above the longer), these abstract concepts are less transparent and necessitate that the group of pictograph users adopt and understand the conventions that allow the symbols to be used. This general approach to denoting referents also becomes increasingly difficult as the concepts become more abstract or complex, making it hard to represent complex thoughts about, for example, human emotions, political concepts, or future events. A second limitation of the inscriptions is that they do not provide direct links to their spoken forms; for example, the symbols for "sun" and "horse" shown in Figure 2.3 provide no indication of how the two words were spoken. Finally, due to their complexity, the symbols can be cumbersome to inscribe and perhaps even require some degree of artist talent to render in a manner that is intelligible to others.

For those reasons, the increasing use of pictographs to represent other types of records (e.g., financial transactions) meant that they were subject to selective pressure to make them easier to use. One of these changes was their simplification and a movement away from the use of true pictographs to the use of more abstract characters. This abstraction of course afforded the depiction of more complex and abstract concepts. Figure 2.4 shows examples of how a few pictographs evolved into their modern equivalents, Chinese characters, during the centuries following the Shang dynasty (sixteenth to eleventh centuries BCE). In tandem with this simplification, another convention that was intended to make reading easier was the adoption of the rebus principle to associate concepts that were difficult to depict with characters that sounded like their spoken counterparts. For example, at one point, the character meaning "wheat" and pronounced /lai2/ was used in substitution for the concept "come," which was difficult to depict but was also pronounced /lai2/. Over time,

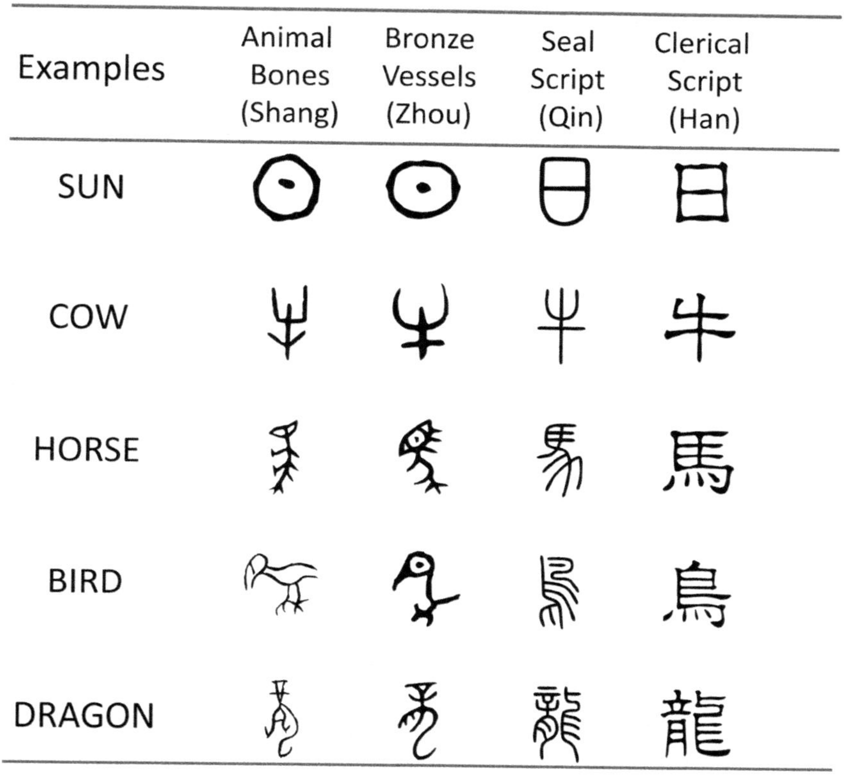

2.2 The History of the Chinese Writing System

Examples	Animal Bones (Shang)	Bronze Vessels (Zhou)	Seal Script (Qin)	Clerical Script (Han)
SUN				
COW				
HORSE				
BIRD				
DRAGON				

Figure 2.4 A few examples showing how early pictographs changed into their modern character equivalents during the evolution of the Chinese writing system These examples were extracted from www.zdic.net.

the character was used exclusively to refer to its new adopted meaning as the spoken word for "wheat" fell out of use. And in a similar manner, other characters were adopted to represent the meanings of concepts that were pronounced like concepts that had originally been associated with the characters. Two consequences of this trend are that it connected the phonology of the spoken language to its written form more directly, and expanded the number of possible referents.

As Figure 2.4 shows, the Chinese writing system continued to change throughout recorded Chinese history. It is worth noting, however, that this evolution did not proceed at a constant rate or with the desired end product in mind; rather, the changes were sporadic and likely emerged unsystematically in various locales, with some of the resulting changes being adopted and spreading to other locales and many (perhaps even most?) either going unnoticed or falling into disuse. The evolution of the writing system was thus analogous to biological evolution in that the retention and proliferation of its features were selected as a function of their utility "fitness," with the changes being made to facilitate the more widespread reading and writing of Chinese.

However, as carefully documented by Norman (1988), there were also at least three significant periods in the development of the Chinese writing system, where the changes were rapid, systematic, and by design. The first was the unification of China under the Qin dynasty (221–207 BCE). This political unification brought about the standardization of units of measurement and legal statutes, and the replacement of various local scripts with a single script that would further consolidate the government's control of its empire. This script was also of two types: a *seal script* that, as implied by its name, was used for official seals and documents, and a *clerical script* that was used by government officials and clerks for commerce, the maintenance of inventories, and so on. Both scripts were highly standardized but with the former being more complex and stylized and the latter being simpler and thus easier to use for everyday purposes.

The second watershed period in the development of the Chinese writing system occurred during the Han dynasty (206 BCE – 24 CE), when the seal script was abandoned in favor of the clerical script, which was further simplified and standardized. For example, previous efforts to preserve the pictographic links between characters and their referents were abandoned in favor of utility. The line segments comprising the characters were also shortened and straightened. The circular lines in the character representing "sun," for example, were straightened to produce its current form, a box bisected by a horizontal line. This simplified clerical script is therefore the basis of the modern Chinese characters that are used today; although native speakers of Chinese would have considerable difficulty reading most characters written in the seal script, speakers with a good understanding of written Chinese can decipher many characters written in clerical script. Finally, an abbreviated, cursive form of the characters were also introduced for informal purposes and for writing draft documents.

The third and final watershed period in the development of the Chinese writing systems occurred in the mid-twentieth century. After their rise to power in 1949, the government of the People's Republic of China began implementing a nationwide reform of the Chinese writing system. Up until 1956, Chinese has been written in the traditional manner, using

Examples	Traditional Script	Simplified Script	Pinyin
SUN	日	日	/ri4/
COW	牛	牛	/niu2/
HORSE	馬	马	/ma3/
BIRD	鳥	鸟	/niao3/
DRAGON	龍	龙	/long2/
FLY	飛	飞	/fei1/

Figure 2.5 A few examples illustrating the similarities and differences between traditional and simplified Chinese characters

relatively elaborate characters and the convention of writing the characters from top to bottom, in columns running from right to left. The reform brought about the simplification of a large proportion of existing characters, a few examples of which are shown in Figure 2.5. The Western convention of writing in rows from left to right was also adopted. Finally, for pedagogical purposes, an alphabetic writing system called *pinyin* was adopted for teaching elementary children in mainland China about the phonology of the Chinese language.[4] This pinyin is still used today as a "scaffold" to support literacy education that is eventually abandoned as the children learn to read characters. It is also worth noting that, although these conventions were adopted in mainland China, the more traditional writing system has largely been retained in Hong Kong, Macau, Taiwan,

[4] Similarly, another phonetic system called *zhuyin* is also used in Taiwan to support early literacy training.

and other geographical regions that have large Chinese diaspora; in these locations, the more complex traditional Chinese characters are often used, and it is not uncommon to see books, newspapers, and signs written in the traditional manner, with columns of characters running from right to left. Finally, modern Chinese is now also written using punctuation to denote clauses and the ends of sentences.[5]

In closing this section, it is noteworthy how the Chinese writing system has influenced the cultures and writing systems of the many countries surrounding China. As the preeminent political and cultural entity in eastern Asia, it is perhaps not surprising that the development of the Chinese writing system and literature had a profound effect on the cultural development of the surrounding regions. The prime example is the fact that the Chinese writing system was borrowed by the Thai, Korean, and Japanese and used for official government purposes for many centuries. Although the Thai developed their alphabet (based on an Old Khmer script) in the thirteenth century CE and the Koreans likewise developed their own alphabetic system (called *hangul*) in the fifteenth century, both countries continued to employ some Chinese characters until the mid-twentieth century. Similarly, although the Japanese also developed their own writing system (a system called *kana* that represents spoken syllables), this indigenous system is still used in combination with Chinese characters (which are called *kanji*) to the present day. The fact that speakers of these vastly different languages could adopt the Chinese writing system to their own languages underscores the point that was made earlier about Chinese characters not being directly linked to the pronunciations of the syllables that they represent – a point that will be raised again in the next section. One immediate implication of this, however, is that native speakers of what are effectively different languages, such as Mandarin and Cantonese and, to a more limited extent, Japanese, can read the same text even though they cannot then talk about its contents. This remarkable situation would be analogous to speakers of English and German being able to read the same newspaper but being unable to discuss its contents.

---

[5] One other historically significant milestone related to the development of Chinese writing warrants mention – the invention of the printing press. The earliest known printed texts were Buddhist scriptures produced in the eighth century CE using inked ceramic blocks carved in relief. The invention of moveable type then occurred sometime later during the Five Dynasties/Ten Kingdoms period (907–959 CE), predating its invention by Johannes Gutenberg in 1440 CE, Germany, by about five centuries (Keay, 2011). As was true in Germany, the mass printing of text allowed for its broad dissemination and likely contributed to the standardization of the writing system.

2.3 The Modern Chinese Writing System

Figure 2.6 shows a sentence written in modern (simplified) Chinese, as is currently the convention in the People's Republic of China. To the Western eye, the feature that is perhaps most salient is the simple fact that the sentence is written as a single continuous line of uniformly sized, box-shaped characters, without the blank spaces between words that, by convention, are used in most alphabetic writing systems. (The use of blank spaces to demarcate word boundaries is not necessarily a feature of *all* alphabetic writing systems, however; for example, Thai is written using an alphabet but, like Chinese, does not use blank spaces to demarcate words; see Reilly et al., 2011.) The absence of between-word spaces is of significant theoretical importance for at least two reasons.

The first is that Chinese words comprise a variable number of characters. For example, estimates of word type frequency derived from large corpus of natural text (e.g., Lexicon of Common Words in Contemporary Chinese Research Team, 2008) indicate that only about 6 percent of Chinese words comprise one character, with an additional 72 percent of words, the large majority, consisting of two characters, 10 percent consisting of three characters, and the remainder consisting of four or more characters. (Chinese words containing four or more characters usually correspond to vocabulary that is slang, proverbs, or borrowed from other

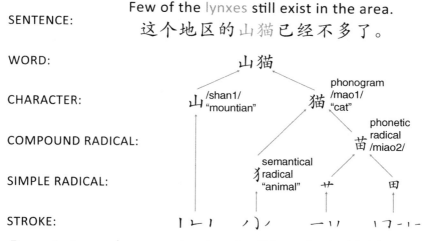

Figure 2.6 An example sentence written in modern Chinese using simplified characters

languages; e.g., 庐山真面目 /lu2 shan1 zhen1 mian4 mu4/ means "the truth of something"; 阿尔卑斯山 /ai er3 bei1 si1 shan1/ means "Alps.") However, token frequency counts, which provide estimates of how often instances of given words occur, indicate that about 70 percent of the words that occur in printed text contain one character, 27 percent contain two characters, 2 percent contain three characters, and only 1 percent contain four or more characters. That the two frequency counts differ reflects the selective pressure to shorten the most used words. Similar pressures exist in English where the most commonly used words also tend to be very short.

As might be guessed from this brief discussion of how text corpora are used to estimate character frequency counts, another important fact is that the sheer number of characters is vast and has continued to grow over the course of Chinese history. For example, Norman (1988) has documented how the number of characters in circulation expanded from approximately 10,000 during the Han dynasty (206 BCE – 24 CE) to more than 50,000 by the Song dynasty (960–1279 CE), but with a significant proportion of those characters now being obsolete and thus only rarely used. Perhaps a better indicator of the number of characters that are still in active use comes from estimates of the number known by the average literate Chinese person. Again, Norman provides these estimates. For example, a study conducted in the 1960s by the Institute of Psychology at the Academy of Sciences suggests that the average university educated person knows approximately 3,500 to 4,000 characters, and that a working knowledge of about 3,000 characters is required to read a newspaper. R. Chang and Chang (1978) provide a similar estimate of 2,800 to 3,000 characters, while W. Wang (1973) provides a considerably larger estimate – that knowledge of 4,000 to 7,000 characters is required to read a newspaper. Finally, the government of the People's Republic of China defines *functional literacy* as knowledge of the 2,000 most common or important characters. Although these estimates clearly vary, they are consistent in showing that – perhaps paradoxically – a well-educated reader of Chinese must devote years of study to learning thousands of characters, but despite this effort ends up knowing only a fraction of the characters that are currently in existence.

Returning now to our discussion of Figure 2.6, the fact that words consist of a variable number of characters in conjunction with the absence of clear word boundaries can result in ambiguity about how any sequence of characters should be grouped together or segmented, thus causing confusion about the boundaries and identities of individual words

2.3 The Modern Chinese Writing System

(Hsu & Huang, 2000; Inhoff & Wu, 2005). To illustrate this point, a somewhat analogous situation can be experienced in English if the spaces between two or more words are removed. For example, consider the letter sequence "catchair." Does it refer to a "cat chair," whatever that might be, or is it instead a directive to "catch air"? Such ambiguities occasionally occur in written Chinese. For example, the three characters "花生长" can be segmented into "花" and "生长," respectively meaning "flower" and "grows," but can also be segmented into "花生" and "长," respectively meaning "peanut" and "grows." Similarly, the four characters "通过去年" contain three overlapping words (i.e., "通过," "过去," and "去年," respectively meaning "through," "past," and "last year"), which can also lead to segmentation difficulty, especially during the initial pass of reading. Indeed, studies in which native Chinese speakers are simply asked to indicate where the word boundaries are in sentences indicate that people find it difficult to define the concept of a word, often disagreeing about precisely where the boundary between two words is located (e.g., Hoosain, 1992; P. Liu et al., 2013). More will be said about this in Chapters 3 and 4.

A second reason why the absence of clear word boundaries is theoretically interesting is that it raises the question of how readers of Chinese "know" where to move their eyes.[6] In alphabetic languages like English and German, for instance, it is generally accepted that readers use information about the length and location of the upcoming or parafoveal word in programming eye movements from one word to the next (Reichle et al., 2012; Schad & Engbert, 2012). Thus, from a fixation on word N, readers simply direct their eyes to the center of word N+1 because this viewing location will afford the most efficient processing of the word (McConkie et al., 1988; O'Regan, 1992); a fixation near the center of word N+1 will allow it to be processed from the center of vision, where visual acuity is maximal (Bouma, 1973; Frey & Bosse, 2018; Normann & Guillory, 2002; Veldre et al., 2023). However, it remains less clear both if and how this strategy might be adapted to the reading of Chinese given the lack of clear information about an upcoming word's length and location. This uncertainty has resulted in different theoretical accounts of saccadic targeting in Chinese reading (e.g., Y. P. Liu, Yu, Fu, et al., 2019; M. Yan et al., 2010; for a review, see Y. P. Liu et al., 2023). These accounts will be discussed at

---

[6] The scare quotes are used here because the decisions that readers make about when and where to move their eyes are not made consciously, but are instead determined by various perceptual, cognitive, and motoric factors that largely operate outside of conscious awareness (see Reichle, 2006).

length later (see Chapter 4), but for now suffice it to say that the main point of this debate is that it has raised questions about long-standing assumptions about the psychology of reading that may eventually be shown to be incorrect (or at least incomplete; e.g., see Y. P. Liu et al., 2019).

Returning to our discussion of Figure 2.6, another striking feature of the Chinese writing system that has not been discussed until now are the characters themselves. As briefly mentioned in the previous section of this chapter, the characters have their origins in pictographic inscriptions (see Figure 2.3), but by the Han dynasty (206 BCE – 24 CE; see Figure 2.4) they had already taken on much of their current form, with each character occupying a uniformly sized, box-shaped area. Closer examination of the characters themselves, however, indicates other important features that differentiate them from words in alphabetic writing systems.

The first is that the characters consist of a variable number of simple line segments that are called *strokes* because, throughout most of China's history, the characters were written using a brush and ink. As shown, both the number and arrangement of the strokes can vary, producing a full range of orthographic complexity that has often quantified using counts of the number of strokes. At one end of the continuum are single-stroke characters like 一 /yiɪ/, which means "one," while at the other end of the continuum are characters having thirty-six strokes, such as 齉 /nang4/, which means "(nose is) blocked." Interestingly, the average number of strokes per character is five or six, like the average number of letters per word in English. Despite the potential variability associated with the shape, size, and location of the individual strokes, their sizes and locations are restricted in that they must occur within the confines of the character. The shapes of the strokes can also be grouped into eight basic types (Y. Hu, 1981).[7] Following the tradition of Chinese calligraphy practice, these eight types of strokes can be illustrated using the single character 永 meaning "forever," as is shown in Figure 2.7. Another integral part of learning to write Chinese is that the order in which the strokes are written within the characters is also explicitly taught through repetition. The order can be described by a set of rules which include writing the strokes from top to bottom and then left to right, rendering horizontal strokes before vertical strokes, and so on. An example showing the order in which the strokes of a character should be written is also shown in Figure 2.7.

---

[7] Note that there are different taxonomies for describing the basic strokes of Chinese characters. For example, the State Language Commission and Ministry of Education China (2001) defines five basic stroke types and thirty-three subordinate stroke types that can be derived from those basic types.

An illustration of the eight basic strokes

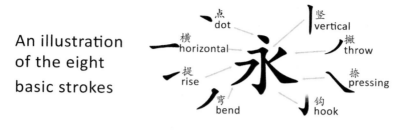

Writing order

Figure 2.7 An example illustrating the eight basic types of strokes and the order in which character strokes are normally written
Note that the second and third strokes in 永 are compound strokes, which consist of a sequence of basic strokes written in a continuous fashion (i.e., without lifting the pen from the page).

A second important fact about the characters is that, in contrast to alphabetic writing systems, where the smallest units are letters that are arranged along a single horizontal dimension, the characters are rendered along two dimensions and often consist of a hierarchy of elements. For example, as Figure 2.6 shows, the character 猫 meaning "cat" is composed of two clusters of strokes, with one on the left side of the character and the other on the right. These stroke clusters are called *radicals* and they are often used to denote information related to either the meaning or pronunciation of the characters in which they are embedded. In fact, about 80 percent of Chinese characters are *phonograms* that consist of one radical that signifies the character's meaning and a second radical that indicates its pronunciation. The semantic radical is most often located on the left or top side of the character with the phonological radical located on the right or bottom side, though this is not always true. Characters can contain up to nine radicals and those radicals are arranged in a variety of different manners (e.g., left-right, above-below, inside-outside, etc.). There are currently about 220 radicals in circulation in the writing system – an admittedly large number but small enough that their redundancy across characters makes the learning of those characters significantly easier.

The Chinese Language and Writing System

With the majority of Chinese characters being phonograms, the remainder can be sorted into three other broad categories:

1. the simple pictographic characters;
2. ideographic characters that represent abstract concepts using symbols whose meanings are suggested by the visual forms of the characters (e.g., the character 上 shown in Figure 2.3 meaning "above");
3. associative compound characters whose meanings are suggested by their constituent radicals (e.g., the character 武 meaning "military force" or "martial arts" and pronounced /wu3/ consists of radicals meaning "dagger-ax" and "stop").

Only the associative compound characters and phonograms remain productive in the modern writing system; the number of pictographic and ideographic characters is largely closed in that most concrete referents and concepts that are easy to depict have already been represented by characters.

Returning now to Figure 2.6 and our discussion of phonograms, it is important to note that the phonetic radicals vary in terms of how diagnostic they are with respect to a given character's pronunciation. Because most phonetic radicals can be characters on their own and thus have a pronunciation,[8] a phonogram can be regular, for example, if its pronunciation is the same as the phonetic radical embedded within it.[9] However a phonogram can be irregular if its pronunciation is different from its phonetic radical. Phonetic radicals can also vary in terms of their consistency, with the pronunciation of some being relatively consistent across the characters that contain them, and the pronunciations of others being relatively inconsistent across their characters. Both properties of characters are respectively illustrated by the examples shown in Panels A and B of Figure 2.8. Finally, because individual characters correspond to monomorphemic syllables, Chinese also exhibits a large amount of homophony, which in turn means that characters can vary in terms of their phonological density. As shown in Figure 2.8C, for example, some pronunciations are common to many characters so those characters exhibit relatively high homophone density, whereas other pronunciations are only shared by a few characters so they exhibit relatively low density.

---

[8] There are also a small proportion of the phonetic radicals that are not standalone characters, but because they consistently appear in characters that share similar pronunciations, are also deemed to be phonetic radicals; e.g., the top (complex) radical in characters 奖 /jiang3/, 浆, /jiang1/, 桨 /jiang3/, and 酱 /jiang4/.

[9] Note that definitions of "phonogram regularity" can either include or ignore tonal similarity. This is also true for definitions of "phonological consistency" and "homophone density" (see Chapter 3).

Phonetic radical	其 /qi2/		(A)
	Regular phonograms	**Irregular phonograms**	
Phonograms	棋, 麒 /qi2/ /qi2/	基, 箕 /ji1/ /ji1/	

Phonetic radical	唐 /tang2/	白 /bai2/	(B)
	Consistent phonograms	**Inconsistent phonograms**	
Phonograms	糖, 塘, 瑭, 搪, 溏 (all pronounced /tang2/)	伯, 帕, 拍, 珀, 泉 /bo2/ /pa4/ /pai1/ /po4/ /quan4/	

	High density	**Low density**	(C)
Homophones:	其, 奇, 齐, 旗, 骑, 歧, 祈, 祁, 哇, 鳍 (all pronounced /qi2/)	乐, 勒 (all pronounced /le4/)	

Figure 2.8 Example phonograms of phonetic radical variation
The example phonograms show how phonetic radicals can vary in terms of their:
(A) regularity; (B) consistency; and (C) homophone density.

The fact that Chinese characters vary in terms of their phonological regularity, consistency, and density is thus similar to what is found in languages with alphabetic writing systems like English, where individual words can vary in terms of their regularity (e.g., "cat" vs. "yacht"), consistency (e.g., "pint" vs. "mint," "hint," "lint," etc.), and density (e.g., "-at" in "cat," "hat," "sat," etc. vs. "-eopard" in "leopard"). However, in the case of alphabetic writing systems, these variables are directly related to the relationships between the individual graphemes (i.e., letter and letter combinations like "sh") and phonemes in a manner that is not possible with Chinese. This difference underscores another fundamental distinction between the two writing systems.

In alphabetic writing systems, the pronunciations of words can be generated in two ways: by retrieving the pronunciation directly from memory, or by "sounding out" the letters (Coltheart et al., 2001). The first method is often referred to as *addressed phonology* because the representation of a word's pronunciation is inferred to be retrieved from some "address" in memory. By contrast, the second method is referred to as *assembled phonology* because the pronunciation is constructed from "rules" that specify the set of *grapheme-to-phoneme correspondences* (*GPCs*) within a language. By this account, addressed phonology is required to pronounce words that do not conform to a language's GPCs (e.g., "yacht" and "colonel" in English), where assembled phonology is required to pronounce unknown letter strings (e.g., "brane" and "flink").[10]

In contrast, the pronunciation of individual Chinese characters cannot be assembled from their constituent parts but must instead be retrieved from memory in a manner similar to what presumably happens with irregular words (e.g., "yacht") in English. The fact that the pronunciations of Chinese characters must be generated using addressed phonology has led to descriptions of Chinese phonology as being available to the reader in an "all or none" manner. For example, as Perfetti et al. (2005) argue:

> ...in an alphabetic system, the word-level units do not wait for a complete specification of all letter units prior to activating word level phonology (i.e., cascade style). In Chinese, the word-level phonology is not activated prior to a full orthographic specification of the character – hence, threshold style. (Perfetti et al., 2005: 55)

Although the distinction between "cascade style" versus "threshold style" phonology as articulated by Perfetti and colleagues (see also Coltheart et al., 1993) is an important one for understanding how Chinese differs from alphabetic writing systems, we hasten to add one important qualifier. Although "threshold style" might accurately describe how the pronunciations of individual characters are generated, the pronunciations of multi-character words can probably also be generated via a process that is more analogous to assembled phonology. That is, the pronunciations of the individual characters might be "sounded out" and then blended to produce the pronunciation of the whole word. Thus, one might argue that, although individual characters play the equivalent of both syllables and morphemes in languages that use alphabetic writing systems, the characters can also play the role of graphemes in that they can be used to assemble the pronunciations of multi-character words. This claim requires one additional caveat, however.

As mentioned previously, an important distinction between alphabetic writing systems and written Chinese is that, in the former, the "building blocks" of words, the individual letters, are arranged along a single horizontal dimension, whereas in the latter, the "building blocks" of words

---

[10] The distinction between addressed vs. assembled phonology also provides a natural account of the two most common types of dyslexia or reading-specific impairment: *phonological dyslexia* is an impairment in the capacity to use assembled phonology whereas *surface dyslexia* is an impairment in the capacity to use addressed phonology (see Castles & Coltheart, 1993). More will be said about dyslexia in the reading of Chinese in Chapter 5.

2.3 The Modern Chinese Writing System

are both hierarchical (i.e., consist of radicals and characters) and arranged along two spatial dimensions. These distinctions are important because having a better understanding of Chinese words will likely inform our understanding of two general issues in the psychology of reading.

The first is called the *alignment problem* and refers to the question: How do readers (most often) perceive the correct order of letters within words? In reading the word "cats," for example, how does the reader know that the word is not "acts" or "cast"? Early models of word identification (e.g., McClelland & Rumelhart's, 1981 interactive-activation model, as discussed in Chapter 1) simply ignored this question by assuming that individual letters are encoded and represented in each of their respective "slots" (e.g., for the word "cats," the letter "c" would be encoded in the first spatial position, "a" encoded in the second, and so on). The fact that certain types of letter-transposition errors are more common (e.g., mistaking "cast" for "cats") than others (e.g., mistaking "cars" for "cats") led to the recognition that the individual letters within a word are not encoded veridically but are instead encoded in some manner that is subject to error. More contemporary models therefore make some attempt to explain these findings by assuming that the positions of letters are subject to spatial uncertainty (Gomez et al., 2008; Norris & Kinoshita, 2012), are converted into temporal codes that are subject to error (Davis, 2010; Whitney, 2001), are affected by the syllabic structure of words as represented in memory (Taft & Krebs-Lazendic, 2013), or also include representations of spatially adjacent letter pairs (i.e., open bigrams; Grainger & van Heuven, 2003).

The second general issue is related to the first and pertains to the question: What are the basic features in visual word identification? In alphabetic writing systems like that of English, for example, there is evidence that the individual letters that comprise words are the basic features that are used in lexical processing. One type of evidence supporting this claim is the letter-transposition effects mentioned earlier, along with the facts that these errors are usually much more difficult to detect than letter-substitution errors but much easier to detect than transpositions involving larger units, such as morphemes (e.g., mistaking "cowboy" for "boycow"). Another type of evidence is that, during natural reading, the individual letters that are initially perceived on the printed page appear to be rapidly converted into abstract orthographic representations that are invariant across fonts, case, or other typographical factors. For example, in eye-movement experiments where participants read text displayed in alternating lower- and upper-case letters (e.g., "LiKe ThIs"), there is no cost associated with changing (e.g., "lIkE tHiS") as compared to not changing ("LiKe ThIs") the case in which the letters are displayed following each successive saccade (McConkie & Zola, 1979). This finding suggests that the lower- and upper-case forms of letters that are as markedly different as "g" and "G" or "a" and "A" are somehow represented in the same manner (i.e., as abstract letters that are somehow devoid of their specific visual features), thereby allowing the set of twenty-six abstract letters in English to function as the invariant features that are used to access a reader's lexicon.

As will be discussed at length in Chapter 3, whether and how this happens during the reading of Chinese is unclear. What is clear, however, is that Chinese words can be decomposed into characters which can then be further decomposed into complex radicals, simple radicals, or strokes (see Figure 2.6). Adding to this complexity is the fact that these units can:

1. play multiple functional roles (e.g., the radical 苗 in the character 猫 /mao1/, meaning "cat," can also be a single-character word 苗 /miao2/, meaning "sprout," which consists of two simple radicals, 艹 and 田);
2. occur in a variety of spatial locations (e.g., the radical 木 occurs in the top half of the character 杰 but the right side of character 休); and
3. undergo some amount of distortion in both their shape and size to accommodate their spatial locations (e.g., compare the radical 土 in the characters 坝 vs. 吐).

Each of these problems lacks a direct analog in alphabetic writing systems, making most models of word-identification (which have been developed around English) of questionable value for finding their solutions. And as we shall see in Chapter 3, although models of Chinese word identification have made valiant attempts to explain key behaviors related to the reading of Chinese characters and words, these attempts have often required a few simplifying assumptions that have sidestepped many of the inherent difficulties discussed here. These issues will be revisited in the upcoming chapters.

2.4 Conclusion

This chapter was intended to provide a brief introduction to the Chinese language and writing system – one that allows a reader who is unfamiliar with either to understand the remainder of this book. Because the focus of this book will be the reading of Chinese, and how it is like but also different from the reading of alphabetic writing systems such as that of English, our discussion of the Chinese language has only been intended to provide a context for any subsequent discussion of the Chinese writing system. Therefore, in the remainder of this book, we discuss in more detail how properties of the Chinese writing system have influenced how readers identify printed characters and words (Chapter 3), the skilled reading of text (Chapter 4), and the development of skilled reading, its impairment, and what has been learned from cognitive neuroscience about reading (Chapter 5). These chapters will each discuss the evidence about their respective topics that has been accumulated from behavioral and brain-imaging experiments and computer models of Chinese reading.

CHAPTER 3

Character and Word Identification

Chapter 2 provided a brief overview of the Chinese language, as well as the historical development and modern features of the Chinese writing system. This chapter will expand upon the latter topic to review what has been learned about what is arguably *the* core mental process involved in reading – the identification of Chinese characters and words. However, due to the unique nature of the Chinese writing system, the review will include some discussion of topics that would not be addressed in a review of what is known about the identification of words in English or other alphabetic writing systems.[1] These aspects of lexical processing are related to the fact that written Chinese:

1. does not use blank spaces or other obvious indicators of word boundaries;
2. consists of words that contain one to four uniformly sized, box-shaped characters and are typically composed of a hierarchy of strokes, radicals, and complex radicals that are rendered along two spatial dimensions;
3. does not provide the means of generating the pronunciations of individual characters using *grapheme-phoneme correspondence* (*GPC*) rules to "sound out" their pronunciations; and
4. has a large character inventory that can readily identified by skilled Chinese readers.

This chapter will therefore review what has been learned about how these four characteristics of the Chinese writing system influence character and word identification, using what is known about the identification of

---

[1] Because it is cumbersome to keep repeating the phrase "words in English or other alphabetic writing systems," we will instead use the abbreviated "alphabetic words" with the understanding that this is shorthand for the former and is meant to encompass (mostly) European languages like English, German, and French that use the Roman alphabet.

alphabetic words as a conceptual "scaffold" to organize the discussion. Our discussion will also be organized around the two general methods that have been used to study word identification: first, behavioral experiments that use tasks that require participants to identify or otherwise process words and that have informed our understanding of the *cognitive* processes that support reading; and second, theories and computational models that have been used to simulate and explain findings from the former. These methods are complementary and together allow for a more comprehensive account of what happens during reading. We therefore now turn to the first method, behavioral experiments, and review what they have taught us about the cognitive processes that support the processing and identification of first alphabetic words and then Chinese characters and words.

3.1 Behavioral Experiments

The topic of how words are identified is one of the most studied in psychology, with a history spanning more than a century (e.g., Huey, 1908). For that reason, and because the volume of research on Chinese character and word identification has dramatically increased during the last decade, our strategy for discussing the latter will be to review what is known about the identification of *alphabetic* words briefly and then use this to highlight how these findings compare to what has been learned about Chinese. Table 3.1 lists the key empirical findings that will be reviewed. This list is not exhaustive but is instead meant to focus our discussion on some of the more important findings that, because they have theoretical implications for our understanding of the mental processes that support skilled reading, have been useful for developing and testing models of word identification (for a review, see Reichle, 2021). For example, findings related to specific types of reading impairment or *dyslexia* might have been included here but are not because they will discussed in Chapter 5. It is also important to note that the findings listed in Table 3.1 are also included because they are robust, having been demonstrated using the different word-identification tasks that were discussed in Chapter 1. And as will be made explicit later in this chapter, a few of the findings (e.g., orthographic-phonological regularity or consistency) differ between the Chinese versus alphabetic writing systems due to fundamental differences in their nature.

As Table 3.1 shows, the findings can be grouped into four broad categories. These categories denote the nature of the processing being considered, and whether it is specific to a word's *orthography* (i.e., spelling), *phonology* (i.e., pronunciation), or *semantics* (i.e., meaning), or to the

48   Character and Word Identification

Table 3.1 *Important findings related to the learning and identification of alphabetic words*

Category	Effects	Brief descriptions
Orthographic	word & pseudo-word superiority	letters in words and pseudo-words are identified more accurately than letters in isolation
	neighborhood density & frequency	density and frequency of orthographic neighborhood facilitates/inhibits lexical processing (i.e., is task dependent)
	letter transposition & substitution	detection of letter transposition/ substitutions varies by within-word position
Phonological	phonological structure	words have phonological structure (e.g., stress)
	phonological priming	access to phonology is rapid and can be cascaded
	orthographic-phonological regularity/consistency	grapheme-phoneme correspondences can vary in terms of their regularity/consistency
Semantic	categorical structure	word meanings have categorical structure (e.g., typicality)
	semantic priming	access to semantics can be cascaded
	morphological structure	word meanings generated via derivation, inflection, compounding, etc.
Learning	word learning	new words can be learned very rapidly (e.g., single exposure)
	repetition priming	repetition facilitates lexical processing
	word frequency	frequency of encounter facilitates lexical processing
	age of acquisition	age of initial learning facilitates lexical processing

learning of words generally. For instance, one paradoxical finding related to the processing of a word's orthographic form is that a letter displayed in the context of a word is more accurately identified than the same letter displayed in isolation (Reicher, 1969; Wheeler, 1970). This *word-superiority effect* is presumably due to the fact the identification of a letter that is displayed in a word receives some type of top-down support from the representation of the word in which it occurs (McClelland & Rumelhart, 1981). Within the framework of the *interactive-activation* model that was introduced in Chapter 1, for example, the processing of the letter "a" displayed in the word "cat" would be facilitated because the node representing the letter "a" would receive some amount of additional activation from the "cat" word node – additional activation that would be absent if the letter "a" is displayed in isolation. That this finding is related to orthographic rather than phonological or semantic processing is suggested by the fact that the identification of letters displayed in *pseudo-words* or letter strings that resemble real words are also facilitated relative to letters displayed in isolation – a *pseudo-word-superiority effect* (Rumelhart & McClelland, 1982). The explanation for this latter finding is that, in the context of a pseudo-word, a letter node will receive some additional activation from those word nodes that the pseudo-word happens to resemble, irrespective of the fact that the pseudo-word itself is not represented in memory. For example, the letter "a" in the pseudo-word "cal" would be supported by the activation of words like "cat," "cab," "pal," and so on. This in turn suggests that orthographic similarity, and not phonology or semantics, is responsible for the word- and pseudo-word-superiority effects.

Another finding related to orthography is that the speed and accuracy with which a word is identified is often affected by its orthographic similarity to other words, as measured by its number of *orthographic neighbors*, or words that differ in spelling by a single substituted letter (Coltheart et al., 1977), as well as the frequency of those orthographic neighbors (e.g., see Andrews, 1997). For example, the word "cat" has many orthographic neighbors (e.g., "rat," "hat," "cap," "cut," etc.), some of which occur more often in printed text (e.g., "car"), whereas a word like "leopard" has only one, less frequently occurring neighbor (e.g., "leotard"). The pattern of findings related to orthographic neighborhood size and frequency is more complicated, however, in that the effects tend to be modulated by the task that is used to measure them. For example, using naming, words having more or higher frequency neighbors are pronounced more rapidly than words having fewer or lower frequency neighbors (Andrews, 1989, 1992; Grainger, 1990; Sears et al., 1995), presumably because words having many neighbors can be pronounced using more common GPC rules or by way of analogy to their neighbors. However, in lexical decision the opposite pattern is sometimes evident, with slower responses to words having many higher frequency orthographic neighbors (Grainger, 1990; Grainger et al., 1989), presumably because such words are more difficult to uniquely identify and thus discriminate from nonwords than are words that have fewer neighbors. At a minimum, these effects collectively show that the efficiency with which a word can be processed is affected by properties of other, similarly spelled words.

One last finding related to orthographic processing is that lexical processing is disrupted in varying degrees by specific types of letter transpositions and substitutions. For example, it is easier to confuse or misperceive "cats" for "cast" than it is to confuse "cats" for "cars" because the former pair of letter strings involve letter *transpositions* while the latter involves letter *substitutions*. These letter transposition or substitution effects have been reported using perceptual-identification (Gomez et al., 2008) and lexical-decision tasks (Perea & Lupker, 2003, 2004; Perea et al., 2005; Schoonbaert & Grainger, 2004), and they provide important clues about how the word-identification system solves the *alignment problem*, which refers to how the relative order of letters within words are perceived and represented in memory. These accounts posit that the spatial positions of individual letters are represented with some degree of uncertainty (Gomez et al., 2008; Norris & Kinoshita, 2012), or are converted to temporal signals (e.g., the first letter in a word propagates its signal first, followed by the second, and so on) that are also subject to noise (Davis, 2010; Whitney, 2001; Whitney & Cornelissen, 2008), or are affected by how the syllabic structure of words is represented (Taft & Krebs-Lazendic, 2013), or due to the fact that pairs of spatially adjacent words are also represented in memory (i.e., open bigrams; Grainger & van Heuven, 2003). These accounts can explain why the mis-ordering of letters sometimes occurs and thus the misperception of words. These accounts also indicate that, contrary to what had been assumed (i.e., that letters simply activate their corresponding representations in fixed "slots"; e.g., McClelland & Rumelhart, 1981), the alignment problem is non-trivial and cannot be ignored by accounts of word identification.

Returning now to Table 3.1, the second broad category of empirical findings is related to phonology, or how words are pronounced. At its most basic level, the capacity to read aloud printed words indicates that their orthographic forms can somehow be used to generate their pronunciations. As was briefly mentioned in Chapter 2, this can happen in two different ways for alphabetic words. The first is that a word's orthographic form is used as a cue to access its pronunciation from memory directly. The second is that knowledge of the language's GPC rules can be used to generate a word's pronunciation from its letters. Note that, by the second account, the word does not necessarily have to be "sounded out" aloud as children often do when they are learning how to read; rather, the GPC rules are assumed to operate below the level of conscious awareness in a rapid, largely automatic manner to convert letters into sounds. These two different ways of pronouncing words are suggested by two simple observations. First, it is possible to pronounce words that do not conform to a language's GPC

3.1 Behavioral Experiments

rules (e.g., "yacht" and "colonel"), suggesting that these pronunciations are accessed directly from memory, perhaps in a manner analogous to how objects are named. And second, it is possible to pronounce nonwords (e.g., "kint" and "pargon") that, by definition, are not stored in memory and thus require the use of some type of assembled phonology. Finally, it is important to note that the phonological information that is available is varied and can be quite complex, including not only the phonemes within the language but also information about spoken stress patterns, how the pronunciations of words are modified when they are contracted, and so on.

A second fact about phonology is that it is rapidly available during lexical processing. Evidence supporting this claim comes from studies (e.g., Lewellen et al., 1993; Van Orden, 1987) in which participants were instructed to make semantic decisions about a sequence of words (e.g., "Does the word refer to a flower?"). Unbeknownst to the participants, some of the words included words that require a "no" response ("rows"), but that happen to be homophones of words that would require a "yes" response (e.g., "rose"), as well as words that were matched for their orthographic similarity (e.g., "robs"). The key finding of these studies was that participants were more likely to (incorrectly) make affirmative responses to the homophones than the spelling-matched control words, presumably because the processing of these items rapidly activated their phonological representations and, in so doing, partially activated the meanings of their homophones – words that *would* require "yes" responses. Such results suggest that phonological processing occurs very rapidly, and that the pronunciations of words provide a means to access their meanings. It is important to acknowledge, however, that this account remains equivocal; for example, Taft and van Graan (1998) have provided evidence suggesting that a word's phonological form is activated even when its orthographic form is inaccessible, and that the phonological information is active in working memory rather than being used to access meaning per se.

One final important fact about phonology is that the pronunciations of words differ in terms of how well they conform to a language's GPC rules. For example, words like "brain" and "toad" conform to the GPC rules of English because their pronunciations can be accurately predicted if one knows how their *graphemes* are pronounced.[2] The two words are thus

---

[2] Graphemes are not the same as letters, and there is not always a one-to-one correspondence between the graphemes and phonemes. This can be illustrated using a few examples from English: (1) the letter pair "sh" correspond to two graphemes but a single phoneme, /ʃ/; (2) the letter pair "ph" is a single grapheme and corresponds to one phoneme, /f/; and (3) the letter "x" is a single grapheme that corresponds to two phonemes, /ks/.

regular. However, words like "yacht" and "colonel" are *irregular* in that they violate the English GPC rules. Using these definitions, words vary categorically with most being regular but some being irregular. However, the pronunciations of words can also vary in terms of their consistency across similarly spelled words. For example, the word "cat" is consistent because other words that share the /æt/ *rime* (i.e., the part of the syllable containing its vowel and any subsequent letters) such as "rat," "bat," and "hat" are all pronounced similarly (i.e., they all rhyme). In contrast, the word "pint" is inconsistent because its pronunciation /paɪnt/ is at odds with its orthographic neighbors (e.g., "hint," "lint," "mint." etc.) that contain the rime /ɪnt/. Using these definitions, words can vary along a continuum of consistency depending on the relative numbers of similarly spelled words whose rimes are either pronounced the same or differently (for excellent discussions of regularity vs. consistency, see Coltheart et al., 2001; Plaut et al., 1996).

As Table 3.1 shows, the third broad category of findings to be reviewed here are those related to the semantics or meanings of words. As shown, the first is that semantic information seems to be structured in memory. For example, information about categories appears to be organized hierarchically, with representations of categories at the *basic level* (Rosch & Mervis, 1975) sharing most features within a given category but also having more distinctive features than the higher-level, superordinate categories to which they belong, as well as fewer idiosyncratic features than the subordinate categories that they subsume. To illustrate this, consider the categories "table" and "chair." These are two basic-level categories. Each category can be readily defined by a set of features that are common to all (or at least most) instances of chairs, on one hand, and of tables, on the other. In contrast, it is much more difficult to specify the features that are shared by all instances of the superordinate category, "furniture," to which they both belong. And similarly, the representations of "chair" versus "table" share fewer features in common than the more specific, subordinate instances within either of the two categories (e.g., "kitchen table" and "coffee table" share most of their features, as do "kitchen chair" and "living room chair"). Finally, although the representations of some categories might be defined by sets of necessary and sufficient features (e.g., "triangle" is a polygon having three edges and three vertices), the representations of most natural categories (e.g., "bird," "planet," "disease," etc.) appear to lack defining features but instead have "family resemblance" structures, with the individual instances within the categories varying in terms of how closely they resemble the central tendency of the category,

3.1 *Behavioral Experiments*

or *prototype* (Rosch, 1973). Members of the "bird" category, for example, vary in terms of how well they resemble the prototypical bird, with robins and sparrows being good examples (i.e., they are small, fly, eat worms, etc.) and penguins and ostriches being poor examples. Importantly, our capacity to access the meanings of words reflects this underlying structure of semantic memory. This is evidenced, for example, in that semantic decisions are faster and more accurate for words corresponding to typical rather than atypical category instances (Rips et al., 1973; Rosch, 1973; Rosch & Mervis, 1975).

Categorical structure can also affect the earliest stages of word identification through *semantic priming*, which is the general phenomenon that processing a specific word like "doctor" can facilitate the processing of words that are related in their meanings like "hospital" or "nurse." Priming has been demonstrated using a variety of tasks including perceptual identification (Marcel, 1983), naming (Hutchinson et al., 2013), lexical decision (Meyer & Schvaneveldt, 1971; Neely, 1976, 1977; but cf. de Wit & Kinoshita, 2015), and semantic verification (de Wit & Kinoshita, 2014), with the basic priming paradigm typically requiring participants to make some type of response to *target* words (e.g., rapidly naming words like "hammer") that, on different experimental trials, are preceded by *prime* words that are semantically related (e.g., "nail") versus unrelated (e.g., "cup"). The key finding is that target processing is facilitated if it is preceded by a related prime as compared to either no prime or an unrelated prime (for reviews, see McNamara, 2005; Neely, 1991). The most widely accepted explanation for this facilitation is twofold. If the interval of time between the prime and target is very brief (e.g., a few hundred milliseconds), then the priming reflects *automatic spreading activation* wherein the process of activating the meaning of the concept corresponding to the prime word partially activates the meanings of semantically related concepts, facilitating the processing of their corresponding words, including the target (Collins & Loftus, 1975). However, if the interval between the prime and target is longer than several hundred milliseconds, then the priming effect can reflect conscious expectations about what the target might be. This slower, expectancy-based account also explains why priming can be observed if participants are instructed, for example, that the primes from a certain category (e.g., birds) are likely to be followed by targets from another, semantically unrelated category (e.g., names of professions); if the prime-target pair is consistent with a participant's expectations, then the normal facilitation in target processing is observed; otherwise, target processing can actually be slower and less accurate (Neely, 1977). Again, the important point of such demonstrations is that access to a word's meaning is rapid and can be facilitated due to how memory is structured, but with lexical processing also being affected in a less rapid and more effortful manner by conscious expectations.

The final finding related to semantics is that the forms of the words themselves are structured to specify meaning. For example, the individual units of meaning, or *morphemes*, can be combined to produce *compound words* (e.g., "snow" + "ball" = "snowball"). Word meanings can also be modified via both *inflectional* and *derivational morphology*. The former refers to the use of affixes and vowel changes that control grammatical agreement between a given word, called the *stem*, and the sentence of which it is part while preserving the core meaning of the stem. Examples would include adding the "s" suffix to a noun like "dog" to make it plural ("dogs") or changing the "u" to an "a" in the verb "run" to make it past tense ("ran"). Inflections therefore do not change the syntactic category of a word, but because they are based on grammatical rules, allow for precise predictions about their forms; for example, if told that "sark" is a singular noun, one can predict that "sarks" will likely refer to a collection of these things.

In contrast to inflectional morphology, derivational morphology is used to generate variants of the base morpheme that differ either in their meaning or grammatical category. An example here is the noun "beauty," which can be modified to generate a number of different derivational forms, including "beautify" (verb) and "beautiful" (adjective). Derivations are therefore productive because they allow new words to be coined; returning to the previous example involving the noun "sark," a verb can be generated by adding "-ify" to produce "sarkify." Again, the key point to be made here is that, in languages and writing systems like English, the relationship between a word's form and meaning is not arbitrary, but instead reflects the constraints among orthography, phonology, and meaning as evidenced by the rules that govern morphological structure.

Turning back to Table 3.1 once again, the final broad category of word-identification findings that have been documented are related to how new words are learned. Perhaps the most obvious but overlooked of these findings is that we are remarkably good at learning new words. For example, if university-educated adults can identify upwards of 70,000 printed words (Segbers & Schroeder, 2017)[3] by the time they are 18–25 years old, then

---

[3] The cited study estimated the number of known *lemmas*, or abstract, base forms of a given word that counted all inflectional variations of a word as a single word.

those same adults have somehow managed to learn eight to ten words per day (on average) across their lives. Even if this estimate is off by an order of magnitude, our capacity to learn new vocabulary is remarkable, as demonstrated by experiments showing that even young children can remember the orthographic forms of new words after a single encounter with those items (Nation et al., 2007). Such demonstrations suggest that, if provided the right context and if properly motivated, a person can learn the spelling, pronunciation, and meaning of a new word after a single encounter with the word (Taylor et al., 2010). Precisely how this happens remains unclear (see e.g., Nation, 2009), but the two findings discussed next provide clues about a few of the cognitive processes that might contribute to word learning.

The first is another priming phenomenon called *repetition priming*. This type of priming refers to the fact that a given word is identified more rapidly the second time it is encountered, even if that second encounter occurs days or weeks later (Feustel et al., 1983; Scarborough et al., 1977). This finding has been demonstrated using a variety of tasks, including perceptual identification (Jacoby, 1983; Whitlow, 1990), naming (Masson & Freedman, 1990), lexical decision (Forster & Davis, 1984; Fowler et al., 1985), and semantic verification (Durso & Johnston, 1979). This finding also suggests that the process of identifying a word somehow changes the word's representation in memory so that it can be processed more easily if it is encountered a second time.

The second finding related to word learning is that words that are frequently encountered in printed text are easier to identify than words that are encountered infrequently. This finding, called the *word-frequency effect*, is ubiquitous in that it is extremely robust and has been both demonstrated using a variety of tasks including perceptual identification (Howes & Solomon, 1951), naming (Balota & Chumbley, 1984), lexical decision (Forster & Chambers, 1973), and semantic verification (Forster & Hector, 2002). (The effect is so reliable that it is often used as a marker of lexical processing during tasks that entail some degree of reading, such as skimming rapidly displayed subtitles in films; Liao et al., 2021.)

As was true of repetition priming, word-frequency effects suggest that the process of identifying a word affects its representation in memory, making it easier to access if the word is encountered again. This conclusion is theoretically important because it might inform our understanding of how printed words are identified. For example, one account of both findings is that, if a word is repeatedly encountered, then its activation threshold decreases, allowing the representation to be more easily activated

(Grainger & Jacobs, 1996; Morton, 1969; Norris, 1994). Alternatively, repetition might cause the resting or baseline level of activation that is associated with the word's representation to increase, thereby making the representation easier to activate (Coltheart et al., 2001; McClelland & Rumelhart, 1981). Yet another explanation is that, through repetition, the connections that link a word's orthographic, phonological, and semantic representations are strengthened, allowing any one of the three to more efficiently activate the other two (Plaut et al., 1996; Seidenberg & McClelland, 1989). Finally, word repetition might result in new instances of the word being encoded into memory (e.g., as discrete memory traces), with the resulting redundancy then allowing more efficient retrieval of a word's lexical information (Ans et al., 1998; Kwantes & Mewhort, 1999; Reichle, 2021; Reichle & Perfetti, 2003). Of course, these accounts of repetition priming and word-frequency effects are not mutually exclusive or exhaustive; the two phenomena may require different accounts or accounts not considered here.

Finally, the last finding listed in Table 3.1 is called the *age-of-acquisition effect*. This finding refers to the fact that, with all else being equal (e.g., frequency of occurrence), words that are learned early in life (i.e., when first learning how to read) are on average easier to identify than words that are learned later in life (Caroll & White, 1973a, 1973b). This age-of-acquisition effect has been demonstrated using naming (Ellis & Morrison, 1998; Gerhand & Barray, 1998, 1999a; Morrison & Ellis, 1995, 2000) and lexical decision (Ellis & Morrison, 1998; Gerhand & Barray, 1999b; Turner et al., 1998), and is mentioned here because it provides evidence that factors other than the number of learning opportunities are also important for vocabulary acquisition. The finding suggests that the manner in which words are learned also plays a role in how readily they can later be identified. Another important example supporting this assertion includes differences in the relative spacing of the learning opportunities; for example, controlling for the number of encounters with a given word, encounters that are more widely distributed over a period of time typically lead to better retention of the newly learned words than the same number of encounters that occur in rapid succession (Wegener et al., 2023). This spacing effect along with the age-of-acquisition effect underscore the point that the mental processes that are responsible for the learning of vocabulary, although seemingly too simple to be worthy of serious investigation, are actually quite complex, and that there is still much remaining to be understood about how words are learned and how this in turn influences their processing and identification.

3.1 Behavioral Experiments

With this abbreviated review of what has been learned about the identification of words in alphabetic writing systems, it is now possible to shift our discussion towards the topic that is the focus of this book – the reading of Chinese and what is known about the identification of Chinese characters and words. This discussion will be organized around the same broad categories listed in Table 3.1, but with deviations as appropriate to describe findings that might be unique to the Chinese writing system (see Chapter 2). To facilitate this discussion, the findings related to the processing of Chinese characters and words are listed in Table 3.2, which is organized similarly to Table 3.1.

If we start this discussion with orthography, then one fact about the Chinese writing system that is so obvious as to almost be overlooked is that its characters can be extremely complex! In contrast to alphabetic writing systems where a small number of letters (e.g., the twenty-six in English or thirty in German) are sufficient to represent an unlimited number of different words, each one of the thousands of characters used in the contemporary Chinese writing system is unique. The fact that thousands of characters can be uniquely rendered is due to the fact that their complexity allows for an almost inexhaustible number of possible characters (e.g., Chang et al., 2018). Any given character can, for example, be used as the base for creating an entirely new character with the addition or substitution of a single stroke. And it is important to add that the type of complexity being discussed here is independent of word length; although words of different lengths can also vary in terms of their complexity, with longer words on average being more complex than shorter words (e.g., "cat" vs. "catacombs" in English, "猫" vs. "猫咪" in Chinese), the complexity of individual characters is mainly determined by their number and type of strokes. Remember that, as discussed in Chapter 2, characters written in the modern simplified Chinese writing system contain up to thirty-six strokes, and that each of these strokes can differ in terms of their location, orientation, length, and shape. Objectively, then, it is possible to quantify character complexity using, for example, the number of strokes, so that characters containing many strokes are defined as being more complex than characters containing fewer strokes. But does such a measure relate in any meaningful way to the intuition that complex characters are probably more difficult to represent or identify in memory?

Of course, this intuition might be subjective and might only be shared by people who are unfamiliar with the Chinese writing system. Several experiments have now provided affirmative evidence, consistent with the hypothesis that, even for skilled readers of Chinese, characters vary in

Character and Word Identification

Table 3.2 *Important findings related to the learning and identification of Chinese characters and words*

Category	Effects	Brief descriptions
Orthographic	complexity	visually complex characters are identified more slowly
	character/word superiority	radicals in characters and characters in words are identified faster than those in pseudo-characters or pseudo-words
	neighborhood density & frequency	density and frequency of stroke/radical/character neighborhood facilitates/inhibits lexical processing (i.e., is task dependent)
	radical/character transposition & substitution	sensitivity in radical position in characters and flexibility in character position in words
Phonological	phonological priming	access to phonology is rapid and obligatory
	orthographic-phonological regularity/consistency	character/word identification can vary in terms of their regularity/consistency
	phonological structure	homophones can be differentiated by sharing the same tone vs. not
Semantic	categorical structure	word meanings have categorical structure (e.g., typicality)
	semantic priming	access to semantics can be rapid
	morphological structure	word meanings generated via compounding, are affected by semantic transparency and other factors
Learning	repetition priming	repetition facilitates lexical processing
	radical/character/word frequency	frequency of encounter facilitates lexical processing but the interplay between units is complex
	age of acquisition	age of initial learning facilitates lexical processing

terms of their complexity and this variable influences the time required for their identification. The experiments have employed a variety of paradigms that generally entail participants naming or making rapid judgments about characters or pairs of characters or pseudo-characters (e.g., "Is this a real character or pseudo-character?" "Are these two characters the same or different?") in order to determine how their complexity affects the decision response times and accuracies. These studies indicate that,

3.1 Behavioral Experiments

with all else being equal, characters consisting of more strokes are more difficult to identify than characters consisting of fewer strokes (Leong et al., 1987; *D. Peng & Wang, 1997; *B. Yu & Cao, 1992; *B. Yu et al., 1995).[4] Perhaps not surprisingly given that characters containing more strokes also tend to contain more radicals (i.e., because radicals are made by strokes, their numbers are correlated), characters constituted by more radicals are also more difficult to identify than characters made up of fewer radicals (Y. P. Chen et al., 1996; *D. Peng & Wang, 1997; *W. Zhang & Feng, 1992; *B. Yu et al., 1995). Furthermore, despite the fact that the number of characters and radicals per character are correlated, the number of radicals per character appears to make an additional contribution to the complexity of a character. For example, controlling for the number of strokes, characters containing more radicals are more difficult to name and make lexical judgment about than characters containing fewer radicals (*D. Peng & Wang, 1997; *W. Zhang & Feng, 1992). Such findings are consistent with the intuition that character complexity affects their processing, but additionally suggests that their representation in memory is hierarchical, with complexity being defined at two levels – that of the strokes and that of the radicals.

As Table 3.2 shows, the next set of findings related to Chinese orthography concerns the word- and pseudo-word superiority effects. Recall that, in alphabetic writing systems, these findings refer to the fact that letters can be more accurately identified when they are displayed in the contexts of words and pseudo-words than when they are displayed in isolation (Reicher, 1969; Wheeler, 1970). Because Chinese words consist of characters and radicals rather than letters, the "markers" of these effects are relative differences in the ease of identifying radicals or characters that are displayed in the contexts of characters or words relative to being displayed in isolation. For example, using a Reicher-Wheeler task (see Chapter 1), *M. Shen et al. (1997) found a character-superiority effect, with radicals displayed in characters being identified more accurately than radicals displayed in isolation, similar to what has been reported in alphabetic languages. However, this effect actually reversed for pseudo-characters, with radicals displayed in pseudo-characters being identified less accurately than radicals displayed in isolation. M. Shen et al. (1997) also found that these effects were modulated by spatial location, being larger for left than right radicals in left-right configured characters and for top than bottom

---

[4] Our convention throughout the remainder of this book will be to indicate with asterisks those research articles that have only been published in Chinese.

radials in top-bottom configured characters. However, using both a Reicher-Wheeler task and a radical-judgment task (i.e., indicating whether a character contains a previously displayed radical), *Luo et al. (2010) failed to replicate M. Shen et al.'s (1997) findings, but instead found that radicals displayed in either two-radical characters or pseudo-characters were identified more slowly than the same radicals displayed adjacent to a non-linguistic symbol, "§." Although the discrepancies between these two studies may reflect methodological differences (i.e., the character or pseudo-character stimuli were displayed for 54–64 ms in Shen et al. vs. 350 ms in Luo et al.), there is additional evidence for the character-superiority effect when directly comparing radical identification in characters versus pseudo-characters. For example, in experiments that required participants to make speeded "same or different?" judgments about pairs of characters or pairs of pseudo-characters (each containing 2–3 radicals), the response latencies and accuracies were affected by both the legality of the characters and the legality of the radical positions within the pseudo-characters; responses to characters were faster and more accurate than responses to pseudo-characters containing radicals in legal positions, with those responses being in turn faster and more accurate than responses to pseudo-characters containing radicals in illegal positions (Y. P. Chen et al., 1996; see also *Cheng, 1981).

Turning now to the identification of characters within words, W. Shen and Li (2012) used a Reicher-Wheeler task and found that character identification was more accurate when a character was displayed in two-character words than in isolation, but that this effect was only evident when the character was the initial character of the word. Other studies similarly showed that characters are more readily identified if they are displayed in words than pseudo-words (*Cheng, 1981; X. Li & Pollatsek, 2011; Mattingly & Xu, 1994; Mok, 2009). Despite some inconsistencies, these findings collectively indicate that the top-down facilitation in the processing of a word's orthographic components that stems from having representations of those words in memory likely reflects at least two sources in the case of Chinese – the representations of individual characters and the representations of words.

Going back to Table 3.2 and the topic of orthographic neighborhood density and frequency, it is important to first note that, due to the hierarchical manner in which Chinese words are composed, the theoretical construct "orthographic neighborhood" can be defined at multiple levels, including using strokes or radicals within characters and characters within words. For example, two characters can be defined as being in the same "stroke neighborhood" if they differ by only a single stroke, whether that difference be a stroke addition, deletion, or substitution. Experiments that have attempted to examine the consequences of stroke neighborhood density or frequency have typically employed masked priming paradigms in which participants respond to target characters that are preceded by briefly displayed prime characters that either are or are not stroke neighbors of the target. These experiments have provided mixed evidence. For example, whereas D. Shen and Forster (1999) observed that stroke neighbor primes facilitated target processing relative to unrelated primes in both naming and lexical decision tasks, J. Wang et al. (2014) observed the oppositive effect employing a lexical decision task, with inhibitory priming. Although the reason for this discrepancy remains unclear, a recent experiment reported by L. Yu et al. (2022) suggests that the priming observed with stroke neighbors is perceptual in origin. In this experiment, primes containing one less stroke than the targets facilitated target processing as much as the targets themselves; however, target identification was slower when it was primed by a neighbor containing one more stroke than the target itself. Also, the amount of priming was not modulated by the frequency of the prime. These findings together suggest that, during visual processing, the perception of the individual strokes is somehow pooled to support the perception of the whole character, with a subset of the information contained in the whole character facilitating its processing more than a superset containing additional information (e.g., a stroke that is not actually present in the whole character).

Although orthographic neighborhood effects can also be defined by the sharing of radicals, it is important to remember that radicals can play different functional roles (i.e., phonological or semantic) in characters, and that these radicals can vary in terms of both their type frequency (i.e., how many different characters they occur in) and token frequency (i.e., how often the character(s) containing the radicals occur overall in printed text). The patterns of effects are therefore complex. For example, a number of experiments have demonstrated that both lexical decision responses to characters and the naming of characters are facilitated for characters that share their radicals with many different characters (i.e., type frequency), and that this pattern holds irrespective of whether the radicals are semantic (M. J. Chen & Weekes, 2004; Feldman & Siok, 1997, 1999; *J. Zhang & Jiang, 2008) or phonetic (Feldman & Siok, 1997, 1999; Q. Li et al., 2011; Taft & Zhu, 1997; *Z. Zhang et al., 2003; *J. Zhang & Jiang, 2008). These facilitatory effects are especially pronounced if the neighbor characters sharing the radicals with the target characters are not higher in frequency (Q. Li et al., 2011). This last finding is similar to what is observed with alphabetic writing systems (Grainger, 1990; Grainger et al., 1989) and likely reflects the fact that the Chinese target characters are also more readily confused with their higher frequency neighbors. This explanation is consistent with the finding that characters having higher frequency neighbors are named more slowly than those that do not (Q. Li et al., 2011; *J. Zhang & Jiang, 2008). However, it is important to emphasize that this explanation is probably not complete and may need to be adjusted in more careful consideration of the radicals' functional roles. For example, effects of neighborhood size or density might be confounded with other properties of the radicals that are related to their functional roles. There is evidence suggesting that this is true in that the size of the neighborhood effect of phonetic radicals is modulated by both the pronounceability of the radicals (*J. Zhang & Jiang, 2008) and the regularity and consistency of the characters in which the radical occurs (*Bi et al., 2006; Q. Li et al., 2011). Future research is clearly required to better understand the nature of these interactions, as well as how they might also be modulated by task demands.

Finally, with the last type of neighborhood effect in Chinese reading, which is defined by multi-character words that share all but one character, the findings are generally quite similar to those just reported in relation to radical neighborhood effects and the orthographic neighborhood effects that have been reported with alphabetic writing systems. So in summary, Chinese words that are similar to many other words by virtue of sharing all but one character with those words tend to be processed more rapidly, although the processing of those words can be slower if many of their neighbors are higher in frequency (H. W. Huang et al., 2006; M. Li et al., 2015, 2017; J. T. Wu et al., 2013).

As Table 3.2 shows, the final category of effects related to orthography are the transposition and substitution effects. As per our discussion of neighborhood effects, transpositions and substitutions can also be defined at the level of radicals and characters. In the case of radicals, the positions of two radicals within a character can be swapped resulting in a transposition, or a radical can be replaced by a different radical, resulting in a substitution. Because radicals can be located literally anywhere within a character, there are more possible kinds of transpositions (e.g., swapping two vertically arranged radicals) than in alphabetic writing systems because letters in the latter are normally arranged along a single (usually horizontal) dimension. However, because the characters in multi-character words

3.1 Behavioral Experiments

are also normally arranged along a single (usually horizontal) dimension, character transpositions are similar to letter transpositions in that they are restricted to the one dimension.

With that background, Taft et al. (1999) found that neither decisions about the lexical status of characters (Experiment 1) nor character-naming responses (Experiment 2) differed between the following two conditions: (1) transposable two-radical characters in which swapping the positions of the radicals would produce another character (e.g., 杏 vs. 呆) versus (2) well-matched but non-transposable two-radical characters (e.g., 寻). These results suggest that there is no discernable cost associated with whatever processing of the transposable characters might be required to avoid confusing them with their transposed counterparts.[5] In another study, Ding et al. (2004, Experiment 4) examined character priming in which the prime characters were either transposed versions of the target characters or completely unrelated to the target characters; for example, the target 杏 might be preceded by the prime 呆 (in which the target's two radicals have been swapped) or the prime 垂 (in which the radicals are completely different from those of the target). The key finding of this experiment was that, relative to the unrelated primes, the transposed primes inhibited target processing, especially if the targets were low in frequency. These findings suggest that readers of Chinese are highly sensitive to the relative positions of radicals within the two-dimensional layout of characters, and that the radicals are probably represented in a position-specific rather than position-invariant manner in memory. By this interpretation, the mental representations of characters consist of information about the identities of their component radicals *and* the correct spatial positions of those radicals; priming is therefore predicted to be effective only if both types of information are provided by the prime.

With respect to transposition effects within words, the available evidence suggests that, in contrast to radicals, the individual characters within multi-character words are represented in a position-invariant manner. For example, Taft et al. (1999, Experiment 5) found that lexical decision responses to multi-character words were slower and more prone to error if those words contained transposable characters (i.e., words in which swapping the order of its characters would generate other words; e.g., 带领

---

[5] The only radical-transposition effect observed in Taft et al.'s (1999) study involved four-radical pseudo-characters wherein transposing two of the radicals produced real characters (e.g., 湖). Taft et al. found that participants were more error-prone and slower to reject the transposable pseudo-characters than non-transposable pseudo-characters. This result suggests that there is a processing cost associated with having to determine the within-character positions of radicals.

and 领带) than if those words contained non-transposable characters (i.e., words in which swapping the order of the characters would generate non-words; e.g., 节目). This finding suggests that there is some degree of uncertainty or flexibility in terms of how the relative positions of characters within a word are represented, with the resolution of that uncertainty requiring additional effort or incurring a small processing cost.

Additional evidence consistent with this interpretation was reported by Gu et al. (2015). Their experiment compared lexical decision responses to two-character target words (e.g., 吝啬) that were preceded by three types of two-character primes: (1) identical primes (e.g., 吝啬); (2) transposed-character primes (e.g., 啬吝); and (3) unrelated pseudo-word primes (e.g., 菠秉). The identical prime facilitated target processing the most, but the transposed prime facilitated target processing more than the unrelated prime. And similarly, H. Yang and colleagues (2019, 2020) compared lexical decisions to four-character target words (e.g., 有所不同) preceded by three types of four-character primes: (1) primes containing center-character transpositions (e.g., 有不所同); (2) primes containing center-character substitutions (e.g., 有扑走同); and (3) transposition primes in which all of the characters were also in the reverse order of the targets (e.g., 同所不有). Target word processing was facilitated following transposition primes relative to substitution primes, and interestingly, priming was also observed in the third condition, with the reserved-order characters (H. Yang et al., 2019, 2020).

These results collectively support our earlier conclusion that, in contrast to radicals, which appear to be represented in a manner that maintains their within-character spatial positions, characters appear to be represented in a manner that is less specific to their within-word positions. Although this conclusion about the orthographic representation of Chinese might not have a direct analog in alphabetic writing systems, one might reasonably argue that the representation of radicals, characters, and words in Chinese can be loosely mapped onto the representation of letter features, letters, and words in English. In the latter, for example, what distinguishes "b" from "d" or "p" from "q" are the relative positions of the constituent letter features (i.e., whether the vertical lines are to the left or right of the circles); as such, one might predict that letter features are represented in a fairly position-invariant way – at least, more position invariant than the representations of letters within words.

Returning to Table 3.2, the next broad category of findings related to Chinese character and word identification are all related to phonology. As the table indicates, the first such finding is simply that access to the

3.1 Behavioral Experiments

pronunciations of characters and words is rapid and largely obligatory during the reading of Chinese. This claim might appear to contradict our earlier discussion of the Chinese writing system in Chapter 2, where we claimed that, in contrast to alphabetic writing systems, the Chinese writing system does not afford a means for GPC rules to be used to convert the written forms of characters into their spoken counterparts directly. However, as will be discussed below, the available evidence strongly suggests that, although the pronunciations of characters are retrieved from memory "threshold style" (to borrow the words of Perfetti et al., 2005: 55), this retrieval is both rapid and obligatory, thereby allowing information about a character's pronunciation and meaning to jointly constrain its identity (for reviews, see Perfetti et al., 2005; Tan & Perfetti, 1998a). As Perfetti et al. (2005: 57) further indicate, this conceptualization of phonological "mediation" is more consistent with the "labor mediation" interpretation of the word in that, in both alphabetic writing systems and Chinese, "phonology stabilizes word identity, even if it does not cause access to word meaning." This claim is supported by the results of a priming study reported by Perfetti and Tan (1998) that will be described at length below, in our discussion of Perfetti and colleagues' lexical constituency model.

However, other evidence consistent with this conceptualization of Chinese phonology comes from a backward-masking experiment reported by Tan et al. (1995). In this experiment, participants viewed briefly displayed target characters that were followed immediately by an experimental mask and then a pattern mask, with instructions to write down the target characters. The target exposure durations were manipulated, as were the relationships between the targets (e.g., 提 /ti2/ meaning "raise") and the experimental masks across three conditions: (1) homophonic (e.g., 啼 /ti2/ meaning "crow"); (2) synonymous (e.g., 抬 /tai2/ meaning "raise"); and (3) unrelated controls (e.g., 鼓 /gu3/ meaning "drum"). The key finding was that participants more accurately identified target characters that were followed by homophonic rather than synonymous or unrelated masks, suggesting that, as argued in Perfetti et al.'s (2005) claim, phonological information is useful in mediating a character's identity. Likewise, in a synonym-judgment experiment reported by Perfetti and Zhang (1995), participants viewed pairs of characters with instructions to indicate as rapidly and accurately as possible whether or not they were similar in meaning. The key finding of this study was that participants were more likely to make slower false positive responses (i.e., erroneously responded "yes") to semantically unrelated, homophonic character pairs, suggesting that there is phonological inference between the characters within a pair. This finding is important because, in performing the synonym-judgment task, it would presumably be advantageous to focus on the meanings of the characters and not their pronunciations. The clear presence of phonological inference therefore suggests that this is not possible – that the generation of the characters' pronunciations is obligatory and an essential part of what it means to "identity" a character.

The next set of findings related to phonology concerns the regularity and consistency of the pronunciations of the characters. Although access to a character's phonology appears to be "all or none" (i.e., threshold-style) and not incremental (i.e., cascaded) as it can be in alphabetic writing systems, a character's pronunciation can be regular or irregular, as well as consistent or inconsistent, as discussed in Chapter 2 (see Figure 2.8). As a reminder, the majority of Chinese characters are phonograms that consist of a pair of radicals, with the one on the left typically signifying the meaning of the character and the one on the right being phonetic and able to provide information about the character's pronunciation. A character that is pronounced the same as the phonetic radical that is embedded within it (ignoring possible differences in tone) is therefore regular whereas a character that is pronounced differently from its embedded radical is irregular. And in a similar manner, a phonetic radical can also be consistent if all of the characters containing it are pronounced the same; otherwise, the radical is said to be inconsistent. Finally, due to the large amount of homophony within the Chinese language, characters can vary in terms of their homophone density, with some characters sharing their pronunciation with a large number of other characters and having high homophone density but other characters sharing their pronunciation with few characters and thus having low homophone density.

As is true with alphabetic writing systems, there is evidence that these phonological variables affect the processing of Chinese characters and words. For example, several experiments have shown that Chinese characters can be named more rapidly and accurately if they are regular or consistent than if they are irregular or inconsistent (Bi et al., 2006, Experiment 2; *Cai et al., 2012; *L. Gao & Peng, 2005; Hue, 1992; Lee et al., 2005; Q. Li et al., 2011, Experiment 1; *Shu & Zhang, 1987; *J. Zhang & Wang, 2001). These findings indicate that accessing the pronunciation of a character by retrieving the pronunciation of its phonetic radical benefits from the two being consistent and from the relationship between the two being consistent across other characters. Furthermore, in experiments where other linguistic properties of the characters (e.g., their frequency) have been controlled, there is evidence that a character's homophone density also affects it processing. For example, both lexical decision and naming responses are faster to characters having higher than lower homophone density (*B. Chen & Ning, 2005, Experiment 1; *G. Yan et al., 2013; Ziegler et al., 2000), especially if those characters are low frequency (H. Chen et al., 2009). However, many specific details of these effects have yet to be worked out. For example, even though many studies have shown that both the character frequency and the position of the phonetic radical within the character (left, right, top, or bottom) modulate the phonological regularity effect, the precise nature of these results are often inconsistent (e.g., *Cai et al., 2012). Similarly, Ziegler et al.'s (2000) study suggests that the phonological frequency (i.e., the average frequency of the homophones) also affects character identification, facilitating lexical decisions to characters having higher phonological frequency while controlling for both homophone density and orthographic frequencies. This result, however, is inconsistent with the results of H. Chen et al.'s (2009) study.

The last findings related to phonology in Table 3.2 concern the phonological structure of characters and words. Like alphabetic scripts, the phonological codes in written Chinese also have internal structure. One unique feature associated with this structure, however, is each character's tone. The fact that each character has a tone quite naturally leads to the question of whether or not tones are integral to the identification of Chinese characters. The research addressing this question is relatively sparse compared to the other two sections reviewed above, in part because the variables of phonological regularity, consistency, and homophone density have not always been consistently defined as to the inclusion of tones along with consonants and vowels. For example, homophonic foils in the masking and priming studies (e.g., Perfetti & Zhang, 1995; Tan et al., 1995) were mostly matched on tones whereas this was not always the case when defining phonologically regular or consistent characters (e.g., Hue, 1992; Q. Li et al., 2011). Despite these limitations, some work has been done to examine the possible role of tone in Chinese character identification.

For example, in an experiment that used a semantic-relatedness judgment task (similar to the one used by Perfetti & Zhang, 1995), Xu et al. (1999) reported significant interference from homophonic distractors of the target characters relative to unrelated distractors, but this interference was only observed with exact homophones (i.e., those that shared the same consonants, vowels, and *tones* as the target characters). The authors attributed this difference between tonal versus non-tonal homophone-interference effects to the phonological representations of Chinese characters – that the tonal information is an essential part of the phonological retrieval in character identification, and tonal information specifically helps narrow down the identity of characters during their identification. *J. Zhang and Wang (2001) similarly found that participants were faster to name characters whose phonetic radicals shared the same tone as their parent characters than those that did not, regardless of the regularity between the radicals and their parent characters.

Finally, a tonal homophone-interference effect was also evident in a Stroop naming study[6] that explored the phonological processing in Chinese character identification (Spinks et al., 2000). In this study, four key types of stimuli were presented to participants: (1) characters representing the names of colors; (2) homophones sharing the same tone as the characters in the first condition; (3) homophones having different tones from the characters in the first condition; and (4) semantic associates of the characters in the first condition. The characters were displayed in different font colors and participants were instructed to name the color of stimuli as rapidly and accurately as possible. Of relevance here, Spinks and colleagues found inflated naming latencies and error rates in the incongruent conditions (e.g., the character referring to the color red and both its homophone and semantic associate when the characters were displayed in green font), and that the homophonic-interference effect was more robust for tonal than non-tonal homophones. This finding is thus also consistent with the hypothesis that tonal information is actively used to identify Chinese characters (see e.g., Taft & Chen, 1992).

Returning once again to Table 3.2, the third broad category of findings concerning the identification of Chinese characters and words is related to semantics. Because the purpose of reading is to understand the content or meaning of the text, it is perhaps not surprising that the main findings related to meaning that are observed with alphabetic scripts have also been reported with Chinese. For example, the semantic representations of Chinese words have categorical structure such that semantic-verification responses to sentences that require knowledge of superordinate categories (e.g., "raven is an animal") are slower when compared to basic or subordinate categories (e.g., "raven is a bird"), and similarly slower

---

[6] In the Stroop paradigm, participants name words displayed in different colored fonts as rapidly as possible. The key finding is that color words displayed in incongruously colored fonts (e.g., "red" displayed in blue font) are named more slowly and less accurately than the same words displayed congruously colored fonts ("red" displayed in red font) (Stroop, 1935).

compared to sentences that require knowledge of atypical (e.g., "crane is a bird") than typical (e.g., "sparrow is a bird") category instances (e.g., *Y. M. Chen & Peng, 1985; see also *B. Chen, 1993; *Miao & Sang, 1991). Categorical structure can of course also influence the identification of words through semantic priming (e.g., *B. Chen & Peng, 2001; *B. Chen et al., 2003; *Y. Guo et al., 2021). However, due to the more direct nature of the links between orthography and semantics in Chinese compared to alphabetic writing systems, there is some suggestion that these semantic priming effects occur more rapidly and reliably in Chinese, with a character's semantic information becoming available as rapidly as its phonological information (e.g., *B. Chen & Peng, 2001; *B. Chen et al., 2003; Perfetti & Zhang, 1995; Tan & Perfetti, 1998b).

As discussed in Chapter 2, however, the Chinese language contains very few grammatical inflections or derivations that necessitate changing a word's form (e.g., the tenses of verbs or numerical agreement between nouns and verbs). Instead, Chinese words are mainly formed through the compounding of morphemes. For example, the compound word 家长们 meaning "parents" is constructed from the stem 家长 meaning "parent" and the suffix 们 meaning "many." This extensive use of compounding has likely contributed to the fact that most studies of Chinese morphology have investigated how compound Chinese words are processed and identified (e.g., via decomposition of their constituent characters vs. direct accessing whole-word representations), and how the semantic transparency of the compound words affects this processing. Despite inconsistency in the reported results, the general pattern seems to be that, with all else being equal, transparent compound words are processed more rapidly than their opaque counterparts (e.g., *B. Gao & Gao, 2005; Tse et al., 2017), and that the meanings of transparent compound words are more readily arrived at through decomposition (D. Peng et al., 1999; Tse & Yap, 2018; *C. Wang & Peng, 1999, 2000).

Turning one final time to Table 3.2, the last category of findings to be discussed is related to the learning of Chinese characters and words. Perhaps not surprisingly given that these findings reflect the basic nature of human memory, which is presumably invariant across different populations of language speakers, the learning-related phenomena that have been observed in the learning English words are mostly evident in the learning of Chinese characters and words. For example, characters and words that are acquired early in life have a processing advantage and are thus identified more rapidly and accurately than characters and words that are learned later (e.g., Y. Chang & Lee, 2020; *B. Chen, You, et al., 2007;

*B. Chen et al., 2004; B. Chen, Zhou, et al., 2007; Y. Y. Liu et al., 2007; Q. Zhang et al., 2022). There are a few interesting findings, however, that appear to be specific to Chinese.

For example, because of the hierarchical nature of Chinese orthography (i.e., radicals embedded in characters which make up words), it is perhaps not too surprising that readers of Chinese are sensitive to the frequency of occurrence of radicals, characters, and words. Experiments support this conjecture. For example, the studies of Taft and Zhu (1997) discussed earlier examined the effect of radical type frequency (i.e., the number of different characters in which a given radical occurs) and found more rapid naming and lexical-decision responses to characters containing high- than low-frequency radicals.[7] Other experiments have likewise examined the token frequency of characters (e.g., Mattingly & Xu, 1994; I. Liu et al., 1996; Y. Y. Liu et al., 2007; Sze et al., 2015; *C. Wang & Peng, 1999; *J. T. Wu et al., 2013; *W. Zhang & Feng, 1992) and words (e.g., M. Li et al., 2017; Xiong et al., 2023; *C. Wang & Peng, 1999; *J. T. Wu et al., 2013; Tsang et al., 2018; Tse & Yap, 2018) and have shown that higher frequency orthographic units are typically responded to more rapidly and accurately than lower frequency units, but with a few theoretical interesting exceptions involving experiments in which, for example, the frequencies of characters versus words have been factorially manipulated.

First consider experiments that have used the lexical-decision task. Although these studies have consistently observed facilitative word frequency effects, the modulating effect of character frequency has been inconsistent (e.g., Xiong et al., 2023; *C. Wang & Peng, 1999; *J. T. Wu et al., 2013). *C. Wang and Peng (1999), orthogonally manipulated the overall frequency of two-character target words as well as the average frequencies of their characters, and observed a facilitatory effect of the (average) character frequency in high- but not low-frequency words. And in two similar studies where the whole word and initial character frequencies were orthogonally manipulated, J. T. Wu et al. (2013, Experiment 2) failed to find a character frequency effect, whereas Xiong et al. (2023) actually observed an *inhibitory* effect of the initial character's frequency when the target words were low frequency. Finally, when the manipulation of initial character frequency was nested within high- and low-frequency words, J. T. Wu et al. (2013, Experiment 3) observed an inhibitory character frequency effect regardless of the word frequency. Similarly inconsistent patterns of results were also observed

---

[7] Note that this definition of frequency makes the radical type-frequency effect equivalent to a radical neighborhood effect in that high-frequency radicals by definition also have more neighbors.

across two lexical-decision mega data sets: Tse et al.'s (2017) data set using two-character traditional Chinese words, and Tsang et al.'s (2018) data set using 1–4-character simplified Chinese words. Of relevance here, although Tse and colleagues observed a facilitatory character-frequency effect, with more facilitation for low- than high-frequency words, Tsang and colleagues reported an inhibitory character-frequency effect in their original regression analysis (Tsang et al., 2018: 1773) that controlled for both the number of words that a character formed and the cumulative character frequency.

Next consider experiments that have used the naming task. Xiong et al. (2023) orthogonally manipulated the whole word and initial-character frequencies of two-character target words and observed additive facilitatory effects of both variables (see a similar finding in J. T. Wu et al., 2013's nested design). In contrast, J. T. Wu et al. (2013; Experiment 2) manipulated the same variables but only observed an interaction such that character frequency facilitated the naming of low- but not high-frequency words.

The types of discrepancies and complex interactions reported here have obviously clouded our understanding of how a key variable related to the learning of characters and words – their relative frequency of occurrence in printed text – affects their processing and identification. Unfortunately, providing a full explanation for such discrepancies and interactions will be challenging because they probably reflect multiple sources, including differences in task demands (e.g., lexical decision vs. naming), and how the experimental stimuli were selected (e.g., differences in the ranges of frequency values used, the presence of uncontrolled covariates, etc.). Of course, these complex patterns of results also probably reflect the inherently complex nature of Chinese lexical processing, including the fact that the Chinese writing system has a complex, hierarchical orthography with most words being formed via the compounding of their constituent characters. To cope with this complexity and to have any hope of understanding the cognitive processes that allow the identification of Chinese words, it is therefore necessary to develop computer models that can explain and simulate at least some of those processes. As the next section of this chapter will show, there have been efforts to develop such models, and these efforts have been met with at least some success. We will now shift our discussion to those models.

3.2 Theories and Models

The preceding review was intended to summarize the most important behavioral findings related to the lexical processing and identification of printed Chinese characters and words. The current section builds upon this work by reviewing the theoretical accounts that have been proposed to explain these findings. These accounts mainly consist of computationally explicit models of the perceptual and cognitive processes that are involved in Chinese word identification. This review will not be exhaustive but is instead only intended to provide some coverage of the types of models that have been developed, focusing on those models that have been influential to the field or that provide some unique insight into the Chinese character or word identification. This section will thus cover four key models.[8]

The first model is not computational per se because it was not implemented as a computer program or set of equations and thus cannot be used to run simulations or generate precise quantitative predictions. It is therefore best thought of as a useful conceptual framework that has been designed to provide qualitative accounts of several experimental findings.[9] It is nonetheless included in this book because of its direct influence on subsequent models. The model was proposed by Taft and colleagues (Taft & Zhu, 1997; Taft et al., 1999) and is illustrated in Figure 3.1. Even a casual comparison of Figure 3.1 to Figure 1.1 suggests that Taft and colleagues' model was directly inspired by the *interactive-activation* model that was originally proposed by McClelland and Rumelhart (1981) and described in Chapter 1. For example, both models consist of a hierarchy of interconnected processing nodes that represent different types of lexical information, with activation being propagated through the network to support the lexical constituents of printed words that are being identified. In the case of Taft and colleagues' model, however, these nodes are organized by the type of lexical information that is being represented, with one collection of nodes corresponding to orthographic information, a second corresponding to phonological information, and a third corresponding to semantic information. The model thus resembles that portion of the interactive-activation model that represents orthography, but with four other notable differences.

The first difference is that, whereas orthographic nodes represent visual features, letters, and whole words in the interactive-activation model, the corresponding nodes in Taft et al.'s (1999) model represent four levels

---

[8] For a concise but more comprehensive review of the Chinese reading models that had been developed c. 2017 (see Reichle & Yu, 2018). For more in-depth descriptions and discussion of the computer models that have been developed to explain the reading of alphabetic writing systems (see Reichle, 2021).

[9] The framework described here is actually a composite of two related but slightly different theories that were first proposed by Taft and Zhu (1997) and subsequently extended by Taft et al. (1999).

3.2 Theories and Models

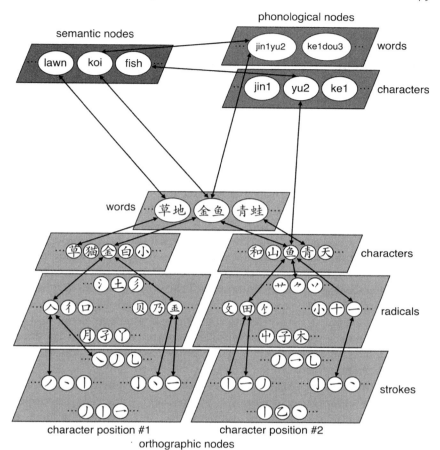

Figure 3.1 Taft et al.'s (1999) Chinese word-identification model
Visual input propagates activation through an interactive network of orthographic nodes (light gray) representing individual strokes, radicals, characters, and multi-character words, as well as nodes representing the pronunciations (medium gray) of single-syllable characters, multisyllabic words, and the meanings (dark gray) of both. For illustrative purposes, only the excitatory connections linking the nodes for a single word, "koi," are shown; excitatory connections similarly link the nodes representing other characters and words and inhibitory connections link nodes within a given type of representation (e.g., all orthographic word nodes are linked via mutually inhibitory connections). Note that the strokes and radicals are represented redundantly, at different spatial locations corresponding to different characters (i.e., first vs. second within a word) and different within-character positions (e.g., left vs. right).

of orthographic information: strokes, radicals, characters, and whole words. Importantly, the model does not include a level of nodes to represent compound radicals (i.e., radicals comprising two or more radicals). Second, whereas feature and letter nodes are arranged along a single spatial dimension in the interactive-activation model, in Taft and colleagues' model the strokes and radicals are arranged along two spatial dimensions. The two models are thus similar in that some of the lower-level lexical information is represented redundantly; in the interactive-activation model, feature and letter nodes are replicated across letter positions; in Taft and colleagues' model, stroke and radical nodes are replicated at different spatial locations within a character. Third, whereas feature and letter nodes are normally activated in parallel across letter positions within the interactive-activation model, the radical nodes are activated serially, from left to right, in Taft and colleagues' model. Finally, whereas the interactive-activation model was limited to explaining how printed words might be identified, Taft and colleagues' model is more ambitious in that it provides a tentative account of how the identification of characters and words interacts with the representations of the pronunciations and meanings of both characters and words. As shown in Figure 3.1, these interactions can occur at two different grain sizes: at the level of individual characters, which represent single-syllable morphemes, and at the level of multiple characters, which in most instances represent polysyllabic, multimorphemic words.

As indicated, because Taft et al. (1999) did not implement their model, it is limited to making qualitative predictions. With that important caveat, the model can explain a number of important findings related to the identification of printed Chinese words. For example, by design, the model provides qualitative accounts of a series of experiments in which participants named or made lexical decisions about single characters and/ or two-character words and in which various properties of those characters and words were manipulated (e.g., type vs. token frequency of the radicals, the number of radicals per character, etc.). The overall pattern of results is complex but key findings explained by the model were as follows. First, in characters consisting of two radicals, the frequency of the left-hand radical did not affect the character identification times but the right-hand character did, suggesting that processing of the left-hand radical starts prior to processing of the right-hand radical, causing the character-identification time to be largely dependent upon the latter. Second, radical frequency modulated character-identification times but only if the radical's frequency was calculated conditional upon its within-character position; for example, a radical that frequently occurs in the left-hand side of some characters but infrequently occurs in the right-hand side of others will function as a high-frequency radical in the former but a low-frequency radical in the latter. Third, the frequency of compound radicals did not modulate character-identification times but the frequencies of their constituent radicals did, suggesting that radicals – but not compound radicals – are represented in the lexicon. And finally, participants were slower and more prone to errors in making lexical decisions about two-character nonwords whose characters could be transposed to make words, suggesting that the coding of spatial position that was evident for radicals is not true for characters.

Each of the aforementioned findings is congruent with the assumptions of Taft et al.'s (1999) model if one assumes that character processing is completed in a serial, left-to-right manner: Radicals, but not compound radicals, are represented redundantly across the different within-character spatial positions, with their resting activation levels being a function of their position-specific frequencies, and with individual characters propagating their activation to multi-character words in a manner that is much less constrained by their spatial positions. These assumptions are sufficient for the model to explain the findings discussed above – at least at a qualitative level of description. This demonstrates the model's utility as a framework for thinking about Chinese character and word identification. But unfortunately, because the model was not formally implemented, its utility is inherently limited because any predictions based on the model will be imprecise and possibly subject to error.[10]

The next model that will be discussed, Perfetti and colleagues' *lexical-constituency* model (Perfetti et al., 2005; Perfetti & Liu, 2006; see also Perfetti & Tan, 1999), extends the previous model because it instantiates a variant of McClelland and Rumelhart's (1981) interactive-activation model that is adapted to the reading of Chinese characters. The model is shown in Figure 3.2. As shown, the model consists of a hierarchy of nodes that are arranged into four layers. The first, input layer consists of two sets of nodes. The first set contains 144 nodes arranged into nine groups, each containing sixteen binary nodes whose overall pattern of activation can represent any one of 623 possible radicals. The first set of input units can thus represent up to nine radicals, the maximum allowable for a given character. The second set of input nodes consists of a pair of binary nodes that, working together,

---

[10] For a discussion of the limitations of verbal theories and how those limitations can be overcome using formal (i.e., computer and mathematical) models, see Hintzman (1991).

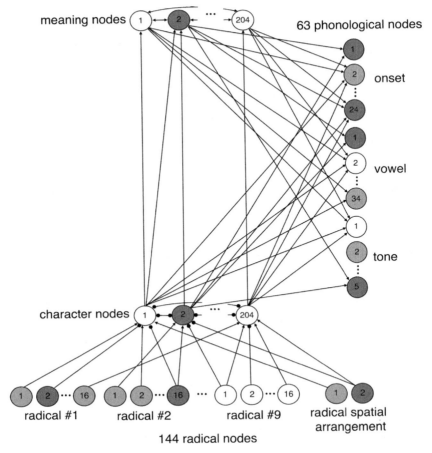

Figure 3.2 Perfetti et al.'s (2005) lexical-constituency model
Only a few connections are shown, with excitatory connections indicated by arrows and inhibitory connections indicated by filled circles. By way of illustration, a distributed pattern of activation across two sets of radical nodes and a pair of nodes that indicate their relative spatial arrangement have activated character node #2, which has in turn activated its meaning and a distributed pattern representing its pronunciation (i.e., the character's onset, vowel, and tone).

can represent four possible common spatial relationships among the radicals: left-right (e.g., 豹 /bao4/, meaning "leopard"), top-bottom (e.g., 苗 / miao2/, meaning "sprouts"), closed outside-inside (e.g., 国 /guo2/, meaning "country"), and open outside-inside (e.g., 医 /yi1/, meaning "doctor/cure").

3.2 *Theories and Models* 77

As Figure 3.2 shows, the input nodes are linked via excitatory and inhibitory connections to a second, intermediate layer of nodes representing the orthographic forms of 204 different characters, with each of those nodes representing one unique character. During the course of lexical processing (i.e., across processing cycles representing increments of time), one or more radicals that are represented by a pattern of active input nodes will propagate their activation to the character nodes, supporting or inhibiting the activation of character nodes to the degree that the radicals match or mismatch the orthographic forms of the characters. Those character nodes that are most consistent with the input will become most active. Because the character nodes are also linked to each other via mutually inhibitory connections, the node that is most consistent with the input will also gradually come to inhibit the others in a "winner take all" manner, as per the interactive-activation model (McClelland & Rumelhart, 1981).

Finally, as Figure 3.2 shows, the orthographic character nodes are linked to the last two layers of nodes: a layer of sixty-three nodes representing the pronunciations of the characters, and a layer of 204 nodes representing their meanings. (These final two layers are also linked so that a character's meaning can be used to generate its pronunciation.) The phonology nodes represent the Mandarin pronunciations of characters using distributed patterns of activation, with twenty-four nodes representing the onset (including the null onset as one possibility), thirty-four nodes representing the vowel, and five nodes representing the tone. Because a character's pronunciation is represented by the distributed *pattern* of activation across *all* of the phonological nodes, the nodes are not linked via mutually inhibitory connections, as are the orthographic nodes. In contrast, the semantic nodes represent the meanings of the 204 possible characters in a one-to-one manner, with the meaning nodes being interconnected via weak excitatory links that allow semantically related words to coactivate each other.

Because the lexical-constituency model has been formally implemented, it provides more precise predictions about the nature of character processing than the model of Taft and colleagues (Taft & Zhu, 1997; Taft et al., 1999). Perhaps the best example to illustrate this is that the model simulates the pattern of character priming that was originally reported by Perfetti and Tan (1998) and that is schematically shown in Figure 3.3. In this experiment, participants viewed two characters displayed in rapid succession, with the interval of time between the onset of the first and second character, or *stimulus onset asynchrony (SOA)* being 43, 57, 85, or

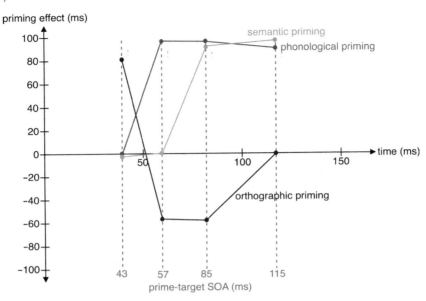

Figure 3.3 The patterns of orthographic, phonological, and semantic priming that have been simulated by Perfetti et al.'s (2005) lexical-constituency model. The four prime-target SOAs are indicated by the vertical dashed lines; the priming effects are indicated as a function of SOA for each of the prime types.

115 ms. The participants' task was to name the second character (i.e., the target) as rapidly and accurately as possible. The similarity between the first character (i.e., the prime) and the target was also manipulated across four conditions:

1. unrelated, with the prime and target being completely dissimilar;
2. graphically similar, with the prime and target sharing a component or being visually similar but not phonologically or semantically similar;
3. phonologically similar but not graphically or semantically similar; and
4. semantically similar but graphically and phonologically dissimilar.

Finally, the specificity of the meanings of the three experimental types of primes was manipulated; those characters were judged by raters to have either vague or precise meanings.

As Figure 3.3 shows, relative to performance in the unrelated condition (which serves as a baseline indicating a 0-ms priming effect), graphic similarity generated rapid facilitatory priming at the shortest SOA that rapidly turned to inhibitory priming before returning to baseline at the longest SOA. In contrast, the phonological and semantic primes only facilitated target processing, but with this facilitation emerging later, at the 57-ms and 85-ms SOAs for the two types of primes, respectively. Finally, not shown in Figure 3.3 is the fact the facilitative priming effects were larger and more rapid for the primes having precise as compared to vague meanings, but only if those primes were semantically similar to the targets.

Although the pattern of Perfetti and Tan's (1998) results is complex and perhaps counterintuitive, the lexical-constituency model provides an elegant interpretation. The key theoretical assumption of this account is that, in contrast to alphabetic languages, where GPCs can be used to generate phonology in a pre-lexical, cascaded manner, phonology in Chinese is generated in a "threshold" manner, with a character's pronunciation only becoming available after its representation has become sufficiently activated in memory. From this assumption, then, it follows that the graphically similar prime would initially facilitate target processing because the two are visually similar; radical nodes shared by the prime and target would partially activate the target's character node. However, with the longer SOAs, the node corresponding to the prime character would exceed its threshold, becoming active and inhibiting the node corresponding to the target character, thereby inhibiting its processing. However, it is precisely at this point in time that the prime character node propagates activation to the phonological nodes corresponding to its pronunciation. In the condition involving phonologically similar primes, the prime character node will activate the same phonological nodes as the target character (because they are homophones), thereby facilitating the processing of the target. Finally, because the mappings between orthography and phonology to meaning are less determinant than the mapping between orthography to phonology, the facilitation that comes from the prime and target being semantically related emerges relatively late and is modulated by the specificity of the prime's meaning (i.e., whether it is precise or vague).

The assumption that competition among active character-level representations plays a central role in the oscillation of priming observed in the graphic- versus phonological-prime conditions also leads to an interesting prediction: Because non-characters are by definition not represented in the lexicon, using non-characters as primes should generate facilitatory and not inhibitory priming. Returning to Figure 3.2, the reason for this prediction is clear: Because non-characters cannot activate character nodes, those nodes cannot actively inhibit the nodes of target characters. A priming experiment reported in Perfetti et al. (2005) tested and confirmed this prediction: Graphically similar characters used as primes facilitated target processing at short SOAs but inhibited target processing at long SOAs, whereas using graphically similar non-characters used as primes facilitated target processing across all of the SOAs.

In closing this discussion of the lexical-constituency model, a few final comments are warranted. The first is that, as discussed, both the model and the theoretical principles that motivated its development provide a compelling account of Chinese character identification and the time course and manner in which orthographic, phonological, and semantic information become available. In particular, Perfetti et al. (2005) have clearly articulated what they see as being the key differences between alphabetic word identification versus Chinese character identification – that the former can happen in a cascaded manner, using sub-lexical units (letters) to access meaning, whereas the latter happens in a threshold manner, with the rampant homophony likely causing a diffuse activation of many characters. Despite these differences, however, the principles of the lexical-constituency model suggest an important role of phonology in both types of writing systems. In Perfetti and colleagues' words:

> In alphabetic systems, phonology stabilizes word identity, even if it does not cause access to word meaning. The role of phonology holds also in Chinese. A character connected to a pronunciation is more definitive (reducing error in identification) than one that is not connected, even if other characters share that pronunciation. (Perfetti et al., 2005: 57)

Thus, according to Perfetti et al. (2005), traditional accounts of word identification based on studies and models of how alphabetic words are identified place too much emphasis on the role of phonology in accessing word identity and meaning. The principles of their model instead suggest that word "identification" corresponds to the actual process of activating a stable configuration of three types of information: a word's spelling, pronunciation, and meaning. By their account, then, one of the main benefits that comes from considering Chinese reading is that it shifts the emphasis from the former to the latter conceptualization of what it means to identify printed words in any writing system.

The next model to be discussed was proposed by X. Li et al. (2009) and it is also a variant of McClelland and Rumelhart's (1981) interactive-activation model as applied to the identification of Chinese words. It

3.2 Theories and Models

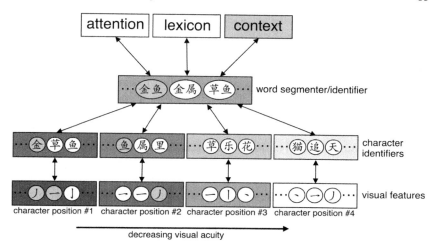

Figure 3.4 X. Li et al.'s (2009) word segmentation and identification model
Bottom-up perceptual information is propagated at a rate determined by visual acuity (indicated by the shading, with darker gray corresponding to more rapid propagation) to the character identifiers, where it is combined with top-down information provided by the lexicon to jointly constrain the likely identity of a word via its segmentation/identification. Attention provides a reference location of the leftmost character of the word being identified. The top-down support from higher-level context has not been implemented but is indicated by a placeholder (the box labeled "context") as an acknowledgment of its necessity.

differs from the preceding models, however, in that its primary goal is to explain how continuous strings of Chinese characters are correctly segmented into groups corresponding to their respective words – a problem that was completely sidestepped by both of the preceding models. This next model also attempts to explain how words are segmented and identified during natural reading, where the high visual acuity that is required to identify the small features of characters is largely restricted to the *fovea*, or central two degrees of visual angle (Normann & Guillory, 2002; see also Veldre et al., 2023). The model is thus committed to the core theoretical assumption that Chinese words are segmented as they identified, with segmentation and identification being constrained by the other perceptual and cognitive systems that support skilled reading.

As Figure 3.4 shows, the model consists of several subsystems that allow for visual perception, the allocation of attention, and the identification of both characters and words. The model thus combines strengths of the two previously discussed models because its explanatory scope includes the identification of multi-character words (like the model of Taft et al., 1999) but has been formally implemented (like the lexical-constituency model of Perfetti et al., 2005). As indicated, the model also instantiates core assumptions of McClelland and Rumelhart's (1981) model. However, rather than being implemented as a hierarchical network of nodes, the model is instead implemented abstractly, using a set of equations that describe how bottom-up information about visual features is combined with top-down information about how words are configured from characters to segment spatially continuous arrays of characters into one–four-character words.

As shown, information about the visual features is spatially localized to four distinct input "channels" corresponding to the spatial locations of four characters. Attention provides a reference location which corresponds to the first character of the word being identified. As each word is identified, attention shifts to the first character of the next unidentified word, causing individual words to be segmented or identified one at a time, in a serial manner. Also note that, because visual acuity decreases to the right of the attentional marker, the rate of visual feature extraction also decreases to the right of the attentional marker.

Information about the visual features from each input channel is used to calculate the likely identity of character at that position. This information is then combined with information from the lexicon about the within-word positions of characters (e.g., 猫 "cat" is the first character in the words 猫咪 "kitten," 猫腻 "trick," and 猫粮 "cat food," but is the second character in 熊猫 "panda," and the third in 三脚猫 "jack of all trades")[11] to calculate the probability that the first character is a word, that the first pair of characters is a word, and so on. As Figure 3.4 indicates, information from the different levels interacts and is mutually constraining; for example, as the likely identity of a word increases, the likely identities of its characters also increase. Finally, although X. Li et al. (2009) cite evidence that contextual factors can influence how characters are segmented into words, their model does not instantiate these higher-level influences, but instead only acknowledges the need to include them by including a "context" placeholder.

The model as described was used to simulate one of five experiments reported by X. Li et al. (2009). In this experiment, participants viewed briefly displayed four-character arrays with the task of naming those characters as rapidly and accurately as possible, with the response times and

---

[11] The literal meaning of this particular word is also "three-legged cat."

accuracies then being the dependent measures. The nature of the displayed characters varied across four conditions:

1. *whole-word*, in which all of the characters belonged to a single four-character word;
2. *two-words*, in which the first pair of characters belonged to one word and the second pair of characters belonged to another word;
3. *half-word*, in which the first two characters belonged to a four-character word but the third and fourth characters were randomly selected (i.e., they did not complete the four-character word); and
4. *non-word*, in which all four characters were randomly selected (i.e., they did not form words).

The key finding from this study was that participants most rapidly and accurately named the third and fourth characters in the whole-word condition, indicating that the processing of those characters received some amount of top-down support by virtue of belonging to a single word – one that included all four characters. In contrast, the third and fourth characters in the other conditions were named less rapidly and accurately due to the fact that they belonged to a second word (in the two-words conditions) or no word (in the other conditions). That this result does not reflect guessing the identities of the final pair of characters in the one-word condition is supported by the fact that performance in the half-word condition was poor, indicating that subject rarely if ever guessed the final pair of characters and thus the word using the first two characters. The experiment demonstrates an analog of the word-superiority effect (Reicher, 1969; Wheeler, 1970) that was discussed earlier in this chapter, with the identification of characters – rather than letters – being facilitated by the processing of the words in which they are embedded.

As indicated, a simulation using X. Li et al.'s (2009) word segmentation and identification model reproduced the basic pattern of response latencies and accuracies reported in their experiment. This demonstration thus provides an existence proof that the type of interactive-activation framework that was originally proposed to explain the identification of English words (McClelland & Rumelhart, 1981) can be adapted to Chinese and thus provide a plausible explanation of one of the most perplexing problems related to Chinese reading – explaining how continuous arrays of characters are segmented to support the identification of individual words. Finally, it is worth noting that X. Li and colleagues' model predicts that, with all else being equal, there is a preference to segment characters into the largest sized units possible. For example, the model prefers to segment the characters 老板娘 into a three-character word meaning "landlady" rather than a two-character word 老板 meaning "boss" because the former segmentation receives extra support from the character 娘. As pointed out by X. Li et al., this preference for how to resolve character-segmentation ambiguity appears to be consistent with the preference of human readers (e.g., J. Wu et al., 2008), further supporting the assumptions of their model.

The last model that will be discussed in this section includes a "family" of related models (Y. Chang et al., 2016; Hsiao & Shillcock, 2004, 2005; Xing et al., 2002, 2004; J. F. Yang et al., 2006, 2009, 2013), all of which are variants of the highly influential "triangle" model of word identification (Harm & Seidenberg, 1999, 2004; Seidenberg & McClelland, 1989; Plaut, 2005; Plaut et al., 1996). Although there are implementational differences among these models, those differences will be ignored for the present purposes because our goal is to only describe how the assumptions of a connectionist model of English word identification have been adapted to simulate the identification of Chinese characters and words.[12] Figure 3.5 is a schematic diagram showing the basic architecture of one of these models (J. F. Yang et al., 2006, 2009). As shown, the models consist of several different layers of interconnected nodes that represent the orthographic form of characters, as well as their pronunciations. In contrast to the models that have been discussed so far, the visual and lexical information is not represented using localist nodes wherein each node signifies a symbol or specific bit of information (e.g., a character or its pronunciation, as per the model of Taft et al., 1999; see Figure 3.1); rather, the information is represented in a distributed manner by the overall pattern of active nodes within each of the layers (as per the phonological representations used in the lexical-constituency model of Perfetti et al., 2005; see Figure 3.2). As shown, all 270 orthographic input nodes connect to each of the 200 hidden nodes, which in turn connect to each of the ninety-two phonological output nodes. Additionally, the phonological nodes are fully interconnected, including auto-connections to themselves, as well as fifty "cleanup" nodes that allow the model to learn attractors or stable patterns of activated nodes (thereby facilitating the learning of more stable representations of the characters' pronunciations).

---

[12] A few of these models will be discussed in Chapter 5 because they provide tentative accounts of reading development (Xing et al., 2002, 2004) or dyslexia (Hsiao & Shillcock, 2004, 2005; J. F. Yang et al., 2013) in Chinese reading.

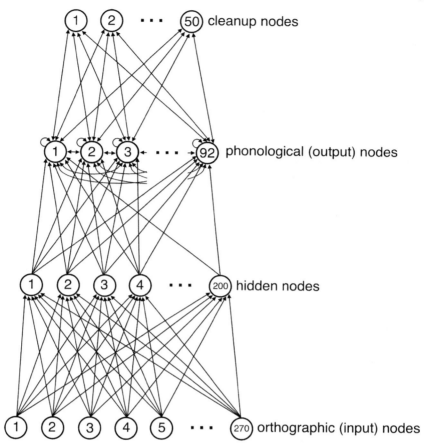

Figure 3.5 J. F. Yang et al.'s (2009) "triangle" model of Chinese character naming
The network's architecture consists of four layers: (1) an input layer of 270 orthographic nodes that represent the features of a character in a distributed manner; (2) 200 hidden nodes; (3) 92 output nodes that represent the pronunciation of a character in a distributed manner; and (4) 50 "cleanup" nodes that function as an attractor.

The precise manner in which orthographic input and phonological output are represented is, however, quite complex. With respect to orthographic input: 270 binary nodes are divided into eight groups, with the first group of twenty-one units representing the overall structure of the character (e.g., its shape, number of radicals, their positions, etc.) and the remaining groups being divided into seven groups that each represent the structure of a single radical (e.g., its strokes, their relative positions, etc.). The input can thus represent characters constituted by one–seven radicals, with each of those radicals being one of 560 unique possible radicals. With respect to phonological output: ninety-two nodes are divided into five groups, with the first representing the onset consonant, the next three representing rime (i.e., any semivowels, the nuclear vowel, and coda), and the final group representing the tone. The phonological information is represented in a distributive manner across these nodes using abstract phonetic features (e.g., manner and place of articulation) to capture the graded similarity of pronunciations among the characters.

The model as described was trained using the back-propagation learning algorithm on a corpus of 4,468 characters from the Modern Chinese Frequency Dictionary (1986). The training was completed in two stages. The first involved (pre)training the phonological-attractor part of the model (i.e., the connections between the phonological and cleanup nodes). The second then entailed training the full model by sampling each character in proportion to the square root of its frequency across three million training trials. Finally, the model was tested by using it to simulate the naming of a set of 120 characters from three conditions:

1. *regular-consistent*, or characters that are pronounced as their phonetic radicals and whose phonetic radicals are pronounced the same (ignoring tone) in other characters;
2. *regular-inconsistent*, or characters that are pronounced as their phonetic radicals but whose radicals are pronounced differently in other characters; and
3. *irregular-inconsistent*, or characters that are pronounced differently than their phonetic radicals.

The characters in each of these conditions could also be high or low frequency.

Key findings from this simulation were, first, that the model accurately named 95 percent of the test characters. Second, the model's naming latencies and accuracies were modulated by the character's condition and frequency: High-frequency characters were named faster and more accurately than their low-frequency counterparts, with performance in naming the latter being especially slow and inaccurate if they were irregular or inconsistent. Importantly, a regularity effect was found even for inconsistent items, suggesting that it reflects the statistical nature of the Chinese writing system rather than the use of categorical "rules" per se. Finally, a follow-up naming experiment that was also reported by J. F. Yang et al. (2009) indicated that the performance of their participants in naming the

3.2   *Theories and Models*   87

same characters followed a similar pattern, with frequency and regularity or consistency interacting to make the naming of low-frequency, inconsistent characters particular slow and prone to error.

Given the model's success in simulating character naming, two final important points about the demonstration warrant discussion. The first is that, in contrast to the models discussed earlier (e.g., Perfetti et al.'s, 2005 constituency model; see Figure 3.2), the model does not presuppose the representation of radicals, characters, or their pronunciations (as per Taft et al., 1999); rather, the architecture of the model in combination with a domain general learning algorithm is sufficient to learn the statistical mappings between simple features making up the orthographic input, on one hand, and the phonological output, on the other. As J. F. Yang et al. (2009: 254) indicate, their model "uses a distributed representation of Chinese characters that eschews any a priori assumptions about the functional units that underlie spelling-to-sound translation."

The second point is related to the lexical constituent that is notably absent in J. F. Yang et al.'s (2009) model – that of character meaning. Several of the same authors reported an earlier simulation (J. F. Yang et al., 2006) using a variant of their model that included an additional layer of 246 semantic nodes and connections linking those nodes to both the orthographic and phonological nodes.[13] This model was trained on a set of 103 characters that included both semantically transparent and semantically opaque phonograms and then tested on twenty-five items of each type. Perhaps not too surprisingly, the model learned the transparent characters more rapidly than the opaque ones. However, contrary to a similar simulation that was reported by Harm and Seidenberg (2004) that involved the learning of English monosyllabic words, J. F. Yang et al.'s (2006) model learned the mapping between orthography and meaning more rapidly than the mapping between phonology and meaning. This result, although perhaps counterintuitive, makes sense if one considers one key difference between English and Chinese. As J. F. Yang et al. (2006) indicate:

> Whereas in English, the development of spelling to sound occurs earlier and more rapidly than the development of spelling to meaning, in Chinese, this pattern is reversed, as mappings from spelling to meaning are learned more readily than spelling-to-sound mappings. ... Whereas the Chinese orthography contains sub-lexical units than prompt lexical meaning, the English orthography contains no such information. (J. F. Yang et al., 2006: 916)

---

[13] Unfortunately, most of the other details about the model and how the simulation was conducted were not provided.

Their model thus illustrates how statistical differences between writing systems, especially the probabilistic mapping between sub-lexical units (i.e., semantic radicals) and the meanings of the characters in which they are embedded, might give rise to important behavioral differences – ones that might, for example, have pedagogical ramifications for the teaching or learning of Chinese versus English.

In closing this section, we hope that our discussion of the models that have been developed to simulate and explain Chinese character and word identification has been useful for showing the interplay between empirical and theoretical research, and how models have provided useful tools for gaining more novel insights into mental processes that would otherwise be difficult to understand. Because this chapter primarily focused on what is known about Chinese character and word identification, our discussion in this section was likewise focused on models that have been used to explain character and word identification. The next chapter will build upon this discussion by first reviewing what is known about the skilled reading of Chinese text using eye-tracking experiments, and then reviewing models that have been developed to explain the results of those experiments and, by extension, the mental processes that support skilled reading.

3.3 Conclusion

This chapter has provided evidence of clear progress in understanding the mental processes that support the processing and identification of Chinese characters and words. This research has demonstrated unexpected similarities in terms of how printed words are identified across writings systems as different as Chinese and English (e.g., top-down facilitation of the processing of a word's orthographic constituents as evidenced by word-superiority effects, the rapid and obligatory access to a word's pronunciation from memory, etc.), as well as notable differences that are likely to be of theoretical importance (e.g., phonological regularity and consistency in Chinese at two different "grain sizes" – the character and word). The research has also demonstrated clear progress as evidenced by the development of sophisticated computer models that both explain and simulate many of the tasks used to study the topic and many of the key findings that have been reported from those studies. Again, this work has been useful in demonstrating points of convergence between word identification in English and other alphabetic writing systems, on one hand, and the identification of Chinese characters and words, on the other.

The best evidence to support this last conjecture is that the basic theoretical principles of one of the most influential models of English word identification, McClelland and Rumelhart's (1981) interactive-activation model, have been so readily adapted to explain the reading of Chinese. The next chapter will see both of these trends continue, with research using eye-tracking methods being used to demonstrate further similarities between the skilled reading of English versus Chinese, and computer models of the former also being adapted to the latter.

CHAPTER 4

Skilled Reading

The previous chapter reviewed what has been learned about the identification of Chinese characters and words using behavioral experiments, on the one hand, and computer models, on the other. This discussion was limited, however, in that it focused only on the identification of characters and words that were displayed either in isolation or in small numbers (e.g., pairs of characters) to examine lexical processing in the absence of the other perceptual, cognitive, and motoric processes that are engaged during the natural reading of text. For that reason, the research that was reviewed in Chapter 3 did not discuss what has been learned from experiments that have examined the natural reading of sentences and more extended passages of text. The section on behavioral experiments, for instance, did not review the various studies that have used eye movements to examine the processing of characters and words in text. The present chapter redresses this limitation and extends the discussion of the previous chapter by reviewing these studies that have examined natural reading. As was true of the previous chapter, this discussion will also be organized around the two "threads" of behavioral experiments and computer models.

Before we begin this discussion, however, it is important to provide a bit more detail about the goals of this chapter. As most readers of this book probably already know, the seemingly trivial task of reading is arguably the single most complex cognitive task that we are not biologically predisposed to perform (compare spoken language). To make this claim a bit more concrete, first consider that a "simple view" of reading (e.g., Gough & Tumner, 1986) would describe it as the sum of two basic activities: the identification of printed words combined with whatever (spoken) language processing is required to convert the meanings of those words into meaningful representations of sentences and larger units of text. Ignoring the fact that the latter is itself an activity of monumental complexity, this simple view belies the fact that both aforementioned activities, identifying printed words and constructing sentence and text

90

representations, cannot be completed independently of the other perceptual, cognitive, and motoric processes that make reading possible. For example, word identification and language processing depend upon the coordinated movement of the eyes and covert attention for the purpose of rapidly and accurately extracting whatever visual features are needed to construct the abstract orthographic representations that are the starting point for lexical processing.[1] Although much of what transpires to move the eyes and attention through a text occurs below the threshold of conscious awareness and with seemingly little or no effort, their movement is surprisingly sensitive to variation in the difficulty associated with lexical and language processing. This is precisely the reason why eye-movement experiments have proven so useful for understanding the psychology of reading (e.g., see Rayner et al., 2012). This coordination of the visual system, covert attention, and lexical and language processing is also a closed loop in that the movement of the eyes (i.e., where the eyes fixate) influences the quality of the visual features that are extracted and thus the rate and accuracy of lexical and language processing.

Another important difference between reading and spoken language comprehension is related to their sensory modalities and how information from those modalities is acquired: Whereas the rate at which spoken language must be understood is largely determined by the speaker's rate of articulation and therefore outside the listener's control (barring the listener asking the speaker to repeat him/herself), in most situations that involve reading the rate is within certain limits under the reader's control (an exception being the reading of subtitles). This is of course not to say that the rate of reading is not modulated by a variety of variables, because it is. These variables include (but are not limited to) one's desired level of comprehension (e.g., full understanding vs. skimming for the gist), the difficulty of the text being read (e.g., a math textbook vs. magazine article), and moment-to-moment differences in the processing difficulty of the text. And there is of course also an upper limit on the rate of reading because all cognitive processes require some amount of time to complete. Although these estimates vary according to reading ability, the nature of the material being read (e.g., fiction vs. non-fiction), and other factors, the best current estimates based on a meta-analysis conducted by Brysbaert (2019) indicate that adults read with

---

[1] This of course ignores the fact that blind people can read braille. But even with braille the same point holds: Reading is an incredibly complex activity that, in the case of braille, would involve finger movements and tactile representations of the dot patterns corresponding to letters that are used to access information about words.

the range of 175–320 words per minute. And Rayner et al. (2016) discuss in detail the many reasons (e.g., limitations of visual acuity) why reading with full comprehension cannot exceed about 400 words per minute.

Although the precise way readers adjust their rate to balance the inherent trade-off between speed and comprehension is still poorly understood, there is evidence that readers *can* rapidly adapt their eye-movement behavior in the service of maintaining some level of comprehension in situations that cause reading to be difficult. For example, in the context of reading subtitles that are displayed very rapidly in film, readers can adjust their reading rate by making fewer, longer saccades and shorter fixations to "skim" as much of the subtitles as possible before they disappear from the screen (Liao et al., 2021). Likewise, instructions to "skim" a text result in a similar pattern of eye movements (Warrington et al., 2023). Reading skill thus entails not only the capacity to comprehend text rapidly and accurately, but some level of volitional control over how the behaviors that support this capacity are coordinated, as well as the capacity to adjust this coordinated activity and thus the rate of reading in a manner that is sensitive to the goals of the reader.

Because of the inherent complexity of reading, it is not possible to provide a definitive review of everything that is known about skilled reading, either of alphabetic writing systems like English or the one that is the focus of this book – Chinese. Therefore, as in the previous chapter, we will begin our discussion of skilled reading with a brief summary of what has been learned from experiments that have been used to study the skilled reading of English and other languages that use alphabetic writing systems. Most of these studies (but not all) involve eye tracking because the method is ideally suited for the task of studying natural reading (e.g., the method is ecologically valid, minimally intrusive, and provides a sensitive, on-line measure of what participants are looking at as they are reading text). We will then review what has been learned from similar studies of Chinese reading, using our earlier discussion of the reading of alphabetic writing systems to compare the two in our attempt to document how reading is both similar and different across the two types of writing systems.

4.1 Eye-Tracking Experiments

To understand how eye tracking has been used to study reading it is first necessary to have a basic understanding of eye-movement control.[2] To facilitate our exposition, though, it is first necessary to provide some

---

[2] For comprehensive reviews, see Rayner (1998, 2009), Rayner and Pollatsek (1989), and Rayner et al. (2012).

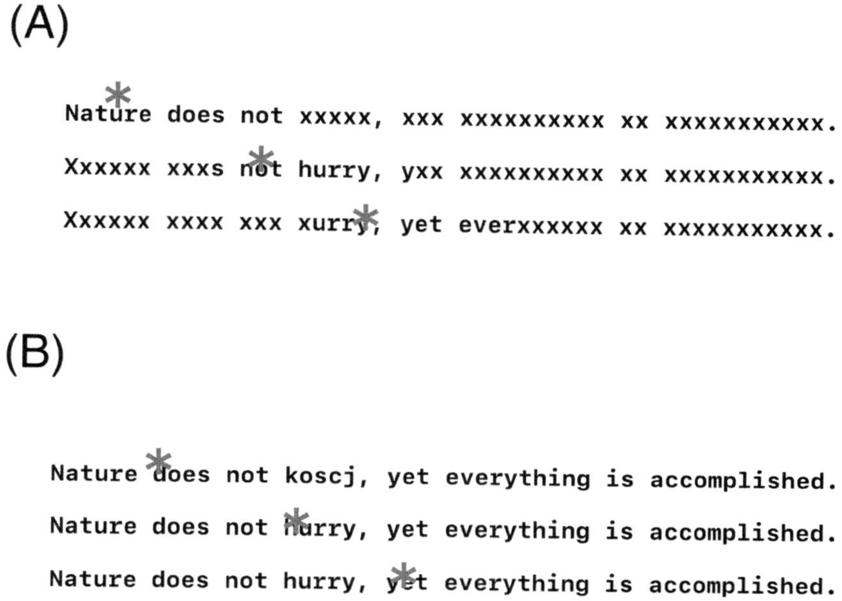

(A)

Nature does not xxxxx, xxx xxxxxxxxxx xx xxxxxxxxxxx.

Xxxxxx xxxs not hurry, yxx xxxxxxxxxx xx xxxxxxxxxxx.

Xxxxxx xxxx xxx xurry, yet everxxxxxx xx xxxxxxxxxxx.

(B)

Nature does not koscj, yet everything is accomplished.

Nature does not hurry, yet everything is accomplished.

Nature does not hurry, yet everything is accomplished.

Figure 4.1   Examples of the gaze-contingent paradigms that are used in
eye-tracking research

Panel A shows the moving-window paradigm. Panel B shows the boundary paradigm.
In both panels, the gray asterisks indicate fixation locations at each point in time.

background on eye-tracker technology and its associated experimental paradigms. As briefly discussed in Chapter 1, eye-tracking devices measure the spatial position of a reader's eye (usually the right, although viewing is typically binocular) with a high degree of spatial and temporal accuracy. At normal reading distances, for example, a single degree of visual angle subsumes about three to four letters, and most eye trackers used for reading research record the position of the eye to within half a degree of visual angle every millisecond. Because the eye tracker interfaces in real time with the computer that both records the position of the reader's eye and controls the text materials that are being displayed to the reader, it is possible to implement *gaze-contingent paradigms* in which what is displayed to the reader at any given point in time is contingent upon where they are looking (Rayner, 1979, 2014). Figure 4.1 provides examples to illustrate two of the more commonly used paradigms.

Figure 4.1A shows a *moving-window paradigm*. In this paradigm, the text inside of a moving "window" is displayed normally around each point of fixation, but with the text outside of this window being distorted in some way. For example, all of the letters outside the window might be replaced by similar looking letters (e.g., "o" substituting for "e," "k" for "h," etc.) or strings of "X"s. The blank spaces that normally separate words can also be retained or filled in with letters. With each movement of the eyes, the window also moves so that, from any given fixation, only a limited amount of normal text is visible. The size and symmetry of the window can also be manipulated. In the example shown, the moving window extends from three letter-sized spaces to the left of the fixation to ten letter-sized spaces to the right of the fixation. By comparing the rate of someone reading normal text (i.e., without a moving window) to their reading rate using various types of windows, it is possible to make inferences about the type and spatial extent of the information that is extracted from each fixation (see McConkie & Rayner, 1975).[3] And because of the inherent trade-off between letter size and visual acuity (i.e., a word that is displayed using a bigger font will also subtend a larger visual angle and thus have to be processed further from the center of vision, where visual acuity is degraded; Veldre et al., 2023), the appropriate metric is letter spaces rather than visual angle (Rayner, 2009).

Another commonly used paradigm is shown in Figure 4.1 Panel B. This *boundary paradigm* employs an invisible boundary located immediately before the blank space preceding a target word (in this example, the word "hurry"). This boundary is not visible to the reader and is only used to trigger a display change. Prior to this change, when the reader's eyes are to the left of the boundary, the target word is not visible; a preview letter string is instead visible at its location (e.g., "koscj"). Because this preview normally differs from the target word in some way, it is referred to as the "invalid preview" condition. As the eyes move across the boundary, the preview is replaced by the target word. One can then measure the looking time on the target word when it is preceded by an invalid preview and compare this to the looking time on the same target word when the preview is valid (i.e., the target word is visible prior to the eyes crossing the boundary). For example, one can compare the looking times on the target word "rose" when it is preceded by the valid preview "rose" versus three different invalid previews: an orthographically similar preview "robs"; a phonologically identical preview "rows";

---

[3] Because the gaze-contingent display changes occur during saccades, when normal visual processing is suppressed (Matin, 1974), readers are often completely unaware of the display changes (Rayner, 2014), even though cognitive processing continues during the saccades themselves (Irwin, 1998).

or a semantically related preview "lily." The reduction in the looking time or *preview benefit* that comes from having a valid as compared to invalid preview of the target word is thus informative about the type of information (e.g., orthographic vs. phonological vs. semantic) that can be extracted during the parafoveal processing that occurs during normal reading (see Rayner, 1975).

Using the paradigms of the type just described, researchers have learned quite a lot about the *perceptual span*, or the "region from which useful information can be obtained from a fixation during reading" (Rayner, 1986: 212). For example, using the moving-window paradigm, researchers have shown that reading proceeds at a normal rate in English as long as all of the letters of the fixated word and fourteen or fifteen letter-sized spaces to the right of the fixation are visible (McConkie & Rayner, 1975, 1976; Rayner & Bertera, 1979; Rayner et al., 1980). However, the type of information extracted from this preview region is not uniform (Rayner et al., 1982). For example, information about the identities of individual letters can only be extracted from a smaller region extending about ten letters to the right of fixation. Beyond this distance, the type of information that is extracted tends to be related to the overall shape of the word and the locations of the blank spaces that demarcate word boundaries (e.g., see Frey & Bosse, 2018). Furthermore, these regions do not just reflect the limitations of visual acuity because the asymmetry that is observed in the reading of English is in the opposite direction during the reading of languages that are written from right to left, such as Hebrew (Pollatsek et al., 1981) and Arabic (Jordan et al., 2014). This suggests that the perceptual span also reflects the allocation of attention, which normally precedes the rightward movement of the eyes during the reading of English but precedes the leftward movement of the eyes during the reading of Hebrew and Arabic. This conclusion is also supported by the results of another gaze-contingent paradigm in which the sizes of the letters to either side of each fixation increased with increasing distance from the fixation (i.e., the sizes of more distant letters were magnified to offset the decline in visual acuity); this manipulation had no effect on the size of the perceptual span, indicating that visual acuity per se is not the only factor delimiting the perceptual span and providing additional evidence about the important role played by covert attention (Miellet et al., 2009). Finally, it is important to note that the size of the perceptual span is smaller in languages like Arabic because the writing system is denser than English (e.g., Arabic is normally written without vowels and sometimes written with small diacritics), making the extraction of detailed visual information from each fixation more difficult than it would be, for example, with English (see Hermena & Reichle, 2020).

With that background on gaze-contingent paradigms, let us now turn to our summary of what has been learned about the skilled reading of English and other languages that use alphabetic writing systems. As one might guess based on what has been said about eye tracking so far, the movement of the eyes through printed text is determined by two decisions that seem to be made largely independently of each other: decisions about *where* to move the eyes and decisions about *when* to move the eyes. One of the first demonstrations of this fact came from eye-movement experiments involving two different gaze-contingent paradigms: one in which a moving window randomly varied in size with each new fixation, and a second in which a random interval of time was introduced between the start of each new fixation and when the text was displayed (Rayner & Pollatsek, 1981). Somewhat remarkably, the size of the moving window affected where the eyes moved, with larger windows on average being followed by longer saccades. But this manipulation did not affect fixation durations. Conversely, the duration of the text-onset delays affected when the eyes moved, with longer delays resulting in longer fixations. But this manipulation did not affect the saccade lengths. The pattern of results was interpreted as showing that information about word boundaries is mainly used to decide where to move the eyes next, whereas lexical-processing difficulty is mainly used to decide when to move the eyes from one word to the next. To the extent that this conclusion is true, it simplifies the exposition of eye-movement control in reading because the two decisions can be treated separately.

For example, research on the "where?" decision suggests that, in English and other writing systems that have clearly demarcated word boundaries, readers most often direct their eyes from the fixated word to the center of the next because this viewing location, called the *optimal-viewing location* (*OVP*), allows the word to be viewed from the center of vision and thus affords the most efficient lexical processing (O'Regan, 1981, 1992; O'Regan & Lévy-Schoen, 1987). This hypothesis is consistent with results from behavioral experiments in which lexical-decision responses to letter strings that were briefly displayed at different locations within the participants' visual field (e.g., with the center of vision on the first letter, middle letter, or last letter) are most rapid and accurate if the OVP is fixated (O'Regan & Jacobs, 1992; O'Regan et al., 1984). Additionally, if one examines the distributions of fixation landing-site positions within a large sample of words, the centers of those distributions tend to be slightly to the left of the OVP

(McConkie et al., 1988, 1989; Rayner, 1979; Rayner et al., 1996), on the *preferred-viewing location (PVL)*. This latter finding has been interpreted as showing that, although readers attempt to fixate the OVP, one or more factors (e.g., differences in the informativeness of initial vs. middle letters within words) cause the fixations to deviate from their intended targets so that the eyes instead fixate the PVL.

Closer examination of fixation landing-site distributions on words also reveals that these distributions are approximately normal in shape, with truncated tails to either side of the words (McConkie et al., 1988; Nuthmann et al., 2005; Rayner, 1979; Vitu et al., 2001). These missing tails reflect instances where, due to saccadic error, the eyes either under- or overshot their intended targets, missing the words completely. The amount of saccadic error is also modulated by the saccade length, with longer saccades resulting in more error, as well as the duration of the fixation on the saccade launch site, with shorter fixations also resulting in more error. Finally, in English, there appears to be some amount of systematic error or bias to make saccades of a preferred length: approximately seven letter spaces (McConkie et al., 1988). For each letter space that the intended saccade is shorter or longer than the preferred saccade length, the saccade that is executed will over- or undershoot its intended target by about half a letter space (McConkie et al., 1988). Thus, in the reading of languages having alphabetic writing systems and well-demarcated word boundaries, the answer to the "where?" question is fairly clear: Readers use parafoveal information about the boundaries of upcoming words to direct their eyes towards their centers because this viewing position affords fast and accurate lexical processing; however, because of both random and systematic motor error, the eyes often deviate from their intended targets, causing the distribution of fixation landing sites to be approximately normal in shape but with missing tails that reflect instances where the eyes completely missed the word being targeted.

Turning now to the "when?" question, the answer is less forthcoming. For example, early accounts of eye-movement control in reading often assumed that the decisions about when to move the eyes were largely decoupled from cognition due to the fact that:

1. words require 150–300 ms to identify;
2. saccades required 125–175 ms to program; and
3. the mean fixation duration during reading is about 225–250 ms (e.g., see Reichle & Reingold, 2013).

These values appear to rule out a simple model in which the identification of one word initiates the programming of a saccade to move the eyes to the next word because, based on the first two points mentioned above, such a model would presumably predict mean fixation durations of 275–475 ms – significantly longer than what is observed. The rejection of this type of simple model resulted in an alternative with two core assumptions. The first of these assumptions is that the oculomotor system causes the eyes to progress through a text at a fixed pace that is sufficient to identify most words being read and that reflects global performance constraints (e.g., the desired level of comprehension, the difficulty of the text, and the skill of the reader). The second assumption is that this forward progression is occasionally interrupted by pauses or regressions as might be necessary to identify a particularly difficult word or resolve problems that might result from failures of higher-level language processing. By this account, then, the "eye-mind link" is very weak because cognition only intervenes when there is processing difficulty, and because the rate of the eyes' progression through text is determined by global parameters.

Unfortunately, this simple account does not provide an adequate explanation of several experimental findings which show that – contrary to what might be predicted by the model – the processing of individual words often has immediate consequences on the time spent looking at those words. The gaze-contingent experiment by Rayner and Pollatsek (1981) that was described earlier, for example, demonstrates that the interval of time between when a fixation begins and when the text being read is initially displayed will have an immediate effect on the fixation duration, lengthening it to a degree that reflects the text-onset delay. And although one might criticize this paradigm for being unnatural, there is now evidence that many lexical and post-lexical variables can rapidly influence the time spent fixating a word (for reviews, see Rayner, 1998, 2009). Two of the most important of these variables include a word's frequency of occurrence in printed text and its within-sentence predictability. Both effects and their significance will be discussed in turn.

A word's frequency of occurrence in printed text can be estimated by simply counting how often each word occurs in some large corpus of text (e.g., Balota et al., 2007; Brysbaert & New, 2009; Francis & Kucera, 1982). These frequency counts are predictive of the number and duration of fixations on the words when they are encountered during natural reading. The key finding is that high-frequency or common words are typically the recipients of fewer, shorter fixations than low-frequency or uncommon words (Inhoff & Rayner, 1986; Just & Carpenter, 1980;

Kliegl et al., 2006; Rayner et al., 2004; Rayner & Duffy, 1986; Reingold et al., 2012; Schilling et al., 1998). As explained in Chapter 3, the standard account of these frequency effects is that they reflect differences in the relative ease of lexical processing, with high-frequency words being easier to identify than low-frequency words. For example, the representation of high-frequency words might have lower activation thresholds (Grainger & Jacobs, 1996; Morton, 1969; Norris, 1994) or resting (baseline) levels of activation (Coltheart et al., 2001; McClelland & Rumelhart, 1981), making the representations of high-frequency words easier to access. Or alternatively, the connections that link the representation of a word's orthographic form to its phonological or semantic representations might be stronger for high- than low-frequency words (Plaut et al., 1996; Seidenberg & McClelland, 1989). A third account might be that, because high-frequency words are encountered more often than low-frequency words, they tend to be represented redundantly in memory, allowing information about high-frequency words to be recalled more readily than information about low-frequency words (Ans et al., 1998; Kwantes & Mewhort, 1999; Reichle, 2021; Reichle & Perfetti, 2003). By any of these accounts, the influence of word frequency on eye movements is argued to demonstrate that the mind is tightly coupled to the eyes in that the movement of the latter often reflects small differences in the relative difficulty of lexical processing (Reingold et al., 2012).

A second important example supporting the hypothesis of a strong eye-mind link is that words that are predictable from their sentence context are also often the recipients of fewer, shorter fixations than words that are less predictable (Balota et al., 1985; Ehrlich & Rayner, 1981; Kliegl et al., 2006; Rayner et al., 2004; Rayner & Well, 1986). Typically, word predictability is defined using a *cloze* procedure (Taylor, 1953) wherein a separate sample of participants read some portion of a set of sentences (e.g., "The orange cat chased the...") with instructions to guess the next word. In the example shown, the word "mouse" is highly predictable and would be guessed by most participants, while a word like "lizard" would be unpredictable and hence unlikely to be guessed by many participants. Thus, with all else (e.g., word frequency) being equal, participants would spend less time fixating and be more likely to skip "mouse" than "lizard" if either of these two words continued the example sentence. Such demonstrations and other examples show that higher-level language processing is important because they provide compelling evidence that even the fairly sophisticated operations that are required to understand sentences can rapidly influence a reader's decisions about when to move their eyes (e.g., see Ferreira & Clifton, 1986; Frazier & Rayner, 1982, 1987; MacDonald et al., 1992; Rayner et al., 1983; for reviews, see Christianson, 2017; Clifton et al., 2007). As indicated earlier, the simple fact that eye tracking is so useful for studying language processing during reading has meant that the methodology has been put to good use for this purpose during the past few decades (Rayner, 1998, 2009; Rayner et al., 2012; Rayner & Pollatsek, 1989). That being the case, we now turn our discussion to what has been learned from eye-tracking studies about the reading of the language that is the focus of this book – Chinese.

Let us then begin this discussion with a global description of eye movements during the reading of Chinese. For example, Sun and Feng (1999) directly compared eye movements of native Chinese versus English speakers when reading semantically equivalent texts in their native language (i.e., short paragraphs of popular science articles from *Scientific American* and their equivalent Chinese translations). Sun and Feng found that the basic eye movement characteristics are highly similar when reading Chinese and English despite the many differences between the two scripts. For example, during the reading of Chinese versus English, respectively, the observed average fixation durations were approximately 257 ms versus 265 ms, the average saccade lengths were approximately 1.71 words versus 1.75 words, and the average reading rates were 386 words per minute versus 382 words per minute. (Converting these estimates based on word units into Chinese characters, the average saccade length was 2.57 characters and the average reading rate was 580 characters per minute.)[4] A similar but more recent study directly compared the eye movements of three cohorts of readers (native speakers of Chinese, English, and Finnish) reading texts in their native scripts that had been carefully constructed to contain equivalent semantic content (Liversedge et al., 2016). This study both replicated and generalized the basic findings of Sun and Feng (1999) in that the total reading speeds across the three types of scripts were highly similar. Additionally, more fine-grained analyses of the eye movements revealed interesting differences; for example, the Chinese readers made fewer overall fixations but they were of longer duration compared to readers of the other scripts, a finding that was attributed to the visually denser Chinese writing system. Thus, although there are likely subtle differences in the eye movements of Chinese readers – differences that reflect the visual density of the Chinese writing system – the evidence suggests that global aspects

---

[4] This conversion assumes that a word is equivalent (in terms of information content) to 1.5 characters.

4.1 Eye-Tracking Experiments

of eye-movement control are similar between the reading of Chinese and the reading of languages that use alphabetic writing systems. Because of this similarity, our discussion of what is known about the skilled reading of Chinese using eye-tracking methods can proceed along the same lines as our previous discussion of what has been learned about the skilled reading of English – by organizing the discussion about the questions of "where?" versus "when?" the eyes move during reading.

As indicated in Chapter 2, one of the most noticeable differences in how decisions are made about where to move the eyes in the reading of Chinese versus English is the degree to which the former appears to be more reliant upon local processing difficulty to determine how far to move the eyes rather than directing the eyes towards specific within-word locations (Y. P. Liu et al., 2015, 2016; Wei et al., 2013). This stands in contrast to what has been observed during the reading of English and other languages that use alphabetic writing systems, where readers appear to direct their eyes towards a few well-specified default targets (e.g., either the center of the upcoming word or the one that follows; McConkie et al., 1988, 1989; Rayner, 1979; Rayner et al., 1996). The evidence for this difference will be discussed at length below because it plays a central role in the development of models that attempt to account for a host of findings related to the targeting of saccades during Chinese reading (see Y. P. Liu, Yu, Fu, et al., 2019; M. Yan et al., 2010).

With that brief background on how readers of Chinese know where to move their eyes, let us now shift to a related topic – that of the perceptual span. Similar to what has been observed during the reading of alphabetic writing systems, the perceptual span in Chinese is affected by a variety of global text characteristics, such as the text difficulty (e.g., perceptual span is larger when reading easy rather than difficult text; *G. Yan et al., 2008; *G. Yan, Zhang, & Bai, 2013) and the types of masks being used to obscure upcoming text (e.g., perceptual span is larger when using visually similar characters rather than ※ symbols; *G. Yan, Zhang, Zhang, et al., 2013; see also *L. Wang & Yan, 2020). The perceptual span in Chinese is similarly affected by the allocation of attention in that the perceptual span is asymmetric, being smaller to the left of fixation (i.e., approximately one character) and larger to the right of the fixation (i.e., approximately three–four characters; H. Chen & Tang, 1998; Inhoff & Liu, 1998), where each degree of visual angle typically equals one character. Although the perceptual span appears to be smaller in size in Chinese compared to alphabetic scripts (presumably because information in Chinese is more visually and linguistically dense than, for example, in English), when using the number of words to measure the perceptual span, the size of the perceptual span similarly equates to one word to the left of fixation and two words to the right of fixation in both English and Chinese (for a review, see Rayner, 2014). The size of the perceptual span in Chinese was perhaps most accurately measured in a study reported by *W. Tong et al. (2014). In this study, the sentences consisted only of single-character words, whereas studies exploring the perceptual span in Chinese often use sentences containing a mixture of words of varying lengths. W. Tong et al. found that the perceptual span extended two characters or words to the right of the fixation, thus providing a slightly more conservative estimate than what had been previously reported. *L. Wang and Yan (2021) likewise used sentences containing entirely two-character words and found that the perceptual span similarly extended one word to the left and approximately two words to the right of the fixation, providing additional evidence to support the view that the perceptual span is not solely determined by visual acuity, and that covert attention also plays an important functional role.

As is true during the reading of English, Chinese readers extract both orthographic and phonological information from the parafovea. However, the depth and extent of parafoveal information extraction may be more extensive than in English, as reflected by two pieces of evidence. First, the evidence for *semantic* preview effects is much more reliable in Chinese than in English (e.g., Tsai et al., 2012; M. Yan et al., 2009; J. M. Yang et al., 2012). In English, for example, semantic preview is only observed when the preview and target words are synonyms and not when they are semantic associates (Schotter, 2013), and evidence of such effects is also likely to be confounded with the plausibility of the preview (e.g., Veldre & Andrews, 2016). Second, there is evidence that Chinese readers can extract information from two words to the right of the fixated word (e.g., J. M. Yang et al., 2009; L. Yu et al., 2016), whereas such word $N+2$ preview effects in English appear to be limited to lexicalized compound words (e.g., Cutter et al., 2014). The more extensive parafoveal processing in Chinese is presumably because Chinese text is visually more compact with its lack of inter-word spaces and denser orthography. However, it may also reflect the fact that there is a more direct link between orthography and semantics in the Chinese writing system.

One point of contrast between Chinese and English, however, is that there are a few studies that suggest that lexical *parafoveal-on-foveal (PoF) effects*, where the lexical properties (e.g., frequency) of a parafoveal word affect the time spent on the fixated word (see Kliegl et al., 2006), might be more prevalent in Chinese than English. For example, Ma et al. (2015; Experiment 1) found that the initial character frequency of a two-character target word affected the fixation duration on the pre-target word (see also *Cui et al., 2010; J. M. Yang et al., 2009). However, this lexical PoF effect was absent when the whole-word frequency of the two-character target word was manipulated (Ma et al., 2015, Experiment 2); nor was it evident in later studies using a similar manipulation. For example, when the word and initial character frequencies of target words were orthogonally manipulated, L. Yu et al. (2021) did not observe character-frequency or word-frequency PoF effects on the pre-target words (see also *Bai et al., 2009; Xiong et al., 2023). Thus, at best, the evidence for PoF effects in Chinese is mixed, and claims of such effects need to be evaluated carefully considering factors that are known to produce patterns of eye movements that resemble POF effects (e.g., poorly calibrated eye trackers, saccadic error, etc.; see Reichle & Drieghe, 2015). Such factors would presumably contribute more to false-positive "evidence" of PoF effects in Chinese than English because the relevant lexical units (i.e., characters and words) are physically smaller in the former than the latter.

With that brief overview of the factors that determine where readers of Chinese move their eyes, let us now discuss the second category of eye-movement decisions, those pertaining to when the eyes move. If one starts with the assumption that, as with the reading of English and other languages that use alphabetic writing systems, lexical processing is the "engine" that causes the forward movement of the eyes, then one obvious question is: What is the functional lexical unit that causes the eyes to progress through the text? Because Chinese characters are orthographically distinct and spatially discrete and, in most cases, correspond to single morphemes, it would seem reasonable to assume that the identification of individual characters (rather than words per se) is what causes readers' eyes to progress.

To examine this question, H. Chen et al. (2003) carried out an eye-movement study in which relatively skilled readers of Chinese (i.e., 6th grade students and older) read text. Their analyses of the eye-movement data used multiple-regression models with both character-level (e.g., character complexity and frequency) and word-level (e.g., word length and word type) lexical variables as predictors. The results of these analyses indicated that a larger proportion of the variance in the eye-movement data was explained by properties of the character than words, suggesting that characters rather than words are the functional units in the reading of Chinese. However, this pattern of results was not replicated in two later sizeable eye-tracking sentence-reading studies (X. Li et al., 2014; L. Yu et al., 2021). These two studies instead indicated that, when including important word-level variables such as whole-word frequency and predictability as predictors along with other character- and word-level predictors in mixed-effect regression models, the properties of words accounted for more of the observed variance in the fixation probabilities and durations. These studies also showed that properties of the characters, such as their frequencies, were less reliable predictors.

A large number of experiments have also demonstrated that properties of words influence their processing and identification in sentences (e.g., frequency: Y. P. Liu et al., 2015, 2016; *X. Song et al., 2022; G. Yan et al., 2006; L. Yu et al., 2021; predictability: Y. P. Liu et al., 2018; *Z. Liu et al., 2020; Rayner et al., 2005; *X. Song et al., 2022; *W. Tong et al., 2022). These results collectively support the hypothesis that the processing of words (and not characters) are the functional units during the reading of Chinese sentences. Further evidence supporting this word-based processing view comes from experiments that have demonstrated that distorting the spatial layout of text (e.g., by adding spaces between characters; Bai et al., 2008; *M. Chen et al., 2022; X. Li et al., 2013) is disruptive to natural reading.

Finally, the assumption that words rather than characters are the important functional units is also supported by experimental evidence that the meanings of words and not individual characters are integrated with higher-level sentence representations during reading. For example, J. M. Yang et al. (2012) manipulated the contextual plausibility of characters that could be single-character words or the first character of a two-character word. A processing cost was only observed if an implausible character was a single-character word but not when the implausible character was a constituent of the two-character word, suggesting that the meanings of words rather than characters are integrated with the sentence representation, and that Chinese readers have a preference to segment words into larger lexical units (e.g., into one two-character word rather than two single-character words). Similarly, J. Zhou and Li (2021) found evidence that readers prefer to segment three-character words as such even in instances where the first two characters of the words could be segmented as a different two-character word.[5]

Given the accumulating evidence that words rather than characters are the functional units of processing during Chinese reading, the next

---

[5] It is worth noting, however, that in a similar study where the frequencies of the embedded two-character words (i.e., the first or last two characters) of three-character words were manipulated, an embedded word-frequency effect was also observed: Three-character words containing higher frequency embedded words were read faster than those containing lower frequency embedded words (J. Zhou et al., 2018). This finding suggests that Chinese readers to some degree process the words that might be embedded within larger words.

4.1 Eye-Tracking Experiments

question then becomes: How are words segmented during the reading of Chinese? This question was discussed in Chapter 3 where behavioral experiments addressing the question were examined. The experiments that will be discussed here attempt to address the question using eye-tracking to examine the segmentation of words during natural reading.

A few eye-tracking studies have attempted to examine how words are segmented and identified during sentence reading by orthogonally manipulating the frequencies of specific target words and their constituent characters to determine how these variables affect various fixation-duration measures on the target words (which are used as proxy measures for the time required to identify the target words). For example, G. Yan and colleagues (2006) manipulated the frequencies of two-character target words and the frequencies of both of their constituent characters and found that both the word and character frequencies influenced the times required to identify the target words. And more specifically, both the low-frequency target words and low-frequency target words containing lower frequency characters were the recipients of more, longer fixations than the high-frequency target words or low-frequency target words containing higher frequency characters. This pattern of results therefore suggests that both character and word frequency influence the time needed to segment characters into words for their identification.

However, this interpretation is equivocal given that G. Yan et al.'s (2006) pattern of results was not replicated in a more recent eye-tracking study reported by L. Yu et al. (2021). This study similarly manipulated the frequencies of two-character target words and their initial characters and carefully controlled for other linguistic properties (including the sentence contexts across the different target word conditions). L. Yu and her colleagues reported a facilitative effect of word frequency but surprisingly also found an inhibitory effect of character-frequency on the target words. The nature of this latter effect was that target words containing high-frequency initial characters were the recipients of *longer* fixations than target words containing low-frequency initial characters. Thus, contrary to what G. Yan et al. (2006) observed, words that have more common initial characters appear to be more difficult to identify. Although L. Yu et al.'s (2021) reverse character-frequency effect was unexpected because it is counterintuitive, it has since been replicated in two other eye-tracking studies (see Cui et al., 2021; Xiong et al., 2023).

The latter pattern of results led the researchers to speculate that frequencies of the characters, and especially the initial characters of words, may provide important cues about or otherwise constrain how continuous arrays of characters are segmented into words. For example, because common characters (i.e., those having high token frequency) tend to occur in many different words (i.e., also having high type frequency or many word neighbors), the characters provide little constraint to narrow down the possible identity of a word in which the characters are embedded, thereby slowing the word segmentation and identification process relative to what would be expected with low-frequency characters. Consistent with this hypothesis, Cui et al. (2013) found that, when the initial character of a two-character word is of low frequency or is predictive of the second character, providing a non-identical parafoveal preview of the second character increased the processing time of the first character and the whole word. However, this finding must be considered with caution because it is important to distinguish between the effects of a character's neighborhood size and frequency in considering neighborhood effects during Chinese reading since the commonly reported neighborhood size effect is often facilitatory, while the neighborhood frequency effect can be inhibitory (e.g., Tsai et al., 2006).

Yao et al. (2022) did precisely this in their investigation of how the predictability of the target words might modulate the neighborhood size (Experiment 1) and neighborhood frequency (Experiment 2) effects observed in Chinese reading. In this study, neighborhood size was defined by the number of words that differ from a target word by a single character, regardless of its spatial position, and neighborhood frequency was defined by two groups, words having high-frequency neighbors versus those without. The authors reported a typical facilitative effect of neighbor size and an inhibitory effect of neighbor frequency when the target words were not predictable from their prior context. However, interestingly, these effects disappeared when the target words were predictable from their prior sentence context, suggesting that, at least during sentence reading where other linguistic cues (e.g., predictability) are not available to facilitate word segmentation and identification, Chinese readers make use of implicit linguistic cues, such as the number of words that are associated with the fixated characters, to help with narrowing down the potential word identity and speeding up lexical processing.

Somewhat similar to studies that have manipulated orthographic neighborhood density, Zang and colleagues (2016; see also *H. Cao et al., 2023; Yen et al., 2012) investigated whether Chinese readers are sensitive to probabilistic cues that might indicate how a sequence of characters should be segmented[6] and whether they then use this information to

---

[6] That is, the ratio of how often a Chinese character appears as a single-character word to how often it appears as the first character of a multiple-character word.

4.1 Eye-Tracking Experiments

facilitate word segmentation and identification. These studies have found a reduced preview benefit from the second character of the two-character target words in conditions where the first character was more likely to be a single-character word. This pattern of results suggests that Chinese readers do in fact make use of the lexical cues to facilitate word segmentation and identification during reading.

Finally, a small number of character-segmentation studies have used ambiguous character strings to examine how words are segmented during reading. An example of such an ambiguous string is the sequence 花生长, which can be parsed and interpreted in two different ways: as 花生|长, meaning "peanut grows"; or as 花|生长, meaning "flower grows." These studies generally show that the processing of such ambiguous strings is more effortful, as evidenced, for example, by longer reading times on such strings as compared to length-matched, unambiguous characters strings (e.g., Inhoff & Wu, 2005; M. Yan & Kliegl, 2016). The fact that Chinese readers are sensitive to character string ambiguity suggests that they may have specific strategies for resolving such ambiguities.

For example, Perfetti and Tan (1999) suggested that readers might adopt a left-prioritized two-character assembly strategy for segmenting words given that most Chinese words are two characters in length. In their experiment, participants read sentences containing ambiguous character strings such as 照顾客, which can be segmented and interpreted as either 照|顾客 (A|BC), meaning "according to customers"; or 照顾|客 (AB|C), meaning "look after customers." This condition was compared to a control condition involving unambiguous character strings like 按顾客 which can be parsed and interpreted in only one way: 按|顾客 (A|BC), meaning "according to customers." Critically, for both conditions, only the A|BC parsing fitted into the sentence context. Perfetti and Tan found that the reading times on the disambiguating region, which consisted of the last character of the ambiguous string and the two subsequent words, were longer in the ambiguous condition than the unambiguous control condition. Additionally, reading times were inflated when the correct segmentation was A|BC rather than AB|C. These findings together thus support the hypothesis that Chinese readers do use a left-prioritized, two-character assembly strategy (see also H. S. Huang & Li, 2020).

However, there have also been a few studies providing evidence against this hypothesis. For example, Inhoff and Wu (2005) examined the reading of sentences containing pairs of spatially adjacent two-character Chinese words that either were or were not ambiguous. For example, in the ambiguous condition, each possible pair of adjacent characters in the string 专科学生 can form a different word (e.g., 专科 meaning "vocational college," 科学 meaning "science," and 学生 meaning "student"), but with the correct within-sentence parsing being to segment the first pair of characters from the second (i.e., AB|CD). However, in the sentences of the unambiguous condition, only the first and last pairs of characters can form words (e.g., 专科毕业 can only be segmented as 专科 meaning "vocational college" and 毕业 meaning "graduate"). A comparison of the reading times in these two conditions indicated a cost associated with processing the ambiguous character strings, seemingly contrary to the predictions of the two-word assembly hypothesis because the first pair of characters are standalone words in both conditions and should thus be equally easy (or difficult) to process (see also M. Yan & Kliegl, 2016). Furthermore, an analysis of the size of the ambiguity cost conditional upon the frequency of the central word in the ambiguous condition (i.e., the word 科学 in the character string 专科学生) indicated that ambiguity was more detrimental to reading if the central word was relatively high as compared to low in frequency, suggesting that the frequencies of the possible words are an important factor that influences how readers parse ambiguous character strings.

To examine the possible interaction between ambiguity and word frequency more closely, Ma et al. (2014) used three-character ambiguous strings (similar to those used by Perfetti & Tan, 1999) and orthogonally manipulated whether the sentence context supported an AB|C or A|BC parsing of the characters, and the relative frequencies of the words in the ambiguous string (i.e., for half of the strings, AB was a high-frequency word and BC was a low-frequency word, and vice versa for the other half of the strings). Importantly, the sentence contexts prior to the ambiguous strings were identical for the A|BC and AB|C parsing conditions, with the strings then being disambiguated by the latter parts of the sentences. Using this design, Ma and colleagues found an interaction between the two experimental factors during re-reading: In the AB|C parsing condition, ambiguous strings in which the characters AB corresponded to high-frequency words received shorter re-reading times and fewer regressions. This pattern suggests that Chinese readers jointly make use of the left-prioritized parsing strategy *and* the frequency of the potential words to facilitate their processing of ambiguous character strings.

Finally, a study reported by L. Huang et al. (2021) further tested if the sentence context prior to the ambiguous character string affects readers' parsing strategies. These experiments also used three-character ambiguous strings (like those used by Ma et al., 2014) and manipulated the degree to which the sentence context prior to the ambiguous string favored an A|BC parsing. (Note, however, that the sentences always supported an AB|C parsing.) Their results showed that, when the A|BC parsing was more plausible (i.e., the prior sentence context supported both the AB|C and A|BC interpretations), readers made longer first-pass reading times and regressed more often back to the ambiguous string compared to when the A|BC parsing was less plausible (i.e., the prior context only supported an AB|C interpretation). This pattern thus lends additional support to the claim that sentence context provides an additional source of constraint on how readers of Chinese parse ambiguous character strings.

Although these studies have collectively provided important insights into how readers segment and identify words in a script that lack explicit word boundaries, these explorations are somewhat limited because they have only examined a few of the variables that might affect word segmentation and identification during natural reading. For example, there has been no work (that we are aware of) examining how differences in the relative probabilities of encountering words of different lengths might be used in conjunction with sentence context and occasional orthographic cues (e.g., punctuation) to guide word segmentation. This limitation, along with the sheer complexity of what must be explained to understand the skilled reading of Chinese and how it differs from the reading of alphabetic scripts, leads us directly to the next section of this chapter, which reviews theories and models that have been developed to explain and simulate Chinese reading.

4.2 Theories and Models

To our understanding, the first serious attempt to simulate eye-movement control in the reading of Chinese text was reported by Rayner et al. (2007). This work adapted an early version of the *E-Z Reader* model (Reichle et al., 2006) of eye-movement control in the reading of English (see Chapter 1) to the reading of Chinese. The adaptions required to do this were quite modest and mainly involved making concessions to accommodate the denser orthographic forms of Chinese sentences (in comparison to English sentences) by adjusting the values of the model's parameters that control the rate of lexical processing. One important new assumption, however, was that, to simulate Chinese readers, it was necessary to provide the model with information about the boundaries of the individual words within the sentences. Saying this another way, the model was completely agnostic about how Chinese characters are segmented into words, with the simulations only being intended to demonstrate that, if such knowledge was imparted upon the model, then the model's other assumptions (which include the serial allocation of attention to words and the dissociation between the shifting of attention and the movement of the eyes; see Chapter 1) would be sufficient to explain the basic patterns of eye movements that are observed during the reading of Chinese.

The model as described was used to complete two simulations: one in which only word frequency, predictability, and retinal eccentricity (i.e., absolute distance from the center of vision measured in character spaces) were used to modulate the rate of lexical processing, and a second in which the same variables along with character frequency modulated the rate of lexical processing. Interestingly and perhaps counter to intuition, the second simulation with its added assumption about character frequency did not improve the model's overall capacity to simulate the observed data. This result is unexpected because of the considerable evidence that character frequency is an important determinant of looking times on words, as reviewed earlier in this chapter (also see L. Yu et al., 2021).

Based on their simulations, Rayner and colleagues (Rayner et al., 2007: 1029) concluded that "the hypothesis that the control of eye movements in reading Chinese is similar to that in an alphabetic language ... is a reasonable one." However, they also acknowledged that their model failed to address one of the key questions in Chinese reading: How do readers segment parafoveal words for the purposes of their identification and saccadic programming? Their simulations had instead presupposed perfect knowledge of word boundaries and adopted E-Z Reader's other assumptions about saccadic targeting: that the oculomotor system uses information about the boundaries of the upcoming words in programming saccades to the middle of those words. The model thus assumed the use of default saccade targets – the middle of upcoming words.

Although the notion of default saccadic targets might make sense in the reading of languages with alphabetic writing systems where the words are most often demarcated by clear word boundaries (compare Thai, an alphabetic script without clear word boundaries; Reilly et al., 2011), the notion is predicated on the assumption that clear word boundaries are normally available to the reader. Although this assumption is perfectly reasonable for English, it is not reasonable for the reading of Chinese, for obvious reasons. Furthermore, there is evidence showing that, in contrast to what has been observed for alphabetic writing systems like English (e.g., see McConkie et al., 1988), the distributions of fixation landing sites on Chinese words are *not* normally distributed with the centers of those

4.2 Theories and Models

distributions being located near the middle of the words. The evidence instead indicates that, in the reading of Chinese, the fixation landing-site distribution tends to be uniform in shape without clear PVLs (Tsai & McConkie, 2003; Y. P. Liu, Yu, Fu, et al., 2019), suggesting that, in moving their eyes from one word to the next, readers of Chinese do not have clear default saccade targets. This then raises the question: How do readers of Chinese know where to move their eyes?

One possible solution to the question was provided by M. Yan and colleagues (2010). They examined the landing-site distributions of initial fixations on words contingent upon the words having been fixated exactly once (i.e., single fixations) versus having been fixated two or more times. Although the distributions were approximately uniform in shape when both types of fixations were included in the analyses, the conditional analyses yielded something unexpected: Whereas the single-fixation distributions were approximately normal in shape and centered near the middles of the words, the first-of-multiple fixation distributions peaked near the beginnings of the words and decreased monotonically over the lengths of the words. The pattern of results led M. Yan et al. (2010) to propose a "flexible" saccade-targeting account in which readers' decisions about where to direct their eyes are contingent upon whether the upcoming word has been segmented from the sequence of characters in the parafovea.[7] As shown in Figure 4.2, Panel A, according to this account, readers will direct their eyes towards the middle of a parafoveal word that has been segmented because this viewing location affords the most efficient identification of the word when it is fixated. However, if the word has not been segmented, then a reader will direct their eyes towards the beginning of the word because this viewing location will allow a second fixation on the word (if necessary) without having to interrupt the progression of the eyes by making a regression. In other words, to avoid having to make unnecessary regressions which would slow the overall reading rate, readers of Chinese opt to be conservative by making mostly progressive saccades, moving their eyes to the middle of words that will most likely be identified from a single fixation but moving their eyes to the beginning of a word that will most likely require two fixations to identify.

---

[7] Although M. Yan et al. (2010) describe their account as allowing for "flexible" or dynamic saccadic targeting, Y. P. Liu, Yu, Fu, et al. (2019) have argued that the account is instead a variant of default targeting because the eyes are always directed towards one of a small number of possible targets – a refixation on the currently fixated word, the beginning or middle of the upcoming word, or in some instances, the beginning of the word that follows. For that reason, we follow Y. P. Liu, Yu, Fu, et al. (2019) and refer to M. Yan et al.'s (2010) account as the "default-targeting" model.

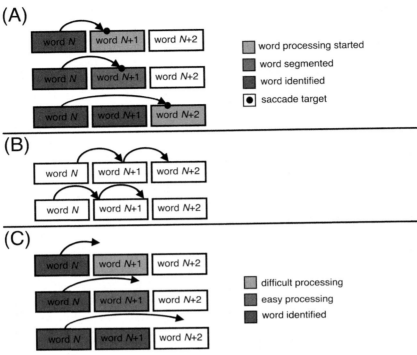

Figure 4.2 The default-targeting (M. Yan et al., 2010) (A) statistical artifact (X. Li et al., 2011) (B) and dynamic-adjustment (Y. P. Liu, Yu, Fu, et al., 2019) (C) accounts of saccadic targeting in Chinese reading
Panel B shows how fixation landing-site distributions that are suggestive of default targets might be due to a statistical artifact reflecting how the fixation landing-site distributions are constructed.

Although M. Yan et al.'s (2010) default-targeting framework provides an elegant account of fixation landing-site distributions that have been observed in the reading of Chinese, this account was not implemented as a formal model. Perhaps more problematic for the account, however, was a demonstration reported by X. Li et al. (2011) using a simple heuristic to simulate eye movements in Chinese reading – a heuristic in which the progressive saccades were of a fixed length but with some amount of saccadic error that was simulated by introducing random (Gaussian) variability to the saccade lengths. When the simulated initial fixation landing-site distributions were analyzed conditional upon those fixations being single fixations versus the first of two or more fixations, the results

4.2 Theories and Models

resembled those observed by M. Yan et al. (2010). And importantly, because the simulation made no assumptions about word segmentation, it demonstrated that the purported relationship between word segmentation and saccadic targeting might be a statistical artifact that reflects how fixation landing-site distributions are constructed. This alternative account is illustrated in Figure 4.2, Panel B. As shown, an initial fixation that (by chance) happens to land near the middle of a given word will tend to be the only fixation on the word because the next saccade (because it is of a fixed length, on average) will move the eyes past the end of the word. But conversely, an initial fixation that happens to land near the beginning of a word will for the same reason be more likely to result in the word being refixated.

X. Li et al.'s (2011) demonstration in combination with a growing body of evidence that readers of Chinese adjust the lengths of their saccades in a manner that reflects the difficulty associated with parafoveal processing (Y. P. Liu et al., 2015, 2016; Wei et al., 2013) resulted in a second account of saccadic targeting in Chinese – one based on the dynamic adjustment of saccade length as a function of parafoveal processing difficulty. This basic hypothesis was formalized by Y. P. Liu et al. (2015) and subsequently used to simulate the findings from several different experiments (Y. P. Liu et al., 2017, 2018; Y. P. Liu, Yu, Fu, et al., 2019; Y. P. Liu, Yu, Reichle, 2019). As Figure 4.2, Panel C shows, the basic intuition of this hypothesis is that, from any given fixation, readers of Chinese are able to monitor the relative difficulty associated with the processing of the parafoveal characters or words and then use this information to adjust the lengths of their saccades accordingly. A saccade into a region will therefore tend to be longer if that region is easier to process, allowing the reader to accommodate differences in local processing difficulty and thereby maximize reading efficiency.

As described in the preceding paragraphs, the key difference between the default-targeting (M. Yan et al., 2010) and dynamic-adjustment (Y. P. Liu, Yu, Fu, et al., 2019) accounts is that, according to the former, any given saccade will be directed towards one of a small number of possible targets, whereas the latter posits that, within some fixed range, the eyes can be directed towards a multitude of different locations. Because of this distinction, it would be easy to discriminate between the two accounts if eye movements were not subject to oculomotor error; one would simply examine the fixations to determine if they are directed to only a few targets (as per the default-targeting account) or a continuous range of locations (as per the dynamic-adjustment account). For that reason, it is necessary to compare the performance of formally implemented versions of the two accounts in their capacity to simulate the data from various eye-movement experiments that have been designed to examine how specific variables (e.g., the frequency of the parafoveal word) influence readers' eye movements. This is exactly the strategy adopted by Y. P. Liu and colleagues (2017, 2018, 2019; Y. P. Liu, Yu, Fu, et al., 2019). Using formally implemented versions of the default-targeting and dynamic-adjustment models, Y. P. Liu and colleagues have shown that the latter consistently outperforms the former in its capacity to provide quantitative accounts of patterns of eye movements observed in several different experiments, with the latter also using fewer free parameters than the former in doing so. Although such demonstrations are not definitive, and although advocates of the default-targeting account might argue that Y. P. Liu, Yu, Fu, et al.'s (2019) implementation of their account overlooks some of its key features, it is fair to conclude that the burden of proof is now on these advocates either to specify how the implementation of their account is deficient, or to provide an alternative implementation.[8]

Apart from X. Li et al.'s (2009) word segmentation and identification model that was discussed in Chapter 3, models of Chinese reading have provided largely separate accounts of character and word identification, on the one hand, and eye-movement control during reading, on the other.[9] The final trio of models that will be discussed in this chapter are thus the first to redress this limitation. As will be discussed, these models attempt to specify how the segmentation and identification of words influence the moment-to-moment decisions about when and where to move the eyes during natural reading. This is particularly true of the first of these models.

The first of these models was developed by X. Li and Pollatsek (2020) and is named the *Chinese reading model* (*CRM*). This model is shown in Figure 4.3. Because of X. Li's central role in the development of this and several other Chinese reading models (X. Li et al., 2009; Rayner et al.,

---

[8] Y. P. Liu, Yu, Fu, et al. (2019) also acknowledged that, in reality, saccadic targeting likely involves both default targeting and dynamic adjustment, since it is weighted towards the former in writing systems that afford clear targets, and is weighted towards the latter in writing systems that do not. To date, this type of hybrid model has not been implemented. However, such an account would explain why, in English, saccades exiting high-frequency words tend to be longer than those exiting low-frequency words (Rayner et al., 2004; White & Liversedge, 2006), and conversely, why fixations tend towards the centers of Chinese words if word boundaries are artificially introduced (e.g., by rending the words in a different color font).

[9] X. Li et al.'s (2009) model is a possible exception here because it attempted to explain explicitly how visual acuity in the context of natural reading might affect the segmentation and identification of words.

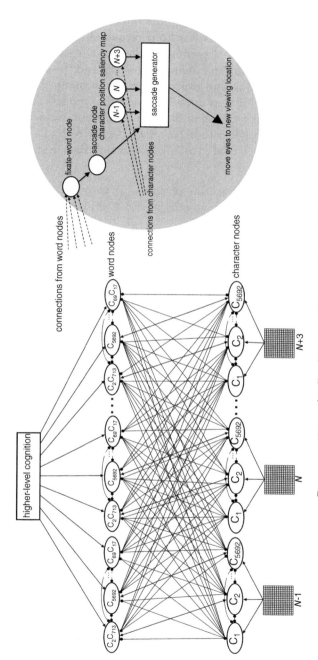

Figure 4.3 X. Li and Pollatsek's (2020) Chinese reading model (CRM)

The model consists of two interacting systems: a word-identification system on the left and an eye-movement control system on the right. The word-identification system consists of character and word nodes, with the latter receiving visual input from 5 spatial locations, N-1 through N+3. Character and word nodes send activation to the eye-movement control system, with a fixate-word and saccade node determining when the eyes move and character nodes in a saliency map determining where the eyes move. For exposition, the character nodes are labeled with unique identification numbers (e.g., C_2 is character #2 of a possible 5,692 characters) and word nodes are labeled with their constituent characters (e.g., the first word node represents a word consisting of C_2 in the first slot and C_{713} is the second slot). Arrows indicate excitatory connections, filled circles indicate inhibitory connections, and ellipses indicate that only a small portion of the network is shown.

2007; Y. P. Liu et al., 2016), it is not surprising that the CRM is the most complete model of Chinese reading that has been proposed to date. As Figure 4.3 shows, the model consists of two interacting subsystems, with one being responsible for segmenting and identifying words and the other being responsible for programming and executing eye movements. The overall architecture of the model is thus quite like two other models that have been developed to explain word identification and eye-movement control during the reading of English text: *Glenmore* (Reilly & Radach, 2003, 2006) and *OB1-Reader* (Snell et al., 2018).[10] All three of these models thus share two core assumptions:

1. words are identified via the propagating of activation through a network of nodes that represent a hierarchy of visual features, letters or characters, and words; and
2. the decisions about when and where to move the eyes are informed by a saliency map that determines the next letter or character to fixate.

As Figure 4.3 shows, the visual input that is fed into the model consists of five 16 × 16 gray-scale images, one for each of 5,692 possible characters in the model's lexicon. The input comes from five separate channels, each corresponding to a unique spatial position and with the total number based on evidence that the perceptual span in Chinese reading typically extends from one character to the left of fixation to three character spaces to the right of fixation (e.g., Inhoff & Liu, 1998). The five channels are thus arranged around the point of fixation, or position N, spanning positions $N-1$ to $N+3$. When a character is displayed to the model, the character's 16 × 16 image will activate a number of character nodes representing the 5,692 different possible character templates at the image's corresponding position. (For the sake of exposition, the character nodes in Figure 4.3 are numbered with their identification number.) The degree to which any given character node becomes active is a function of both the degree of similarity between the image and the node's character template (with similarity being quantified using proportional feature overlap) and retinal eccentricity, which degrades the input as a function of the absolute distance between the input and the center of vision, position N. The influence of eccentricity itself is also modulated by the processing difficulty of

[10] The word-identification system is also very similar to X. Li et al.'s (2009) word identification-segmentation model that was discussed in Chapter 3. But in contrast to that earlier model, the word-identification system in the CRM is implemented as a network of interconnected nodes (as per the interactive-activation model; McClelland & Rumelhart, 1981) rather than using equations to estimate the probabilities of a given set of characters belonging to a word.

4.2 *Theories and Models*

the fixated word, becoming more severe and thus restricting parafoveal processing as foveal processing difficulty increases.

The character nodes then propagate their activation to word nodes to the degree that they are consistent with each word's position-specific configuration of characters. For example, as Figure 4.3 shows, the first word node in the first spatial position corresponds to a two-character word, consisting of character #2 in the first position and character #713 in the second; this word node thus receives excitatory activation from character #2 in position N-1 and character #713 in position N. For the sake of exposition, most of the character and word nodes and their excitatory and inhibitory connections are not shown. But as is true of the interactive-activation model (McClelland & Rumelhart, 1981), the word nodes are mutually inhibitory so that, at any given point in time, only one word can be identified. The rate at which this happens is dependent upon the amount of character-node activation that it receives, the frequency of the word (which determines each node's resting or baseline level of activation), the amount of inter-word competition that results from multiple words sharing characters, and each word's within-sentence cloze predictability. The latter is approximated via top-down activation from a "high-level cognition" module that activates word nodes to a degree that is proportional to their cloze predictability. Finally, notice that the words are represented both redundantly and dynamically across all the possible spatial positions within the perceptual span. As X. Li and Pollatsek (2020) indicate:

> When the eyes move, new slots corresponding to the new characters in the perceptual span are added into the word-processing module. When a word is identified, all the slots corresponding to the recognized characters are removed from the word-processing module. (X. Li & Pollatsek, 2020: 9)

As Figure 4.3 shows, the second main component of the CRM is the eye-movement control system. In this system, the decisions about when to move the eyes are determined by activity of the word nodes. As a word is being identified, it propagates activation to a fixate-word node that in turn propagates activation to a saccade node. As the activation of the latter increases, it will eventually exceed a threshold which then causes the saccade generator to move the eyes. The timing of the eye movements is thus coupled to lexical processing, but only loosely so.

The decisions about where to move the eyes are determined by a saliency map that consists of nodes corresponding to each spatial position in the perceptual span, with each node receiving activation from its corresponding character nodes. When a decision to move the eyes has been made, the saliency nodes are scanned serially from left to right and the first node having activation less than some threshold is selected as the saccade target. This heuristic allows the model to move its eyes just beyond the current focus of lexical processing (e.g., the characters of the word that was just identified), consistent with the processing-based strategy of Li et al. (2011) and Wei et al. (2013). However, the saccades themselves are subject to motor error which often causes the fixations to deviate from their intended targets.

The CRM's architecture as described above provides natural accounts of word frequency, predictability, and length. For example, because high-frequency words are represented by word nodes having high resting levels of activation, they require less time to identify than low-frequency words and are thus (on average) the recipients of fewer, shorter fixations. The model was thus able to accurately simulate the pattern of results of an eye-movement experiment reported by Wei et al. (2013), in which high-frequency target words were fixated less often and for shorter durations, and were also followed by longer (exiting) saccades, than were the lower frequency target words. Moreover, as mentioned above, the model assumes that parafoveal processing is modulated by foveal processing difficulty, thereby allowing the model to predict the interaction between foveal load and parafoveal preview (Henderson & Ferreira, 1990; Kennison & Clifton, 1995; Kliegl et al., 2006; White et al., 2005). This also allows the model to simulate the amount of preview that comes from having a valid preview of a parafoveal word accurately (Gu & Li, 2015).

Similarly, in the model, predictable words receive some additional amount of top-down activation from the "higher-level cognition" module and thus take less time to identify, causing them to be the recipients of fewer, shorter fixations. This design feature allowed the model to simulate accurately the results of another eye-movement experiment in which target words varied in terms of their predictability (high vs. medium vs. low; e.g., Rayner et al., 2005). The CRM reproduced the graded effect of predictability that was observed: As the predictability of the target words increased, they received fewer fixations, were fixated for shorter amounts of time, and were followed by longer (exiting) saccades.

Finally, according to the model, shorter words are less subject to the influence of retinal eccentricity than longer words (i.e., the characters of shorter words are on average closer to the center of vision than are the characters of longer words). This design feature of the model allowed it to simulate accurately an eye-movement experiment that directly compared two- versus four-character words (X. Li et al., 2011). As was observed, the model predicted no difference in the first-fixation durations between the two types of words but predicted more fixations and longer gaze durations on the longer words, as well as longer exiting saccades from those words. Additionally, the fixation landing-site distributions on the target words followed the observed pattern: Initial fixations were more likely near the beginnings of the words and declined monotonically across the words, with no differences between longer versus short words. This last finding is important because it supports a processing-based account of saccade targeting (i.e., an account in which saccade lengths are modulated by local processing difficulty rather than the eyes being directed towards default targets; e.g., Wei et al., 2013).

In addition to the basic effects related to eye-movement control in reading, the CRM simulates and explains a few more experimental findings related to the preferences that readers seem to exhibit in how they segment continuous sequences of characters into words. For example, in encountering the two-character sequence 野猫 meaning "wild cat," where 野 "wild" and 猫 "cat" can both be single-character words or 野猫 "wild cat" can be a two-character word and both ways of segmenting the characters provide equally good continuations of a sentence, the model tends to segment the characters into one two-character word because its word node out-competes the two nodes representing single-character words. This tendency is consistent with demonstrations that readers of Chinese exhibit the same preference to segment characters into longer words (e.g., J. M. Yang et al., 2012; Wei et al., 2013; J. Zhou & Li, 2021). Similarly, in encountering an ambiguous three-character sequence 花生长 that can be alternatively segmented into the words 花生 meaning "peanut" and 长 meaning "grow," on one hand, or the words 花 meaning "flower" and 生长 meaning "grow," on the other, the model prefers the former (i.e., a left-prioritized two-character assembly strategy) unless the latter sequence (e.g., 生长 meaning "grow") happens to correspond to a higher frequency word. As discussed, these preferences have also been documented with readers of Chinese; with all else being equal, readers tend to segment the ambiguous character sequence 花生长 as the words 花生 "peanut" and 长 "grow" (e.g., L. Huang & Li, 2020), unless 生长 "grow" happens to form a higher frequency word (e.g., Ma et al., 2014). The CRM thus provides a viable account of Chinese word segmentation and at least some of the documented preferences that Chinese readers exhibit in parsing ambiguous strings of characters into words.

Even with this brief discussion of the CRM, it should be apparent that the model has a large explanatory scope and accurately simulates a wide range of findings related to the skilled reading of Chinese. The model also very nicely demonstrates how theoretical assumptions that have been widely used to explain the reading of English and other languages that use alphabetic writing systems (e.g., the framework of the interactive-activation model; McClelland & Rumelhart, 1981) can be adapted for the reading of Chinese, with detailed specification of precisely how those assumptions must be adapted (e.g., the top-down propagation of activation to segment characters into words). For these reasons, it should also be clear that the CRM provides a gold standard against which other models of Chinese reading will need to be compared. Let us therefore continue this discussion of Chinese reading models by introducing two final models.

The first of these models deviates quite considerably from X. Li and Pollatsek (2020) CRM in that it returns to the earlier effort (see our previous discussion of Rayner et al., 2007) to adapt the E-Z Reader model to the reading of Chinese text. Remember that Rayner et al.'s earlier effort was limited in that the simulations suggested that there was little if any role for character processing, and the model was provided with information about how characters were segmented (i.e., their boundaries) for the purposes of word identification and saccadic targeting. To address these two limitations, L. Yu and colleagues (2021; see also Y. P. Liu et al., 2023) developed a version of E-Z Reader with additional assumptions specific to the reading of Chinese – the *Chinese E-Z Reader*, or *CEZR*.[11] Figure 4.4 shows the model's architecture, which is almost identical to that of the E-Z Reader model on which it is based (see Figure 1.2). Like E-Z Reader, the CEZR model assumes that attention is allocated in a serial manner to support the processing and identification of only one word at a time, and that the completion of an initial stage of lexical processing, called the *familiarity check*, is what triggers the programming of a saccade to move the eyes to the next word. The key difference between the two models is that, in CEZR, the familiarity check is also used to assess the relative differences in the levels of familiarity of the four characters immediately to the right of the word that has just been identified. In other words, upon segmenting the characters of and successfully identifying word N, attention shifts to the next four characters to segment them and identify word $N+1$. Relative differences in the familiarity of those characters (and more specifically, the possible groupings of those characters), in combination with two new model parameters, are then used to make inferences about the likely grouping of the characters. The character-segmentation heuristic and parameters that are used to do this are illustrated in Figure 4.5.

[11] Although Wu et al. (2008) proposed a similar heuristic for segmenting Chinese characters into words within the framework of the E-Z Reader model, this heuristic was not formally implemented or tested.

4.2 Theories and Models

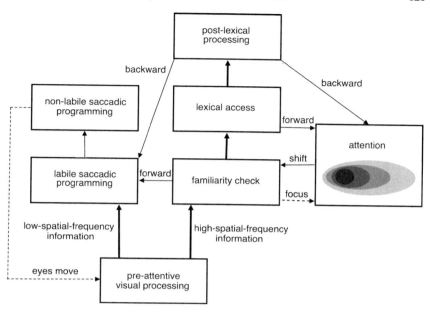

Figure 4.4 Y. P. Liu et al.'s (2023) Chinese E-Z Reader (CEZR) model
This model's architecture is identical to that of the standard E-Z Reader model (see Figure 1.2) with one exception: Relative differences in the familiarity of different possible groupings of characters are used to segment continuous lines of characters into their corresponding words, using the heuristic illustrated in Figure 4.5. The dashed arrow suggests how this segmentation heuristic is used to focus attention on whatever group of characters that is most likely to belong to the next unidentified word.

As Figure 4.5 shows, if the first unidentified character is familiar and the time required to complete its familiarity check exceeds a processing deadline (represented by the parameter θ_1), then the model infers that that character corresponds to a single-character word, allowing lexical processing of that word to continue and causing the oculomotor system to begin programming a progressive saccade. (These saccades are not directed to specific targets but are instead dynamically adjusted to accommodate parafoveal processing difficulty, as per the dynamic-adjustment model that was discussed earlier; Y. P. Liu, Yu, Fu, et al., 2019). However, if the familiarity check on the first character completes more rapidly than θ_1 and more rapidly than the familiarity check on the first two characters by some amount (represented by the parameter θ_2), then the model instead infers that the first pair of characters corresponds to a two-character word, again allowing lexical processing and saccadic programming to continue. And by

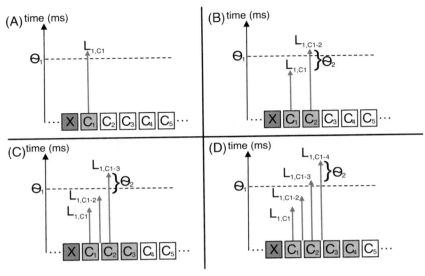

Figure 4.5 A schematic diagram illustrating the character-segmentation heuristic used by Y. P. Liu et al.'s (2023) Chinese E-Z Reader (CEZR) model
X indicates the final character of a word that has been identified, and C_1 through C_5 indicate the first five characters belonging to the next unidentified word(s). Attention is diffusely focused on the first four of these characters. The familiarity check time for the first character is indicated by the vertical arrow labeled L_{1,C_1} in the four panels; similarly, the familiarity check time for the first pair of characters is indicated by the arrow labeled L_{1,C_1-C_2}, and so on. Panel A shows that if the time required to complete L_{1,C_1} exceeds the first parameter θ_1, then the first character is segmented as a single-character word. However, as panel B shows, if L_{1,C_1} completes more rapidly than L_{1,C_1-C_2} by some amount of time, represented by the second parameter θ_2, then the first pair of characters are segmented as a two-character word. Panels C and D show how this heuristic generalizes, allowing the model to (respectively) segment and identify three- and four-character words.

extension, if neither of the two preceding situations happens but the time required to complete the familiarity check for the first pair of characters is faster than the first three by θ_2, then the model infers a three-character word. Finally, if none of the first three situations happens then the model will by default infer that the next four characters correspond to a word.

The model as described above was used to complete simulations from a corpus of eye-movement data that were collected during the reading of sentences containing high- and low-frequency two-character target words in which the first character was also factorially manipulated to be either high- or low-frequency (L. Yu et al., 2021). As discussed earlier in this

4.2 Theories and Models

chapter, this experiment replicated the standard word-frequency effect, with high-frequency target words being the recipients of fewer, shorter fixations than the low-frequency target words. However, the novel contribution of this experiment was the finding that the frequency of the initial character generated the opposite effect, with target words containing high-frequency initial characters being the recipients of more, longer fixations than targets containing low-frequency initial characters. Although this finding was unexpected and counter to intuition, it has subsequently been replicated (e.g., see Cui et al., 2021; Xiong et al., 2023). And perhaps more importantly, in relation to the present discussion, the CEZR model provides an account of this interaction, as well as accounts of a host of other findings from the study, including the influence of word frequency, word predictability, and word length on fixation-duration and fixation-probability measures, fixation landing-site distributions, and the lengths of saccades into and out of words. Finally, the model predicts levels of word-segmentation accuracy that are comparable to those observed with native Chinese speakers (see P. Liu et al., 2013) – 95 percent for the target words and 89 percent for all of the other (i.e., non-target) words in the corpus.

One final benchmark of the model's success is the results of a simulation 2 × 3 "experiment" in which the basic framework of the CEZR model was used to evaluate the explanatory adequacy of two different saccade-targeting assumptions and three different word-segmentation heuristics. The two saccade-targeting assumptions were default targeting versus the dynamic-adjustment of saccade length (as per Y. P. Liu, Yu, Fu, et al., 2019). The three word-segmentation heuristics were:

1. simply providing the model with information about the length of each upcoming word (as per the simulations reported by Rayner et al., 2007);
2. using the relative proportions of words of each length (e.g., 72 percent of words are two characters long; Lexicon of Common Words in Contemporary Chinese Research Team, 2008) to guess the length of each upcoming word; and
3. using the patterns of character familiarity to infer word length, as assumed by the CEZR model that was described previously.

The results of these simulations were informative. For example, the model variant that had perfect knowledge of word boundaries performed poorly, suggesting that human readers also lack perfect word-boundary knowledge. Additionally, the variant of the model corresponding to the CEZR (i.e., the variant using dynamic-adjustment of saccade length and the familiarity-based segmentation heuristic) outperformed the other five models in its capacity to simulate the various eye-movement measures derived from the L. Yu et al. (2021) experiment. This latter result reaffirms earlier claims (e.g., Y. P. Liu, Yu, Fu, et al., 2019) about the dynamic nature of saccadic targeting and further supports the feasibility of the familiarity-based word-segmentation heuristic.

Because the different measures that were used to evaluate the CEZR model were collected from a single experiment (L. Yu et al., 2021), the simulation demonstrates that the model can provide a comprehensive account of behaviors that likely reflect complex, non-linear interactions (see Engbert et al., 2005: 788). This aspect of the model stands in contrast to X. Li and Pollatsek's (2020) CRM, which to date has only provided accounts of key results that have come from separate experiments. It thus remains unclear if the CRM could simultaneously explain the wide variety of findings that are explained by the CEZR model. However, in fairness, it is also important to point out that, in contrast to the CRM, the CEZR model does not provide a detailed, process account of word identification, but instead only specifies how variables related to lexical processing (e.g., a word's frequency in printed text) affect the times required to identify words. This limitation is of course shared with the E-Z Reader model on which the CEZR is based. Future work will thus be required to develop a more detailed, process-based account of word identification within the framework of the CEZR model, perhaps along the lines of what was done with E-Z Reader in developing the *Über-Reader* model of reading (see Reichle, 2021). We now turn now to the final model of eye-movement control in Chinese reading.

This last model that will be discussed in this chapter was recently proposed by Fan and Reilly (2022) and is an adaption of the *Glenmore* model (Reilly & Radach, 2003, 2006) that was mentioned earlier, in our discussion of X. Li and Pollatsek's (2020) CRM. Like the CRM, Fan and Reilly's model has as its core a variant of the interactive-activation model (McClelland & Rumelhart, 1981) that has been adapted to the identification of Chinese words, as well as a saliency map that is used to inform the model's decisions about both when and where to move the eyes. The model's architecture is shown in Figure 4.6. As can be seen, the architecture is very similar to that of the CRM (see Figure 4.3).

Unfortunately, Fan and Reilly (2022) do not provide a detailed description of their model or many of the details about how its implementation differs from the standard version of Glenmore.[12] Their description does make it clear, however, that there are two main adaptions of the model as

---

[12] For detailed descriptions of the standard version of the Glenmore model, see Reilly and Radach (2003, 2006), or Reichle (2021: 419–24).

4.2 Theories and Models

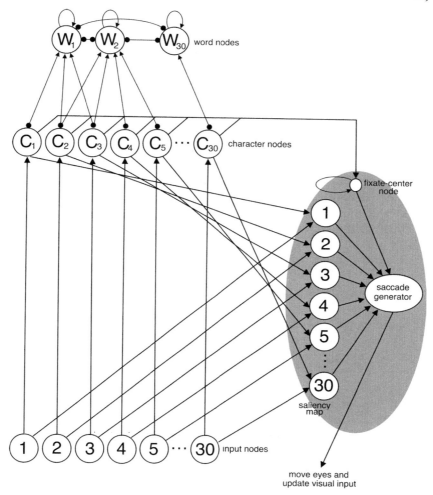

Figure 4.6 Fan and Reilly's (2022) variant of the Glenmore model adapted to the reading of Chinese
Thirty input nodes provide visual information to a bank of nodes representing characters, with each node C_1 through C_{30} representing a set of possible characters at positions 1–30, respectively. Character nodes connect to word nodes, a fixate-center node that determines when the eyes move, and a bank of nodes in the saliency map that determine where the eyes move.

applied to the reading of Chinese. The first is that the letter nodes of the standard model are replaced by nodes representing characters. The second is that character complexity, as quantified by the number of strokes within a character, plays a crucial functional role in the saliency map and thus influences the model's decisions about where to move the eyes. With all else being equal, lower frequency characters require more time to identify and are more likely to be saccade targets. And likewise, complex characters (i.e., characters constituted by more strokes) tend to be more salient and more likely to be saccade targets. Thus, according to the authors (Fan & Reilly, 2022: 7), eye-movement control in the reading of Chinese involves two "complementary" mechanisms: "a default, long range mechanism that progresses the eyes left-to-right, targeting successively visually complex characters," and "a lexically driven short-range mechanism that targets word centers." As implemented within the framework of Glenmore, these two mechanisms operate by modulating the saliency of potential saccade targets.

Finally, although Fan and Reilly's (2022) adaption of the Glenmore model provides an interesting new account of saccadic targeting with the potential to explain a variety of findings related to eye-movement control in Chinese reading, the model's utility in this regard is difficult to evaluate because no detailed simulations of the type reported by both X. Li and Pollatsek (2020) and L. Yu et al. (2021) are provided. The authors do, however, describe one novel prediction of their model. This prediction concerns the relative weighting of word frequency and character complexity in situations where one of the two variables might be more influential in determining where the eyes move. Fan and Reilly also provide at least some evidence confirming this prediction in an analysis of their eye-movement corpus; this evidence lends support for the basic claim that saccadic targeting reflects the interplay of lexical and visual variables. Their model thus shows promise as an account of eye-movement control in reading.

In closing this discussion of the models that have been proposed to explain the skilled reading of Chinese, we share our suspicion that researchers will likely adapt other such models (e.g., SWIFT; Engbert et al., 2005) to the reading of Chinese, as well as develop new models like the CRM of X. Li and Pollatsek (2020). As has been demonstrated, however, many of the basic perceptual, cognitive, and motor processes that determine how skilled readers of Chinese move their eyes through text are not unique to that language or writing system. Indeed, the fact that the basic frameworks of several models (e.g., the interactive-activation model of McClelland & Rumelhart, 1981; E-Z Reader; Reichle et al., 2012) have already been adapted to Chinese strongly suggests that the broad outlines of these models are applicable to languages and writing systems as different from each other as English and Chinese. It is important to emphasize, however, that these demonstrations also indicate that there are also substantial differences that must be explained, both in terms of the nature of what is represented in the lexicon (e.g., letters vs. characters) and how this information might be used during both lexical processing (e.g., segmenting characters into words) and eye-movement control (e.g., relying more upon local processing difficulty in deciding where to move the eyes). The models discussed in this chapter indicate that researchers are making progress in understanding these issues. But we suspect that the real challenge will be to develop models of reading that are general enough to accommodate any language and writing system to which it is exposed – a reading model that, for example, can simulate the skilled reading of native English or Chinese speakers equally well if it is provided with the appropriate "experience" (as might be simulated, for example, by adjusting a few key parameter values). Such modeling efforts of course hint at the important role of reading development, and in the next chapter we will briefly discuss this issue and what is currently known about the developmental trajectory of skilled Chinese reading. We will also briefly discuss one computer model of Chinese word identification that simulates key aspects of this developmental trajectory.

4.3 Conclusion

Like the previous chapter, this chapter has also provided evidence of clear progress in our understanding of the mental processes that support the skilled reading of Chinese. Again, there are unexpected similarities in terms of how native speakers of Chinese and English read text in their respective languages (e.g., perceptual spans that allow for a similar amount of information to be extracted per fixation), as well as several theoretically interesting differences (e.g., saccades lengths are dynamically adjusted rather than being directed towards specific targets). This research also shows clear progress in that sophisticated computer models have been developed that both explain and simulate many of the perceptual, cognitive, and motoric processes that support the skilled reading of Chinese text. As was true in the previous chapter with models of character and word identification, these reading models often adapt existing models that were designed to explain the reading of English (e.g., E-Z Reader; Reichle et al., 2012) to the Chinese writing system, using the frameworks of the former to demonstrate the ways in which the mental processes that support the reading of the two languages are similar or different. The next chapter of this book will extend our discussion of Chinese reading to three topics that have been central to the science of reading:

1. the development of reading skill that occurs as pre-literate children become skilled adult readers;
2. the patterns of reading-specific impairment that are indicative of specific types of dyslexia; and
3. what is currently known from cognitive neuroscience (and in particular, experiments that use brain-imaging methods) about how the human brain supports skilled reading.

CHAPTER 5

Reading Skill Development, Dyslexia, and Cognitive Neuroscience

The previous chapters have reviewed the empirical and theoretical research that has been done to understand the identification of Chinese characters and words both when they are viewed and processed in isolation and in the context of sentences, during skilled reading. In the present chapter, the goal will be to examine research on what is in essence the complement of skilled reading by reviewing studies related to three topics:

1. the normal developmental trajectory that occurs when someone who is illiterate (usually a child) learns to identify some number of characters and words and, usually through years of formal education and practice, becomes a skilled reader;
2. the atypical developmental trajectory that occurs when someone who has adequate access to education and resources nonetheless fails to become a skilled reader, often due to reading-specific impairment, or *dyslexia*; and
3. what is known about the neural underpinnings of the reading of Chinese and how it is similar to and different from the reading of alphabetic writing systems.

All three of these topics will be examined using the same organizational "threads" that were used in the previous chapters: behavioral experiments and computer models. The third topic will of course also review work that has been done using a variety of different methods for understanding the neural basis of cognition – most notably, the different methods that have been developed to image the brain during reading and other reading-related tasks, such as word naming and lexical decision (for a brief overview of these methods, see Chapter 1).

5.1 Reading Skill Development

Because lexical processing is arguably the most important component of skilled reading, it is perhaps not surprising that most research on reading development has been focused on how children learn this critical skill. Although some of this research has started to focus on the development of higher-level reading comprehension skills, this section will focus exclusively on the former topic of how children learn to read Chinese characters and words. This will be done by way of comparison to what is known about how children learn to identify words in alphabetic writing systems like English. As will become evident, although children learn to read in a similar manner across writing systems, the process of learning to read is also affected by the unique properties of a given script (for reviews, see Castles et al., 2018; Landerl et al., 2022; McBride, 2016; Share, 2021).

The process of learning how to read English or other alphabetic languages typically emphasizes the development of *decoding* skill, or the ability to rapidly and accurately "translate" or convert individual letters into their corresponding sounds. This is especially true during the initial stage of learning how to read, where letter knowledge and phonemic awareness are critical skills that develop in a reciprocal manner with reading skill (see Castles et al., 2018; Ehri, 2005; McBride & Wang, 2015; Rayner et al., 2001). As reading skill develops, children also gradually transition from reading words via grapheme-to-phoneme decoding to being able to identify words more directly and thus more rapidly and accurately, especially if those words are frequent or have irregular pronunciations (see Brysbaert et al., 2018; Nation, 2017). As reading skill continues to develop, children become sensitive to the morphological structure of complex words, gaining awareness of the underlying regularities between spelling and meaning (e.g., "un" + "clean" = "unclean," "clean" + "er" = "cleaner"; see Carlisle, 2000; Treiman & Cassar, 1996).

Research has also indicated that the orthographic *depth* of a writing system, or the degree to which graphemes map onto phonemes in a one-to-one, unambiguous manner, influences the initial stage of learning to read, with "deep" scripts like English resulting in slower reading skill development than "shallow" scripts like Spanish or Czech (e.g., Caravolas et al., 2013; Spencer & Hanley, 2004). And relative to alphabetic writing systems, the initial stage of learning to read Chinese characters is more effortful and proceeds at an even slower pace: Estimates suggest that an additional two–three years are required (McBride-Chang, 2004) because of both the large inventory of radicals (around 600; *Han, 1994) and characters (several thousand; see Chapter 2) that must be learned to attain functional literacy, and because phonetic radicals provide relatively unreliable information about the pronunciations of characters. Perhaps for those reasons, the government of mainland China adopted the use of an

5.1 Reading Skill Development

alphabetic writing system called *pinyin* in the 1950s to help increase the literacy rate of its citizens. This system is still used today in early reading education to teach phonological awareness to children as they are also being introduced to Chinese characters.[1] This obviously complicates any discussion of reading skill development because children in mainland China receive two types of reading instruction (first pinyin and then characters), but it also affords an interesting contrast between children in mainland China (where pinyin is used) and children from other Chinese-speaking areas like Hong Kong (where pinyin is not used and reading instruction begins with characters).

Because of the importance of phonological knowledge in alphabetic writing systems, many early studies on learning to read Chinese also explored the role of phonological awareness. These studies employed phonological awareness tasks and demonstrated that awareness of syllables and rimes develops relatively early, but that awareness of onsets develops relatively late (e.g., C. Ho & Bryant, 1997a, 1997b; Shu et al., 2008; *Tang & Wu, 2009). Phonological knowledge and skill then continue to develop with age and grade, but with the rate of development also being influenced by instructional experience (McBride-Chang et al., 2004; Shu et al., 2008). For example, McBride-Chang and colleagues (2004) compared the development of phonological awareness in Chinese kindergartners and first graders sampled from Hong Kong and Xi'an, a large city in mainland China. This comparison indicated that Xi'an children outperformed Hong Kong children on both the syllable and phoneme-onset tasks, suggesting that the pinyin that is used in teaching the Xi'an but not the Hong Kong children facilitated the development of the former group's phonological knowledge. However, C. Ho and Bryant (1997a) observed a phonological regularity effect (i.e., phonologically regular characters were named faster than irregular characters) and phonological errors (i.e., overregularization in pronouncing irregular characters) in Hong Kong first and second graders, indicating that these children were also aware of and could make use of the implicit phonological regularities in Chinese characters. (For evidence of an awareness of phonological regularity in Beijing primary schoolers, see *Shu & Zeng, 1996; and *Shu et al., 2000.)

Research has shown that the use of pinyin facilitates reading-skill development, presumably because it helps children visualize and thereby gain awareness of both phonemes (because individual pinyin letters are

---

[1] Pinyin also allows for easy-to-use keyboard interfaces for electronic devices like computers and smartphones.

used to spell out the phonemes of syllables and their corresponding tones) and the pronunciations of the whole characters, and because it allows children to self-teach themselves unknown characters that exist in their oral vocabulary (e.g., *Shu & Liu, 1994). For example, *Ren et al. (2006) compared two groups of Chinese kindergarteners across a nine-month period during which they received reading instruction either with or without the use of pinyin. The results of this comparison indicated that the children who learned using pinyin gained more phonological knowledge, with significant improvements in their knowledge of Chinese syllables, onsets, and rimes. Similarly, Lin and colleagues (2010) found that Chinese kindergarteners' pinyin spelling scores predicted their subsequent character reading performance a year later, even controlling for other core cognitive skills (e.g., phoneme-deletion performance, pinyin letter-name knowledge, initial character reading scores). Finally, a recent experiment conducted by L. Li et al. (2018) indicated that the use of *zhuyin* (the equivalent of pinyin that is used in Taiwan) alongside text facilitated several measures of the reading performance of Grade 2 students. Relative to a baseline condition that did not entail the use of zhuyin, the students using zhuyin were better at phonological decoding (i.e., accurately reading aloud) novel characters that had been embedded in three-character words. The use of zhuyin did not enhance the orthographic learning of these compound words, however, as measured using both orthographic-choice and spelling tasks.

The studies that have just been reviewed indicate that there is a relationship between phonological knowledge and the development of reading skill in students whose education includes explicit phonological training using either pinyin or zhuyin. This work has been informative because it demonstrates that phonology plays an important role in learning to read Chinese, just as it does in learning how to read English or other alphabetic scripts. The work is limited, however, in that it remains silent about what happens with children who are learning to read Chinese without the additional support that comes from the use of pinyin or zhuyin, as is common outside of mainland China, where reading instruction often begins with the introduction of characters.

Studies investigating the relationship between children's phonological knowledge and their literacy development in the absence of pinyin or zhuyin training also collectively suggest that the children's phonological knowledge, and especially their speech segmentation (i.e., syllables, onsets, and rimes) and suprasegmental (i.e., tones) knowledge, is associated with their character and word reading measured both concurrently

5.1 Reading Skill Development

and longitudinally (e.g., C. Ho & Bryant, 1997b; C. Hu & Catts, 1998; McBride-Chang & Ho, 2000; Siok & Fletcher, 2001). For example, C. Ho and Bryant (1997b) examined the link between Hong Kong children's visual-spatial and phonological skills and their future success in reading. This was done by first measuring various visual-spatial (e.g., eye-motor coordination, shape detection, visual memory) and phonological (e.g., rhyme-tone detection, partial homophone detection, phonological feature detection) skills of a group of three-year-old preschoolers. The reading ability of those same children was then measured two–three years later using the reading of single characters, two-character words, and pseudo-characters, with successful performance in the last of these requiring the use of phonetic radicals. In a statistical analysis that controlled for the children's age and IQ, as well as the education of their mothers, the visual-perception skills were predictive of the children's early character reading performance, whereas children's phonological skills were predictive of their later word reading, presumably because phonological knowledge facilitated the use of phonetic radicals to help read unknown characters. McBride-Chang and colleagues (2008) further demonstrated a strong and unique association between children's tone awareness and their ability to identify characters, even after controlling for syllable knowledge and other variables (see also Shu et al., 2008; X. Tong et al., 2015). And more recently, Y. Zhou and colleagues (2012) conducted a training study in which Hong Kong kindergarteners were provided with:

1. phonological training that was designed to improve awareness of syllables, rimes, and tones;
2. homophone training which helped children differentiate the morphemes that share the same pronunciation; and
3. morphological training that taught the children how to combine morphemes into compounds words.

Relative to the no-training condition, morphological training improved the children's character and word reading, and both morphological and homophone training also improved the children's vocabulary, whereas phonological training only improved the children's phonological awareness, with little or no improvement in either character and word reading or vocabulary.

As noted earlier, many early studies of Chinese reading development focused on the role of phonology because this variable was known to play such an important role in the reading of alphabetic scripts. And for precisely the opposite reason, many other early studies of Chinese reading development have focused on another feature of the writing system because it differs so markedly from alphabetic scripts – the fact that Chinese characters are two-dimensional configurations of strokes that vary in terms of their complexity. This has led researchers to explore the possible relationship between children's visual processing skill and their reading ability.

For example, C. Ho and Bryant's (1997b) longitudinal study showed that children's visual-spatial skills were positively associated with their early character reading performance. Similarly, H. S. Huang and Hanley (1997) compared the relative importance of visual-spatial skills (visual-form discrimination and visual pair-associate learning) and phonological awareness (rhyme and phoneme detection) for the reading ability of eight-year-old primary school children in Hong Kong, Taiwan, and Britain. Their results showed that the children's visual-spatial skills, particularly their performance in visual paired-associate learning, were the best predictor of Chinese reading ability for both Hong Kong and Taiwanese children, but not for the British children. This study and others to be reviewed thus indicate that the role of visual-spatial skill in learning to read Chinese remains inconclusive.

For example, a meta-analysis of thirty-four studies published between 1991 and 2011 suggested only a low-to-moderate positive correlation between children's visual-spatial skills and early (i.e., prior to Grade 2) character acquisition, with this relationship being much attenuated after Grade 2 (L. Y. Yang et al., 2013). And similarly, Li et al. (2012) conducted a study of children from mainland Chinese spanning kindergarten through Grade 3. A key finding was a lack of correlation between the visual-spatial skills and character identification of the kindergartners after statistically controlling for other phonological and morphological skills as well as speeded naming. (There *was* a positive correlation, however, between kindergartners' visual-spatial skills and character reading performance before the other variables were controlled.) Interestingly, H. Li et al. (2012) found a unique positive relationship between primary schoolers' orthographic knowledge (measured using an orthographic judgment task) and their character reading performance when other cognitive skills were statistically controlled, suggesting that orthographic awareness plays a more important role than visual-spatial skill in children's reading development, especially for primary school students who are just starting to receive formal reading instruction.

In line with H. Li et al.'s (2012) latter finding, several other recent studies also suggest a more important role of children's orthographic knowledge (i.e., awareness of the internal orthographic structure of Chinese

5.1 *Reading Skill Development*

characters), especially radical knowledge (e.g., phonetic radicals providing clues about how to pronounce characters, semantic radicals are often on the left of compound characters while phonetic radicals are on the right, etc.), in reading development (X. Tong & McBride-Chang, 2010; X. Tong et al., 2009; Yeung et al., 2016). For example, X. Tong and colleagues (2009) conducted a one-year longitudinal study on Hong Kong kindergarteners that explored the relative contributions of orthographic, phonological, and morphological knowledge, as well as differences in ability to name numbers rapidly, on the children's performance of three reading tasks both at the start of the study and after the intervening year:

1. naming two-character Chinese words;
2. spelling two-character Chinese words; and
3. reading comprehension.

There were two sets of findings from this study. First, both orthographic knowledge (i.e., the ability to discriminate characters from visual symbols, noncharacters, and pseudo-characters) and morphological knowledge (as measured via lexical compounding and homophone production) uniquely explained performance on all three reading tasks, with orthographic knowledge also predicting word identification and spelling one year later, and with morphological knowledge also predicting word identification and reading comprehension one year later. Second, although phonological awareness did not explain performance on any of the three reading tasks, it did predict later spelling performance.

Studies have also suggested that Chinese children become aware of the orthographic structure of Chinese characters from a young age. For example, using variations of a character-decision task, researchers have demonstrated that kindergartners can already differentiate both patterns of strokes from patterns of straight lines (*H. Li et al., 2006; *Zhao & Li, 2014) and radicals from digits or distorted radicals (Qian et al., 2015), probably because these children have been exposed to print prior to starting school. Other studies have likewise demonstrated that primary school children are able to differentiate characters from random stroke patterns, as well as characters and pseudo-characters from non-characters containing illegal radicals or radicals in illegal positions, and that this orthographic awareness continues to develop with age and grade, with knowledge of the positions of radicals developing earlier than knowledge of the radicals themselves (*H. Li et al., 2006; *J. Li, Fu, & Lin, 2000; Shu & Anderson, 1999; *Zhao & Li, 2014).

Children also develop an awareness of the functions of semantic versus phonetic radicals. For example, Shu and Anderson (1997) asked first, third, and fifth graders in Beijing to select characters (from among four foils) to complete distorted two-syllable words that were in the children's oral vocabulary. One of the syllables in the distorted words was presented as a known character, in written form, and the other in pinyin; children were asked to choose the correct character to replace the pinyin. Third and fifth graders were more likely to choose characters containing the semantic radicals that were relevant to the meaning of the whole words, suggesting that these children made use of the semantic radicals and were sensitive to their function. Similarly, C. Ho et al. (1999) conducted two experiments in which Hong Kong first and third graders received instruction on the phonetic (Experiment 1) and semantic (Experiment 2) functions of radicals. Both experiments demonstrated a training benefit for both groups of children, suggesting that even first graders can exploit the internal regularity of Chinese characters, generalizing the pronunciations of phonetic radicals and the meanings of semantic radicals to unknown (i.e., new) characters. Other studies have provided additional evidence that explicit training on the functions of radicals facilitates reading and writing development (Anderson et al., 2003; X. Chen et al., 2003; Packard et al., 2006).

In addition to orthographic knowledge, several studies indicate that the actual act of writing (i.e., the hand movements required to write characters as well as the order in which the strokes are written) also plays an important role during the initial stage of learning how to read, possibly because the act of writing helps in the decomposition of characters and radicals into their constituent parts, the individual strokes. For example, Tan et al. (2005) found that children's writing skill as measured by the speed and accuracy of a character-copying task was uniquely associated with the character reading performance of both beginning (seven- and eight-year-olds) and intermediate (nine- and ten-year-olds) readers, even after statistically controlling for IQ and phonological skills (see also McBride-Chang et al., 2011). And a two-year longitudinal study reported by Lo et al. (2016) found that children's semantic radical knowledge measured at the first grade significantly predicted their later word reading and spelling performance. This study also found that, after controlling for other important cognitive skills (e.g., rapid naming, phonological, morphological, and semantic-radical awareness), the children's knowledge of strokes and their order (as measured by the children's accuracy at filling in the next strokes of partially rendered characters) also contributed to their spelling performance.

Although the studies that have just been discussed suggest that writing and the knowledge of strokes and their order that this entails contributes to the development of reading skill, it is important to note that, in another study, Lam and McBride-Chang (2013) directly compared the effectiveness of two types of training (stroke order writing vs. radical knowledge) in Hong Kong kindergarteners. This study found that the radical-knowledge training significantly improved the children's semantic knowledge and dictation, while the stroke-writing-order training had no effect. Although it is difficult to interpret null findings, this lack of a training effect may simply reflect the fact that eight weeks of training was insufficient to influence how kindergarteners learn to write complex (i.e., traditional) characters, especially if the trained stroke order conflicts with the order in which the children may have already learned to write those characters (e.g., prior to any training received in the experiment).

Finally, given that the phonological cues are not very reliable in Chinese, along with the fact that there are many homophones in Chinese and the majority of Chinese words are formed through the compounding of morphemes, it is perhaps not surprising that an increasing number of studies have consistently shown that children's morphological knowledge is critical in learning to read Chinese, and especially the identification of words (e.g., Ku & Anderson, 2003; W. Li et al., 2002; H. Li et al., 2012; McBride-Chang et al., 2003; X. Tong et al., 2009; Yeung et al., 2013). There is also an ongoing debate (e.g., see McBride, 2016) about whether the skill of using semantic radicals to learn new characters (because a semantic radical is often indicative of its character's meanings; see Chapter 2) reflects *orthographic* awareness (because semantic radicals are orthographic constituents of characters, as are phonetic radicals) or instead reflects morphological awareness (because semantic radicals are often indicative of a character's meaning even if they cannot be pronounced). We have already discussed findings related to the former interpretation above and will discuss findings related to the latter interpretation here, reviewing studies that inform our understanding of how children might learn to use their knowledge of morphology to make inferences about words.

For example, McBride-Chang and colleagues (2003) explored the relationship between morphological awareness and reading skill in Hong Kong kindergartens and second graders. They measured children's morphological awareness using two tasks:

1. a morpheme identification task in which the children selected pictures corresponding to the correct meanings of morphemes in two-character words; and
2. a morpheme construction task in which the children generated new compound words for novel objects and concepts using a previously learned morpheme.

Reading skill was also measured using both character and word identification. The results showed that performance on both morphological awareness tasks uniquely predicted these children's reading skill even after statistically controlling for the children's age, visual processing speed, phonological awareness, and number naming speed. And consistent with this finding, a longitudinal study by X. Tong et al.'s (2009) found that children's morphological skills (as measured via lexical compounding and homophone production) were also uniquely predictive of their word identification skill and reading comprehension.

A few studies have also suggested that explicit morphological training facilitates children's learning to read. For example, X. Wu and colleagues (2009) conducted a large scale two-year intervention for 169 Beijing first graders that entailed both orthographic training (i.e., teaching students the orthographic structure of characters) and morphological training (i.e., teaching students how to generate new words using known characters). About half of the students received the orthographic and morphological intervention during their first and second grades, while the remainder received no training. X. Wu and colleagues showed that the intervention significantly improved children's literacy development across the duration of the study, engendering significant vocabulary development and improving sentence reading comprehension early in the second grade, and improving word dictation, reading fluency, and paragraph reading comprehension early in the third grade. Similarly, in the study by Y. Zhou et al.'s (2012) where Hong Kong kindergarteners received phonological, lexical compounding, and homophone training, the lexical compounding training significantly improved the children's character and word reading.[2]

Finally, as is true in learning how to read an alphabetic script, the amount and quality of learning experience matters in Chinese reading development. For instance, low-frequency characters and words are read more slowly and less accurately than higher frequency characters and words, and this frequency effect tends to be more pronounced with younger than older children (e.g., *J. Chen & Zhang, 2005; C. Ho & Bryant, 1997a; Shu & Anderson, 1999). This finding, along with the others reviewed so far in this section, underscore our earlier claim that the differences in how children learn to read Chinese versus alphabetic scripts are arguably overshadowed

---

[2] At this point, it is important to acknowledge that several of the studies that have been discussed also suggest that the rapid naming of digits or letters is an important predictor of children's reading skill. Because the mechanism mediating this effect remains unclear (see McBride & Wang, 2015 for a review), we will not discuss this result here.

by the similarities. As will be discussed later in this chapter, these similarities likely reflect a common set of brain structures that support the development of skill reading that is largely invariant across writing systems. For now, however, we will shift our focus to discuss another method that has been used to understand the development of Chinese reading.

This discussion of reading skilled development has shown that rapid progress is being made in understanding how children become skilled readers of Chinese. This empirical work has been complemented by its theoretical counterpart. One example is the model that was proposed by Xing et al. (2002, 2004) and that is depicted in Figure 5.1. As shown, this model is a connectionist network that simulates the speeded naming task of Chinese characters. The architecture of the model is relatively simple in that it consists of a single layer of connections that link nodes representing both the orthographic and phonological forms of characters on the input side, and nodes representing the pronunciation of those same characters on the output side. As shown, both the input and output nodes represent simple orthographic and phonological features. For example, the orthographic input consists of a large number of nodes representing the number of radicals in a given character and their spatial arrangement, as well as the features of up to seven different radicals. Similarly, two groups of phonological input nodes represent the features of a character's pronunciation and the pronunciation of its phonetic radical. Finally, a group of output nodes represents the phonological features of the character's pronunciation.[3]

During the training of the model, all of the input nodes corresponding to the orthographic and phonological features of a character are turned on (i.e., activated), as are the nodes corresponding to the features of the character's pronunciation. The connection weights between all co-active nodes are then increased or strengthened so that, across multiple iterations of learning, the model learns to map a character's orthographic form onto its pronunciation accurately. The model is thus a *self-organizing map* (Kohonen, 1995; see also Miikkulainen, 1997) because, if trained on some type of training corpus, the model will learn to abstract out whatever statistical structure happens to be in that corpus and then generalize this knowledge to new instances if they share the same structure as the corpus.

---

[3] Xing et al. (2004: 49) acknowledge that it might be "strange to mix phonological information with orthographic information in one [input] representation," but justify this design by citing evidence (e.g., Yang et al., 2000) suggesting that "sound information of whole characters and their phonetics is included into [sic] the orthographic representation of phonograms."

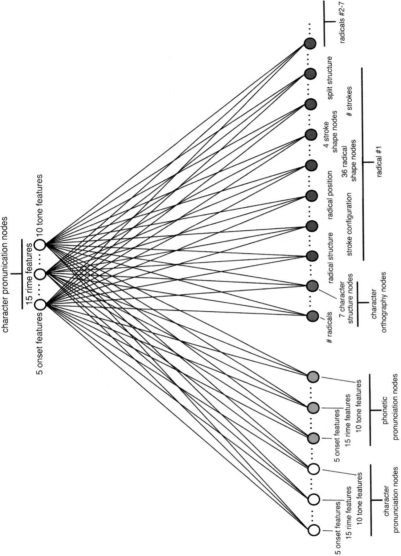

Figure 5.1 Xing et al.'s (2002, 2004) connectionist model of Chinese character pronunciation

At the bottom of the figure going from left to right are: (1) thirty nodes (white) representing features of the character's pronunciation; (2) thirty nodes (light gray) representing features of the pronunciation of the character's phonetic radical; (3) eight nodes (medium gray) corresponding to the number of radicals and their arrangement with the character; (4) seven groups of forty-five nodes (dark gray), with each group representing the orthographic features of a radical. The thirty features at the top of the figure represent features of the character's pronunciation. (Note that all of the connections are bi-directional with the strength of the connections being adjusted by strengthening the connections between co-active nodes.)

5.1 *Reading Skill Development*

This type of learning is "unsupervised" because the model is able to learn about the structure of the corpus from specific examples, without any type of explicit instruction about the nature of the structure (compare back-propagation, where an error signal must be provided to the model; e.g., see Reichle, 2021, Appendix C). For that reason, the model is a useful tool for examining the type of statistical knowledge that beginning readers of Chinese *might* extract from their experiences in school, after they have received some amount of formal instruction about the most commonly used Chinese characters.

This was precisely the approach adopted by Xing et al. (2002, 2004). They did this by first selecting a textbook corpus that was compiled from materials that make up the reading curriculum for Grade 1–6 children in mainland China. Detailed statistical analyses of the corpus indicated that, with the progression from Grade 1 to 6, children are taught about 3,306 characters, with an increasing number of those characters being phonograms and about 75 percent of the total corpus consisting of phonograms. The overall token frequency of those characters also decreases across grades because the most commonly used characters (which also consisted of a higher proportion of non-phonograms) are taught in the earlier grades. And because characters having regular pronunciations (i.e., characters that are pronounced the same as their phonetic radicals) also tend to be lower in frequency, the proportion of regular characters that are learned also increases across grades. Finally, because the total number of known characters increases with grade, so do the number of characters that share a phonetic with one or more other characters. Although both the number and size of these character "families" increase with grade, as children learn more characters, the number of inconsistent families increases more rapidly than the number of consistent families. In other words, children learn an increasing number of characters that share a common phonetic, but one or more of those characters are pronounced differently. Therefore, these analyses collectively indicate that the materials used to teach Chinese children how to read have a fairly complex statistical structure – one that reflects the intrinsic properties of the characters themselves, but one that also reflects the curriculum and the order in which the characters are taught across grades.

Xing et al. (2002, 2004) then completed a series of simulations using their model. Each of these simulations first entailed training their model on a randomly selected sample of characters from the textbook corpus, using only those characters that would have been taught by Grade 2, 4, or 6, and sampling those characters proportional to their frequency of occurrence in the textbooks. This was done to approximate the learning history

Reading Skill Development

(i.e., lexical knowledge) of beginning readers at three different points in their education, and to ensure that the model would receive more training on the commonly occurring characters. Each simulation then tested the model's capacity to name some number of trained characters accurately as well as some number of new, untrained characters. Across the simulations, the model was quite accurate in generating the correct pronunciations of previously learned characters (more than 93 percent correct), with its overall performance improving with grade level. The model also exhibited effects of character frequency, regularity, and consistency in that it was more accurate naming those characters that occurred more often, were pronounced like their phonetic radicals, and/or were pronounced similarly to other characters sharing the same phonetic radicals. However, these effects interacted with grade level: Going from Grade 2 to 6, the sizes of the frequency and regularity effects decreased but the size of the consistency effect increased. Finally, the model was able to generate the correct pronunciations of novel characters, with an increasing reliance upon the use of phonetic radicals to do so going from Grade 2 to 6.

Based on the results of their statistical analyses and simulations, Xing and colleagues (2002, 2004) argue that children who are learning to read Chinese do not simply commit new characters to memory via rote memorization (as might be assumed), but instead rely upon the inherent statistical structure of what is being learned. This conclusion is important given the marked differences between Chinese and writing systems like English and German, where the statistical regularity between orthography and phonology is more readily apparent. The simulations also strongly suggest that learning plays an important role in moderating the regularity or consistency effects that have been interpreted as evidence favoring one or another set of mechanisms for identifying printed words (e.g., the debate about whether word vs. pseudo-word naming requires one "route" or two; see Coltheart et al., 2001; Seidenberg & McClelland, 1989); the magnitude of these effects instead varies as a function of learning in complex ways that seemingly require the use of computer models to understand fully. And as will become clear in the next section, this complexity only increases with efforts to understand why the acquisition of reading skill sometimes deviates from its normal trajectory, as happens with different types of reading impairment.

5.2 Dyslexia

This section will discuss *dyslexia* or reading-specific impairment. Although dyslexia can result from head trauma, disease, or stroke, most of the research that has been conducted on dyslexia among readers of Chinese has not focused on this type of *acquired dyslexia*, but has instead focused on *developmental dyslexia* – a reading-specific impairment that is characterized by delayed or poor literacy skills despite having no obvious neurological or sensory deficits, and despite having adequate intelligence and an adequate opportunity to learn how to read (e.g., Bishop & Snowling, 2004; Snowling, 1987). Because a core component of this impairment is inaccuracy and dysfluency in reading isolated words, it is most often diagnosed using performance on standardized tests that have been designed to measure accuracy and/or speed in identifying or spelling words, rather than, for example, using performance in reading actual text. Using such measures, a child who performs 1.5 or more standard deviations below the mean performance of their same age or grade peers might be deemed as dyslexic (e.g., L. P. Yang et al., 2022).

Because learning how to identify words in alphabetic languages entails the learning of *grapheme-to-phoneme correspondences* (*GPCs*) (e.g., Bishop & Snowling, 2004; Peterson & Pennington, 2012) whereas learning to read Chinese does not, early studies examining the prevalence of dyslexia tended to underestimate its rate of occurrence in Chinese-speaking countries (e.g., Makita, 1974). However, more recent studies have adopted the same diagnostic criteria that have been used to study dyslexia with alphabetic languages and have consequently reported similar rates of dyslexia among children who are learning to read Chinese versus alphabetic writing systems.[4] For example, Stevenson and colleagues (1982) compared the reading levels of fifth graders in Taiwan, Japan, and the United States. The students' reading skill was measured using culturally appropriate reading tests that spanned seven grade levels of difficulty (kindergarten through the sixth grade). Other tests were also included to measure vocabulary and the reading comprehension of textual materials, as well as both verbal and non-verbal tests of general cognitive functioning. The key finding was that approximately 2 percent, 8 percent, and 3 percent of the Taiwanese, Japanese, and American children respectively lagged their own grade (the 5th) by at least two full grades. And when dyslexia was defined to include those children who obtained the lowest 10 percent of reading scores and scored one or more standard deviations below the mean for verbal ability, the percentages of dyslexic children were approximately equivalent across the three countries: 7.5 percent, 5.4 percent and 6.3 percent for Taiwan,

---

[4] Although standardized criteria are available for diagnosing dyslexia in Hong Kong and Taiwan, this is less true in mainland China (see McBride et al., 2018).

Japan, and the United States respectively. The two findings thus suggest comparable levels of reading impairment across the three languages that were studied. A recent meta-analysis similarly estimated the mean prevalence rate of dyslexia to be 7.10 percent (95 percent confidence interval = 6.27 percent to 7.97 percent), with this estimate being invariant across both writing systems and differences in their orthographic depth (L. P. Yang et al., 2022).

Although word identification is obviously the core component of reading, researchers and educators have long recognized that skilled reading requires the fluent coordination of many different mental processes and skills. This insight has resulted in considerable effort to both identify the processes and/or skills that fail to develop in children who have been diagnosed with developmental dyslexia, and to design a taxonomy for classifying the different types of dyslexia that might result from these failures. These efforts have historically conformed to one of two different general approaches that will now be discussed in turn.

The first approach has been directly informed by the *dual-route model* of reading that was developed by Coltheart and his colleagues (2001, 2013). As its name suggests, the model's core theoretical assumptions are that words can be identified using one or both of two processing "routes":

1. a *lexical route* in which a word's orthographic form is used to retrieve its pronunciation and meaning directly from memory, and
2. a *sub-lexical route* in which a word's pronunciation is first assembled using GPC rules so that its meaning can then be retrieved using the word's phonological representation.

The theoretical distinction between these two processing routes thus provides an elegant account of the two most common types of developmental dyslexia. By this account, impairment of the first, lexical route can cause difficulty in naming or identifying irregularly pronounced words (i.e., *surface dyslexia*) because such words cannot be named or identified using assembled phonology. And conversely, impairment of the second, sub-lexical route can cause difficulty in naming or identifying nonwords or regularly pronounced words (i.e., *phonological dyslexia*) because these items are often named or identified using assembled phonology. Thus, according to this first approach, it should be possible to identify the locus of a dyslexic child's difficulty using a naming task: poor performance naming irregularly pronounced words is indicative of an impaired lexical route and surface dyslexia, whereas poor performance naming nonwords is indicative of an impaired sub-lexical route and phonological dyslexia.

5.2 Dyslexia

Although the dual-route model has provided a useful framework for understanding dyslexia among children who are struggling to read English, the approach has arguably proven less useful for understanding reading impairment among children who are struggling to read Chinese. This limitation is probably due to the simple fact that – as mentioned previously – the Chinese writing system does not allow for the use of GPC rules. And although the phonetic radicals that are embedded within many characters provide useful clues about a character's pronunciation, those clues are often not reliable.

The inherent limitation of the dual-route model as an account of Chinese developmental dyslexia was demonstrated by a study reported by C. Ho et al. (2007). This study examined the incidence rate of surface versus phonological dyslexia in Hong Kong primary school children. Three groups of children were included in the study: children diagnosed as dyslexic using a standardized test; chronological age-matched children; and reading-skill-matched children. All three groups were evaluated in terms of their ability to accurately name two types of stimuli: exception characters (i.e., phonologically irregular and inconsistent characters), and pseudo-characters constructed from semantic and phonetic radicals in legal positions (with their correct pronunciation taken to be that corresponding to their phonetic radical). Using the regression method of Castles and Coltheart (1993) to classify the children as having surface versus phonological dyslexia based on their relative performance in the two naming tasks, C. Ho et al. (2007) found that the majority of their sample (62 percent) performed particularly poorly at naming irregular characters and were thus classified as surface dyslexics, while none of the children were classified as having phonological dyslexia. This pattern was markedly different from what has typically been reported in samples of English-speaking dyslexic children, where phonological dyslexia is more common (e.g., Castles & Coltheart, 1993; Manis et al., 1996). The children that were identified as having surface dyslexia also exhibited more severe reading impairment (e.g., lower word reading scores) than the original (i.e., full) dyslexic sample, performed worse on other literacy and cognitive tests than their age-matched group, and were slower at naming the exception characters and pseudo-characters than their reading-skilled-matched group. These findings are also contrary to previous findings which indicate that English-speaking children with phonological dyslexia exhibit more impairment (e.g., Manis et al., 1996). Finally, the children's performance in naming the exception characters was positively correlated with their performance in naming the pseudo-characters, suggesting that the lexical versus sub-lexical routes posited by the dual-route model might not be as independent in the reading of Chinese as they are in the reading of English and other alphabetic languages, and that the two main types of dyslexia that are predicted by the dual-route model might not be valid for the reading of Chinese.

Other studies appear to support these conclusions. For example, using a similar methodology, F. Ho and Siegel (2012) reported a higher proportion of surface than phonological dyslexics (26 percent vs. 13 percent, respectively) in their sample of Hong Kong children, although it is important to note that their participants were diagnosed using a Chinese language test and not the normal standardized test (see C. Ho et al., 2007). And likewise, Shu et al. (2005) reported instances of surface but not phonological dyslexia in their case studies (which were conducted in mainland China).

The apparent consistency of this evidence, however, was seemingly violated by a study reported by L. C. Wang and Yang (2014). This study examined two groups of Taiwanese sixth-graders: 60 dyslexic children who had previously been diagnosed using learning disabilities criteria and poor word-identification performance, and 45 age-matched, typically developing children. Both groups were examined using a battery of tests that were designed to measure their orthographic, phonological, and semantic knowledge and skills. Using the same regression method as both Castles and Coltheart (1993) and C. Ho et al. (2007), L. C. Wang and Yang (2014) found that 20 percent of their dyslexic sample were classified as having phonological dyslexia, while 18.3 percent were classified as having surface dyslexia. (An additional 20 percent of their sample was found to have *deep dyslexia* or semantic-processing deficits.) Furthermore, the children with surface dyslexia were more impaired on the orthographic tests (which measured the children's radical positional and functional knowledge), while the children with phonological dyslexia were more impaired on the phonological tests (which mainly tested the children's phonological awareness). These findings suggest that the surface versus phonological dyslexia criteria may measure Chinese children's general orthographic versus phonological knowledge rather than their ability to assemble phonology or effectively use phonetic radicals as cues to pronounce whole characters. Although the reason(s) for the discrepancies between L. C. Wang and Yang's (2014) results and those reported by C. Ho et al. (2007) remains unclear, it might be due to the fact that L. C. Wang and Yang's dyslexic children were older (12 years) than C. Ho and colleagues' (9 years) and/or that zhuyin is used to facilitate phonological awareness in Taiwan (the site of the L. C. Wang & Yang, 2014 study) but not in Hong Kong (the site of the C. Ho et al., 2007 study). It is also worth noting that L. C. Wang and Yang failed to observe a significant correlation between their dyslexic children's pseudo-character and irregular character naming (i.e., the regression line was flat) and that this may have distorted their classification results. However, irrespective of the reason(s) for these discrepancies, one might reasonably conclude that the first theoretical approach to understanding developmental dyslexia – the approach motivated by the dual-route models of word identification (Coltheart et al., 2001, 2013) – appears to be less applicable to the reading of Chinese. This conclusion thus brings us directly to the second approach.

The second main approach for understanding and diagnosing dyslexia has used increasingly sophisticated psychometric tests to identify the specific cognitive deficits that underlie different types of reading impairment. As discussed in Section 5.1 (on reading skill development), the available evidence suggests that a large number of component skills, including visual-spatial, orthographic, phonological, morphological, and rapid naming, contribute to the capacity to identify characters and words rapidly and accurately. A large amount of research has therefore been directed towards identifying those component skills and understanding how their impairment might impede normal reading development (see L. Zhang et al., 2023, for a review). Thus, in contrast to the first approach that has been used to understand dyslexia, which is perhaps more theory driven, this second approach is more data driven.

One example to illustrate this second approach is a meta-analysis reported by P. Peng et al. (2017). This meta-analysis included 81 studies that had previously examined the cognitive profiles of Chinese dyslexic children from 1964 to 2015 across mainland China, Hong Kong, and Taiwan.[5] The results of this meta-analysis showed that, compared to the age-matched, typically developing children, dyslexic children exhibited deficits in a wide range of cognitive skills, including significant impairments in visual-spatial skills, orthographic knowledge, phonological awareness, morphological awareness, speeded naming, and working memory, as well as more moderate impairments of motor skills. However, when compared to reading-ability-matched, typically developing children, dyslexic children only showed a modest deficit in orthographic knowledge and a moderate deficit in speeded naming. These patterns together suggest that, despite the dyslexic children having developmental delays in several cognitive skills,

---

[5] The study by C. Ho et al. (2007) was included in this meta-analysis.

orthographic knowledge and rapid naming deficits are the main sources of their reading difficulty. This conclusion requires two important caveats, however. The first is that the second of two comparisons involved fewer studies because many of the studies in the meta-analysis did not include reading-ability-matched control groups. The second is that the conclusion is at odds with evidence from other studies suggesting that morphological skill is a particularly important variable in discriminating between children who do versus do not have difficulty reading Chinese (e.g., Shu et al., 2006; S. Song et al., 2020).

P. Peng et al.'s (2017) meta-analysis also examined the potential roles of four moderating variables:

1. the age of the children;
2. the location of the study (mainland China vs. Hong Kong);
3. the severity of the dyslexia as measured using the diagnosis cut-off (ranging from the bottom 5th to the 35th percentile); and
4. the diagnostic screening method (i.e., character identification vs. character identification and reading comprehension).

Of these four variables, only the severity of the dyslexia modulated the extent of deficits in visual-spatial skills, phonological awareness, morphological awareness, and rapid naming; children who were diagnosed using more conservative criteria showed more severe deficits in these skills. This finding suggests the importance of adopting more conservative diagnostic criteria if the goal is to accurately describe a child's deficit profile. The rapid naming deficit was also jointly moderated by children's age and the screening method such that younger children tended to have a more severe rapid naming deficit if they were screened using both character identification and reading comprehension, suggesting that rapid naming somehow taps into reading skill beyond the identification of isolated characters.

P. Peng et al.'s (2017) meta-analysis also found that Chinese dyslexic children have a more general pattern of impairments in their phonological awareness and working or short-term memory. For example, their syllable awareness, onset-rime awareness, phoneme awareness, and tone awareness were equally impaired, as were both their verbal and non-verbal short-term or working memory. However, they showed more severe deficits in speeded letter and digit naming than character naming. This last finding should be interpreted with caution, however, because it is contrary to the results of another meta-analysis which indicated that both speeded digit and character naming were more strongly associated with reading performance than either object or color naming (S. Song et al., 2016). Clearly,

5.2 Dyslexia

more research is required both to establish the reliability of these relationships and to understand their theoretical and practical significance.

More recently, a small but increasing number of studies have started to examine the neural systems that support the reading of Chinese, and how atypical development of these systems might result in dyslexia. For example, a recent meta-analysis conducted by Y. Li and Bi (2022; see also X. Yan et al., 2021) cataloged the abnormalities in brain-activity patterns that were exhibited by dyslexic children who were native speakers of Chinese versus alphabetic languages. This meta-analysis showed that the dyslexic children exhibited hypoactivation in two brain areas (left inferior frontal cortex and anterior cingulate cortex) which suggests that there are universal phonological-processing and attentional deficits across writing systems. The Chinese dyslexic children also exhibited hyperactivation in three brain regions (right postcentral gyrus, left rectus, and right middle temporal gyrus) which further suggests the use of writing-system specific compensatory strategies. These patterns are obviously complex and for that reason have yet to be interpreted definitively. But studies of this type promise to advance our understanding of not only dyslexia but also the neural systems that support skilled reading, as will be discussed in Section 5.3. First, however, we will once again shift our focus from the empirical work that has been done on dyslexia to discuss recent efforts to understand reading impairment using computer models of reading.

There have been a few attempts to use connectionist models of character naming to understand the patterns of behavioral deficits that are observed in dyslexic Chinese readers. This discussion will be limited to one of those efforts: Two sets of simulations were reported by J. F. Yang et al. (2013) using the models shown in Figure 5.2. These models are attractor network models similar to the ones that have previously been used by J. F. Yang and colleagues (J. F. Yang et al., 2006, 2009) to examine the speeded naming of Chinese characters in typical readers (as discussed in Chapter 3; see Figure 3.5). The models in Figure 5.2 have the same basic architecture as those earlier models, but in the first set of simulations the number of input and output nodes were adjusted to accommodate the orthographic and phonological differences between English and Chinese, as shown in panels A and B of the figure respectively. And in the second set of simulations, the architecture was further modified to create a bilingual version of the model – one that could simultaneously name English words and Chinese characters, as shown in Figure 5.2 Panel C. Each of these simulations will be discussed in turn.

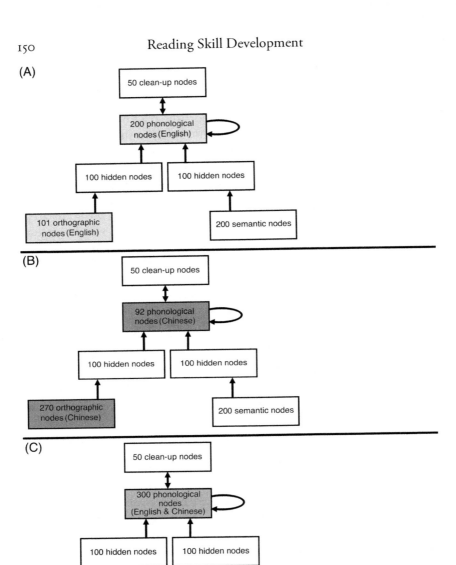

Figure 5.2 The attractor network models used by J. F. Yang et al. (2013) in their simulations of English word and Chinese character naming and how performance in these tasks might be impaired by phonological vs. surface dyslexia Panels A and B respectively show the architectures of the English vs. Chinese models, while Panel C shows the architecture of the English-Chinese bilingual model. The arrows indicate connections between successive layers of nodes, with the double-headed arrows indicating bi-directional connections.

5.2 Dyslexia

The first set of simulations directly compared two variants of the model (as shown in Figure 5.2 Panels A and B) in their capacity to name English words versus Chinese characters accurately. Both variants had identical architectures with a few minor modifications that were necessary to accommodate between-language differences in orthography and phonology; otherwise, both variants used the same learning algorithm to learn the mappings among the orthographic, phonological, and semantic nodes, and used exactly the same set of distributed patterns across the semantic nodes to represent the meanings of individual words and characters. The simulations examined the performance of both models in generating the pronunciations of words and characters whose pronunciations varied in terms of their regularity or consistency, with this performance also being evaluated as a function of learning (i.e., number of training trials). Additionally, naming performance was compared across three conditions:

1. a "typical reader" condition that used the models' standard assumptions and thus served as a baseline condition;
2. a "phonological dyslexia" condition in which the strengths of the connections between the orthographic and phonological nodes were reduced, causing phonological impairment; and
3. a "surface dyslexia" condition in which the strengths of the connections between the semantic and phonological nodes were reduced, causing semantic impairment.

The key findings of this first set of simulations were that the typical versions of both the Chinese and English models performed equally well learning their materials (99 percent correct), but that the English version required about half as many training trials as the Chinese version to do so, suggesting that the English writing system affords an easier mapping between orthography and phonology. Although the naming performance of both models was reduced in the two dyslexia conditions, the nature of the impairment was different for English versus Chinese. For example, phonological dyslexia reduced naming accuracy more in English (81 percent correct) than Chinese (89 percent correct), but surface dyslexia reduced naming accuracy more in Chinese (85 percent correct) than English (99 percent). This dissociation indicates that naming performance in English is more dependent upon the orthography-to-phonology mappings than it is in Chinese, with naming in the latter being more dependent upon the semantic-to-phonology mappings. These differences were also differentially affected by regularity and consistency. For example, surface dyslexia in the English model did not impair the naming of regular-consistent words but did impair the naming of irregular-inconsistent words, while phonological dyslexia impaired the naming of both types of words. However, in the Chinese model, both types of dyslexia impaired the naming of both types of characters. Finally, the English variant of the model was tested on its ability to pronounce untrained nonwords; surface dyslexia did not impair performance (86 percent correct) relative to that of the typical model (86 percent correct), but phonological dyslexia did (77 percent correct).

The second set of simulations reported by J. F. Yang and colleagues (2013) used a third variant of the attractor network that is shown in Figure 5.2 Panel C. This variant instantiated a bilingual reader of English and Chinese in that it had two sets of orthographic input units (one for English and one for Chinese) and a sufficient number of phonological nodes to adequately represent the pronunciations of both English words and Chinese characters. After training this model on both languages, the model was tested as per the first set of simulations. These tests essentially replicated those of the first simulations, showing the model learned English more rapidly than Chinese but with equivalent asymptotic performance and differential patterns of impairment between the two languages for phonological versus surface dyslexia. As with the first set of simulations, phonological dyslexia reduced naming accuracy more in English (59 percent correct) than Chinese (72 percent), whereas surface dyslexia reduced naming performance more in Chinese (90 percent correct) than English (99 percent correct). Additionally, surface dyslexia impaired the naming of English irregular-inconsistent words but not regular-consistent words, whereas phonological dyslexia impaired the naming of both types of words and non-words. However, both types of dyslexia impaired the naming of both types of Chinese characters.

The results of this first simulation obviously replicate earlier efforts to show that a learning model can abstract the statistical structure that is inherent in the orthography-to-phonology mappings of both English words (e.g., Plaut et al., 1996; Seidenberg & McClelland, 1989) *and* Chinese characters (Xing et al., 2002, 2004; J. F. Yang et al., 2006, 2009). However, these new results also extend these earlier efforts by demonstrating that a single functional architecture is capable of learning writing systems as different as English and Chinese, or even (as demonstrated in the second set of simulations) the simultaneous learning of *both* writing systems. Perhaps more importantly, the simulations demonstrate how specific patterns of behavioral impairments that have been argued to be indicative of phonological versus surface dyslexia can result from degradation in the quality of the mapping between orthography and phonology in the case of the former, or semantics and phonology in the case of the latter. Finally, the simulations demonstrate how the statistical structures of English versus Chinese can differentially affect the severity of the behavioral deficits observed with phonological versus surface dyslexia – not because of any underlying differences between the functional systems that support the reading of the two writing systems, but instead because of the writing systems themselves and differences in the statistical structures that can be abstracted from them.

Taken at face value, the simulations described in this section suggest that, despite of the many significant differences between the Chinese and alphabetic writing systems that have been reviewed in this book, the underlying mental "machinery" that supports skilled reading is largely invariant across languages. This was perhaps most explicitly suggested, for example, by J. F. Yang et al. (2013), who claim that:

> When the same functional architecture is trained to read English and Chinese, distinct patterns of typical and atypical development are observed across languages. Gross differences in the rate of learning of the two writing systems are clearly captured by the models, as are differences in the patterns of deficits that are observed in reading disability ... suggesting that these patterns are driven by statistical properties of the writing systems themselves, and not by differences in the basic architecture of reading across languages. (J. F. Yang et al., 2013: 360)

This is obviously a strong claim and for that reason warrants careful consideration. But additionally, the claim might be unwarranted because the simulations motivating it are based on the presupposition that any between-language differences in the nature of their orthographic or phonological representations play only a minor functional role and can thus be ignored in deciding whether or not two reading architectures are functionally the same. For example, in their reported simulations of English word and Chinese character naming, J. F. Yang et al.'s (2013) models included different numbers of orthographic input and phonological output nodes across the two languages, and those nodes often represented features without equivalents across the two languages (e.g., additional nodes for representing tones in Chinese but not English). For that reason, and because most of the research that has motivated the development of computer models of reading has been behavioral in nature (see Reichle, 2021), it is important that any strong claims about the functional equivalence of the reading architecture across writing systems be informed by what is known about the actual neural systems that support reading. In other words, it is important to answer the question: Is there any evidence that the neural

154   Reading Skill Development

systems that support reading are fundamentally different in readers of Chinese versus English? The final section of this chapter will attempt to provide a (tentative) answer to this question.

5.3   Cognitive Neuroscience

The previous sections of this chapter reviewed what has been learned from behavioral experiments about the mental processes that are involved in both the typical and atypical development of Chinese reading skill. This section will now discuss experiments that have used brain imaging (see Chapter 1) to inform our understanding of the *neural* systems that are involved in reading. Because both the technology and methods used to image the brain have undergone rapid improvements since their use first became prevalent in the 1990s, brain-imaging research is both exciting and tentative in that our understanding of the brain mechanisms that support reading is advancing very rapidly. For that reason, and because of the obvious complexity of the subject matter, this review will by necessity only provide a high-level summary.[6]

To start off, it is important to note that efforts to understand "the reading brain" are not independent of the previously discussed behavioral experiments in two important respects. The first is that brain-imaging experiments generally employ the same tasks that are used in the behavioral experiments. This means that the experiments described in this section are directly motivated by and extensions of earlier behavioral research, with the main objective to date being to provide evidence about *where* some cognitive process occurs in the brain rather than the precise nature of that process per se (e.g., whether it is completed using symbolic or distributed representations). Or saying this the other way around, the main goal is to understand the functions of different cortical areas to gain a better understanding of how they contribute to tasks like reading. The second way in which behavioral and brain-imaging experiments are co-dependent is that the results of both types of experiments have been interpreted within the frameworks of reading theories and, in at least one instance that will be discussed below (Hsiao & Shillcock, 2004, 2005), have informed the development and evaluation of computer models of reading.

Figure 5.3 shows images of the human brain and several key cortical regions and pathways that have been implicated in reading. Because skilled reading

---

[6] For an in-depth but accessible review of many of the basic findings related to the cognitive neuroscience of reading, see Dehaene (2009).

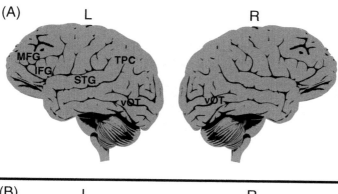

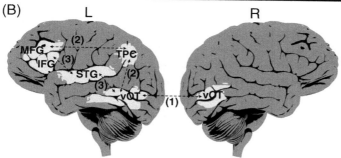

Figure 5.3 Images showing the left (*L*) and right (*R*) cerebral hemispheres of the human brain and the major cortical regions and anatomical pathways that are involved in the identification of printed words
Panel A shows the regions that appear to be universal across writing systems: (1) bilateral ventral occipital-temporal cortex (*vOT*), which supports orthographic processing; and the left (2) temporal-parietal cortex (*TPC*); (3) middle frontal gyrus (*MFG*); (4) inferior frontal gyrus (*IFG*); and (5) superior temporal gyrus (*STG*), which collectively support semantic and/or phonological processing. Panel B shows the main pathways that link the nodes of the reading network: (1) the corpus callosum integrates orthographic processing across the left and right vOT; (2) the dorsal pathway spans the left vOT, TPC, and MFG and supports phonological processing; and (3) the ventral pathway spans the left vOT, STG, and IFG and supports semantic processing.

entails coordinating the neural systems that subserve vision and attention with those that subserve spoken language, it is not surprising that so many different cortical areas are active during reading (Cohen & Dehaene, 2009). For example, Figure 5.3 Panel A shows those areas that are known to support the identification of printed words, along with frontal and parietal regions that are involved in executive control and attentional selection.

Many brain-imaging experiments (a few of which will be reviewed below) have consistently shown that these areas are involved in reading, largely irrespective of the language or writing system but with the activation of some regions being modulated by the writing system (as will also be reviewed).

For example, one of the first studies to demonstrate the functional roles of the different cortical areas was reported by Pugh et al. (1996). This experiment used fMRI to measure brain activity of participants while they made four types of same-different judgments about pairs of visually displayed stimuli. These tasks were designed to evoke specific types of processing:

1. judgments about line orientation (e.g., "//\/ – //\/") requiring visual-spatial processing;
2. judgments about letter case (e.g., "BtBT-BtBT") requiring both visual-spatial and orthographic processing;
3. rhyme judgments (e.g., "lete-jeat") requiring visual-spatial, orthographic, and phonological processing; and
4. category judgments (e.g., "corn-rice") requiring visual-spatial, orthographic, phonological, and semantic processing.

The brain activity generated during these tasks was compared against a resting baseline condition, and between-task contrasts allowed more specific types of processing to be isolated; for example, subtracting the activation observed during the case-judgment task from that observed during rhyme-judgment task would presumably isolate the regions involved in phonological processing because visual-spatial and orthographic processing are common to both tasks and thus cancel out in the contrasts. The baseline contrasts confirmed the involvement of the regions shown in Figure 5.3 Panel A. The between-task contrasts provided additional clues about the putative roles of these regions, with bilateral ventral occipital-temporal regions and the left fusiform gyrus, for example, being more responsive to the processing of letter case than line orientation, suggesting that the regions are involved in orthographic processing. Similarly, the left frontal regions were mainly implicated in phonological processing, while the left temporal and parietal regions appeared to support both phonological and semantic processing.

Although subsequent studies have improved upon Pugh et al.'s (1996) methodology and clarified the interpretation of their findings, those basic findings have been replicated across a large number of experiments involving both English and other languages and writing systems, including Chinese. For example, Bolger et al. (2005) conducted a meta-analysis of forty-three experiments that used either PET or fMRI to examine the identification of printed words in alphabetic writing systems (n = 25), Japanese kana (n = 5) or kanji (n = 4),[7] and Chinese (n = 9). The results of this meta-analysis were remarkably consistent with the results reported by Pugh and colleagues and broadly consistent with two other meta-analyses conducted around the same time (Pammer, 2009; Tan et al., 2005), although some important script-related differences were also identified (as will be discussed below).

More recently, the claim that a single network of cortical regions supports the reading of different writing systems has been more directly tested and confirmed by Rueckl and colleagues (2015). Their experiment used fMRI to examine the patterns of cortical activation that were evident when four groups of participants made semantic categorization decisions in response to words that were spoken or written in one of four different languages: Spanish, English, Hebrew, or Chinese. The observed patterns of cortical activation again indicated a remarkable degree of consistency across both the presentation modality (i.e., spoken vs. written words) and the languages and writing systems that were examined. In the words of the authors:

> All four languages show convergence ... with observed differences representing relatively minor variation in the degree to convergence, demonstrating how the reading network is deeply constrained by the organization of the brain network underlying speech. (Rueckl et al., 2015: 15513)

This invariance across writing systems is perhaps not too surprising given that, as has already been discussed (see Chapter 1), our capacity to read is a recent cultural invention that, up until the last few centuries, has remained the privilege of a small minority of well-educated individuals (Robinson, 1995). For those reasons, our capacity to read has not been around long enough or prevalent enough to have influenced human evolution, and this then provides a natural account of why a single network of cortical regions appears to support reading across writing systems as different as English and Chinese (Dehaene & Cohen, 2007; see also Perfetti & Tan, 2013). By this account, the capacity to read is mediated by a network of cortical regions that have evolved over millennia to support spoken language and vision, bolstered by regions that have likewise

---

[7] Japanese is written using two writing systems. The first, *kana*, actually consists of a pair of syllabaries in which graphemes are used to represent spoken syllables: *hiragana*, which is used mostly for grammatical elements and native Japanese words; and *katakana*, which is used mostly for foreign words and names. The second writing system, *kanji*, consists of characters borrowed from Chinese and is used to represent most content words.

evolved to perform more general computations that are "recycled" during literacy development to support skilled reading.

A prime example of the latter is a region that has been identified as playing a critical role in printed word identification – a portion of the left lateral occipital-temporal region (see Figure 5.3 Panel A) alternatively called the *fusiform gyrus* or *visual word-form area* (*VWFA*; Cohen et al., 2000, 2002; McCandliss et al., 2003). Several brain-imaging experiments have demonstrated that this region is both responsive to the orthographic forms of letter strings, and that its level of activation is modulated by the degree to which those letter strings are orthographically similar to real words. For example, Binder et al. (2006) reported an fMRI experiment in which participants viewed five-letter nonwords with the task of indicating the presence of letters containing ascenders (e.g., "b," "d," "k," etc.); the amount of fusiform activation that was observed during this task increased as the nonwords became more word-like (i.e., as the mean bigram frequency of their constituent letters increased). And similarly, Vinckier et al. (2007) reported an fMRI experiment in which participants viewed both nonwords (that varied in terms of how closely they resembled words) and words with the task of detecting a target letter string (i.e., "######"). The amount of fusiform activation observed in this task also varied as a function of how closely the letter strings resembled words, being minimal for nonwords and maximal for words, but also increasing monotonically as the nonwords became more word-like.

These observations and others (for reviews, see Cohen & Dehaene, 2009; and McCandliss et al., 2003) indicate that the left fusiform gyrus plays a central role in the identification of printed words. However, given the argument that was made earlier against an evolutionary basis for reading, this role may not be specific to the processing of words per se, but is probably related to the processing of complex visual stimuli that require configural processing of their component features (e.g., faces; for a review, see Kanwisher & Yovel, 2006) and that require high-resolution foveal vision for their identification (Dehaene & Cohen, 2007). For the purpose of this chapter, what is critical is that the VWFA appears to play an important role in identifying words across languages and writing systems (Bolger et al., 2005; Rueckl et al., 2015), with a sizeable body of evidence now specifically implicating the region in the processing of Chinese characters and words (Kuo et al., 2003; Lee et al., 2004; Perfetti et al., 2007; Tan et al., 2001; see also Perfetti & Tan, 2013).

However, as discussed earlier, Rueckl and colleagues (2015) have shown, despite this invariance, that there are also a few reliable differences across languages and writing systems that may reflect, for example, the alphabetic versus logographic nature of the writing systems, the degree of transparency between their written and spoken forms, and so on. These differences provide important clues about the cortical mechanisms that support language- and writing-system-specific aspects of reading. The remainder of this section will therefore focus more closely of what has been specifically learned about the cognitive neuroscience of *Chinese* reading. Unfortunately, as W. Guo and colleagues (2022: 2) noted, "cognitive and neuroimaging studies are largely focused on alphabetic writing systems, while exploration of the Chinese writing system is relatively lacking." Additionally, most of the research that has been done on the Chinese writing system has used the reading of English as the contrasting or "baseline" condition – a comparison that may be less than ideal considering arguments that English itself may be an "outlier orthography" that is unrepresentative of most alphabetic scripts (e.g., Share, 2008). With those caveats in mind, here is a summary of what has been learned.

A recent meta-analysis reported by W. Guo and colleagues (2022) attempted to identify the brain *connectome*, or main functional regions of the cortex along with their "structural or connectivity patterns" (W. Guo et al., 2022: 2) using brain-imaging methods and graph-theoretic approaches. The goal in doing this is to understand better how those cortical regions, or functional *nodes*, are coordinated during reading, and how this coordination might vary across different languages and writing systems. The results of this analysis were largely consistent with the ones discussed earlier (e.g., Bolger et al., 2005; Pammer, 2009; Tan et al., 2005), providing additional confirmation of the network of cortical regions that seem to support word identification irrespective of writing systems (see Figure 5.3 Panel B). This analysis also extended the earlier efforts by documenting several potentially important between-script differences. Two of these findings will be discussed here because they are consistent across a larger number of studies, and because they lend themselves to interpretation using the results of earlier behavioral studies and models of Chinese reading.

The first of these findings is that, as indicated earlier, the identification of Chinese characters to evoke more extensive bilateral activation of the ventral occipital-temporal cortex and the VWFA (F. Cao et al., 2009; Kuo et al., 2003; Lee et al., 2004; Nelson et al., 2009; Perfetti et al., 2007), with the activation of the latter sometimes being more pronounced in the right than left analog (e.g., Tan et al., 2000, 2001). W. Guo et al. (2022) suggest that this pattern might reflect the fact that, in contrast to alphabetic words, which might be represented by simple linear arrays of abstract letters, Chinese characters must be represented holistically, as two-dimensional configurations of strokes and radicals. Because of this representational difference, the right VWFA might, during literacy development, become more specialized for the kind of configural processing that is required to identify whole characters (see Perfetti et al., 2007).

The second major finding of significance is that Chinese character identification is associated with more activation of the left middle frontal gyrus (F. Cao et al., 2009; Kuo et al., 2003; Lee et al., 2004; Nelson et al., 2009; Perfetti et al., 2007; Tan et al., 2000, 2001), with some evidence that this activation may be bilateral (e.g., Dong et al., 2005). One interpretation of this finding is that it reflects the fact that Chinese is more dependent upon a "threshold style" access to phonology, whereas English also allows for assembled phonology (Perfetti et al., 2005), and that the middle frontal gyri play a prominent role in learning the direct associations between character forms and their pronunciations (Perfetti et al., 2007). Alternatively, the frontal gyri may represent the motor actions that are involved in writing Chinese characters (F. Cao et al., 2013; F. Cao & Perfetti, 2016), as suggested by the evidence reviewed earlier that character writing skill seems to be predictive of reading skill (Lo et al., 2016; McBride-Chang et al., 2011; Tan et al., 2005). One final interpretation is that the identification of Chinese characters places greater demands on visual-spatial working memory (Kuo et al., 2003; Tan et al., 2001), one of the possible functions that has been attributed to the middle frontal gyrus (Courtney et al., 1998). Of course, these alternative accounts are not necessarily mutually exclusive.

In addition to these two differences, it is important to note that W. Guo et al. (2022) identified several other processing nodes that appear to play roles in Chinese reading (e.g., left anterior temporal lobe). We will describe those areas or their purported roles here because many are speculative, having been inferred from a small number of studies or from experimental paradigms that are not representative of natural reading. There are, however, a few other notable findings that have emerged from this collective body of work – findings that are theoretically interesting and that might have some pedagogical importance.

The first appears to be a direct consequence of the fact that reading Chinese requires more support from the bilateral occipital and fusiform regions and the left middle front gyrus than does the reading of English. This difference suggests an interesting asymmetry with respect to how native speakers of either English or Chinese might learn to read the other language. As articulated by Perfetti et al. (2007), the asymmetry can be expressed in terms of two fairly specific hypotheses. The first is the *assimilation* hypothesis, or the idea that the cortical network that has been established to read one's native writing system is sufficient to handle the second writing system. By this account, the same network of cortical regions would support the reading of both writing systems, although the amount of work done by the different regions might vary across the two writing systems. The second hypothesis is *accommodation*, or the idea that the cortical network that has been established to read one's native language is insufficient to handle the second writing system, and that additional cortical regions might be recruited to meet the functional requirements of the second writing system. If these hypotheses are correct, then bearing in mind the asymmetry in the cortical networks that support the reading of Chinese versus English, one might make the following prediction: In learning to read English, the cortical networks of native Chinese speakers should readily assimilate the cognitive demands that must be met to read an alphabetic script. Reframing this prediction: In learning to read Chinese, the cortical networks of native English speakers cannot meet all of the cognitive demands required to read the Chinese script; they must instead accommodate the new writing system by recruiting additional cortical areas that are specifically required to read the Chinese script.

These two predictions were tested by Nelson and colleagues (2009). Their fMRI study examined the patterns of brain activation that are evoked when two groups of participants, native Chinese speakers who were fluent speakers of English and native English speakers who were learning Chinese, passively viewed Chinese characters and English words. The observed patterns of brain activity were broadly consistent with the predictions outlined above. First, native Chinese speakers exhibited bilateral activation of the occipital and fusiform areas, as well as activation of the left middle frontal gyrus, when viewing either Chinese or English words, suggesting that a single cortical network – one that was originally configured to read Chinese – is sufficient to support the reading of Chinese and English. In other words, the Chinese-reading network appears to have assimilated the reading of English. Second, native English speakers exhibited activation of the left occipital and fusiform areas but no activation of the left middle frontal gyrus when viewing English words. However, they showed bilateral activation of the occipital and fusiform areas as well as activation of the left middle frontal gyrus when viewing Chinese words. In other words, the English-reading network appears to have accommodated the reading of Chinese by recruiting additional cortical areas – the right occipital and fusiform areas and the left middle frontal gyrus.

Although the pattern of results and its interpretation are tentative (Nelson et al., 2009 discuss alternatives which they provide arguments against), it is worth noting that several other studies using EEG (see Chapter 1) and fMRI broadly support the assimilation and accommodation hypotheses (e.g., see Geng et al., 2023).[8] For example, one of the most compelling is a Chinese character-training study in which native speakers of English were provided with three days of training on Chinese characters (Y. Liu et al., 2007). After completing the training, those participants passively viewed the trained characters and English words while their brain activity was measured using fMRI. The patterns of brain activity observed as a function of language replicated what has been previously reported, with activation of the left occipital and fusiform areas during the reading of English as well as right occipital and fusiform areas and left middle frontal gyrus during the reading of Chinese. This pattern lends additional support to Perfetti et al.'s (2007) accommodation hypothesis in showing how the computational demands that are required to identify Chinese characters recruit cortical areas that are capable of meeting those demands. And as discussed by Perfetti et al. (2007), the computational demands and purported function of the left middle frontal gyrus, that it "supports a memory for a character so that a constituent stored with the character can be retrieved" (Perfetti et al., 2007: 142), are also broadly consistent with the basic principles of Perfetti et al.'s (2005) lexical constituency model, which was discussed in Chapter 3.

Returning now to the second significant finding that has emerged from cognitive neuroscience research on Chinese reading: that the physical act of writing, as discussed earlier in the section of reading skill development, plays an important role in the identification of Chinese characters (Perfetti & Tan, 2013). In that section, we reviewed evidence from behavioral studies which suggest that the hand movements associated with writing characters, and in particular the order in which the individual strokes within a character are written, is predictive of reading skill in children (Lo et al., 2016; McBride-Chang et al., 2011; Tan et al., 2005). The significance of this finding is supported by a few recent fMRI experiments. For example, F. Cao and Perfetti (2016) conducted a training study in which native English speakers learned two sets of Chinese characters either via writing the characters or writing their pinyin equivalent. The participants' brain activity was then measured

---

[8] Many of these studies are reviewed by Perfetti et al. (2007).

5.3 Cognitive Neuroscience

as they performed each of two tasks: passive viewing versus imagined writing of the newly learned Chinese characters and English words. The observed pattern of brain activity replicated previous findings with the Chinese characters, with bilateral occipital and fusiform activation and activation of the left middle frontal gyrus. The latter activation was more pronounced with Chinese than English in both tasks, and was more pronounced with imagined writing than passive viewing in both languages. And perhaps most importantly, left middle frontal gyrus activation was more pronounced for Chinese characters that had been learned via their writing than the writing of their pinyin equivalents.[9] F. Cao and Perfetti (2016) provide the following interpretation of their findings:

> Chinese [writing] places greater visual memory demands on reading than does alphabetic writing, because it requires discrimination among thousands of characters. Writing-specific motor information can support orthographic processing against the high demands of written Chinese. Native Chinese speakers learn to read by repeatedly copying and writing characters in specific sequences of strokes, providing this support and leading to activation, by reading, of writing-related brain areas. (F. Cao & Perfetti, 2016: 16)

By this account, the motor commands that are involved in writing characters by hand might be conceptualized, for example, within the framework of Perfetti et al.'s (2005) lexical constituency model, as being additional lexical constituents, similar to the orthographic, phonological, and semantic codes that become co-active when a Chinese character has been "identified." Irrespective of whether or not this interpretation is correct, however, the findings themselves are congruent with the behavioral evidence reviewed earlier (e.g., Tan et al., 2005) showing that reading and writing are more intrinsically linked in Chinese than in English and other alphabetic writing systems.

Turning now from our discussion of the empirical work that has been carried out to understand the cognitive neuroscience of Chinese reading, we now want to provide an example of how this work has influenced the development of reading models. This example and the final model that will be discussed in this book was developed by Hsiao and Shillcock (2004, 2005) and is shown in Figure 5.4. This model is similar to the other connectionist models that were discussed earlier in this chapter (e.g., J. F. Yang et al., 2013) and Chapters 3 and 4 (e.g., X. Li et al., 2009;

---

[9] The pattern of findings was replicated in a second fMRI experiment. In this second experiment, native Chinese speakers were the participants, thereby addressing any possible concern that the pattern is specific to less proficient second-language learners.

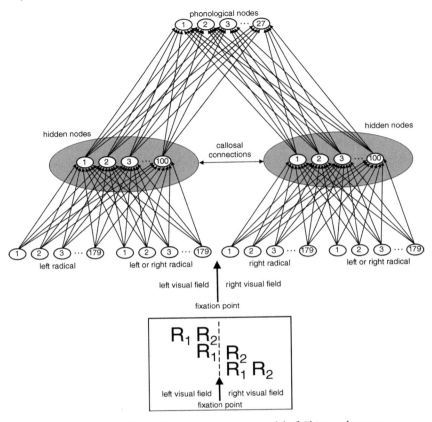

Figure 5.4 The "split fovea" connectionist model of Chinese character pronunciation proposed by Hsiao and Shillcock (2004, 2005)

The model generates the pronunciations of characters from the four banks of input nodes representing a given character's radicals in four possible spatial positions that are defined relative to the point of fixation. As shown, the visual field is bisected by the point of fixation. The gray ovals indicate groups of hidden nodes within the two cortical hemispheres that are completely interconnected to themselves and to the hidden nodes in the opposite hemisphere via the excitatory bi-directional callosal connections. The inset shows how the two radicals within a phonogram character, designated here as "R_1" and "R_2," can be located in either or both visual hemifields so that information about the radicals is initially available to only one or both groups of hidden nodes.

J. F. Yang et al., 2006, 2009). It differs from these earlier models, however, in that its architecture incorporates a key attribute of the human cortical system – the fact that the cerebral cortex is divided into two hemispheres, left and right, with information from each of the visual hemifields being initially propagated to the contralateral hemisphere before the information is shared between the two hemispheres via a large bundle of neural fibers called the *corpus callosum* (e.g., for a comprehensive overview, see Wurtz & Kandel, 1991). As Figure 5.4 shows, this feature is captured by the model's architecture; input about the orthographic forms of radicals is initially propagated via feedforward excitatory connections to one of two groups of hidden nodes that are indicated within the figure by the gray ovals. These hidden nodes then propagate their activation both forward to a common set of phonological output nodes that represent the pronunciations of characters, and to each other via the "callosal" connections that are the functional equivalent of the corpus callosum in the model.[10] The input to the model is thus "split" or divided at the point of fixation or center of vision, with input from one visual hemifield only initially being available to one set of hidden nodes. The implication of this is that information about the orthographic forms of characters can under different circumstances (depending on where a character is located relative to the point of fixation) can be initially propagated to either or both of the two sets of hidden nodes, as illustrated in the Figure 5.4 inset. As shown, a given character might be displayed in one visual hemifield so that information about both radicals (denoted by "R_1" and R_2" in the figure inset) is propagated to only one of the two sets of hidden nodes, or the character might be bisected so that each set of hidden nodes only receives information about one of the two radicals.

Other aspects of Hsiao and Shillcock's (2004, 2005) model are very similar to those of the other connectionist models that were discussed in this book (e.g., Perfetti et al., 2005). For example, the orthographic input at each of the four possible spatial locations (defined relative to the point of fixation) is represented by a set of 179 nodes that represent the most common radicals in Chinese characters. Likewise, a set of the twenty-seven output nodes represent the pronunciations of characters using a distributed coding scheme. And like many of the models that have been previously discussed (e.g., J. F. Yang et al., 2013), the network was trained on a large corpus of two-radical characters (phonograms) that varied in terms of both their token frequency and the regularity of their pronunciations, and that were displayed in each of the three possible locations during training

---

[10] Figure 5.4 indicates that the input nodes are directly connected to hidden nodes on the ipsilateral rather than contralateral side; the figure was rendered this way for the purposes of simplifying the exposition and maintaining consistency with the figures in Hsiao and Shillcock (2004, 2005). However, it would be more accurate to depict each of the two sets of hidden nodes as contralateral to the input nodes to which they are connected.

(as per the Figure 5.4 inset). This exercise was completed using two variants of their model: the model as depicted in Figure 5.4, and a second without the callosal connections but with added recurrent connections among the hidden nodes to (roughly) equate the two variants in terms of their computational power.

Hsiao and Shillcock (2004, 2005) reported several key findings from these simulations. The first is that, as might be expected from similar efforts (e.g., J. F. Yang et al., 2006, 2009, 2013), the model's naming performance was affected by both character frequency and regularity: the model more accurately named frequent characters and characters that had pronunciations the same as their phonetic radicals, and these two effects interacted such that the regularity effect was larger for low-frequency characters. However, more interesting because of its possible relevance to this section on the neuroscience of reading, the standard, split-fovea variant of the model learned more rapidly than the variant without the callosal connections, particularly with respect to the learning of characters having irregular pronunciations. The latter variant also tended to regularize the pronunciations of those characters that it mispronounced, similar to what has been reported with Chinese surface dyslexics (e.g., Yin & Butterworth, 1992). Based on these findings, Hsiao and Shillcock draw two main conclusions. The first is that the split-fovea architecture facilitates the "discovery of the relationship between character substructure and pronunciations" (Hsiao & Shillcock, 2004: 605). The second is that the variant of their model without the callosal connections provides an account of surface dyslexia if the absence of such connections is viewed as being an extreme form for hemispheric desynchronization, consistent with Shillcock and Monaghan's (2001) more general account of dyslexia. Although this claim is obviously inconclusive, it does illustrate how the convergence of computer modeling and behavioral and neuroscience research has been used to inform our understanding of how Chinese characters are identified and how this process might be impaired with surface dyslexia. We will therefore close this discussion with this final example but add that such efforts also illustrate the ingenuity of the researchers who manage to combine the use of these different methods to their advantage.

5.4 Conclusion

Previous chapters of this book reviewed what has been learned from a variety of different experimental paradigms about the identification of

Chinese characters and words and the skilled reading of Chinese. This chapter has focused on three topics that have direct bearing on the skilled reading of Chinese: how the skill develops and why it sometimes does not, and what has been learned from cognitive neuroscience about the reading of Chinese. The first two of these topics have obvious pedagogical implications in that, as we indicated in Chapter 2, around 1.3 billion people speak and (at least to some degree) read Chinese. So having a better understanding of typical and atypical reading skill development may provide new insights into the teaching of this critical life skill. Additionally, the research that has been done to understand the neural basis of Chinese reading and how it is (dis)similar to the reading of other languages and writing systems also informs our basic understanding of the human brain and mind. This advancement occurs through the natural progression of science; as an experiment provides a tentative answer to some question, the answer often raises new questions that await the next round of experimentation. As we will argue in the next chapter, this is currently the state of affairs with Chinese reading research: it is rife with opportunities to make significant contributions to the science of reading in that there are many "loose threads" that remain in our current accounts of the cognitive and biological processes that support Chinese reading. The final chapter will therefore describe a few of those opportunities by sharing what we believe are the most important of those unanswered questions.

CHAPTER 6

Future Directions

The previous chapters of this book provided a brief overview of the Chinese language and writing system. More specifically, we have attempted to document:

1. how the Chinese writing system differs from alphabetic writing systems (Chapter 2);
2. what has been learned about the identification of Chinese characters and words from behavioral experiments and computer models (Chapter 3);
3. what has been learned about the skilled reading of Chinese from eye-tracking experiments and computer models (Chapter 4); and
4. what is known about the acquisition of skilled Chinese reading and its impairment, and the neural underpinnings of Chinese reading and how the brain systems that support this skill are similar to and different from those that support the reading of alphabetic scripts (Chapter 5).

This final chapter will have two main objectives. The first is to list the main similarities and differences between the reading of English versus Chinese, in an attempt to provide clear points of theoretical contrast. Our reason for doing this should be obvious to anyone involved in reading science – to focus attention on unresolved questions that warrant further investigation. The second objective is closely aligned with the first – to suggest specific areas of research that we believe are timely for investigation given what is already known about the reading of Chinese and how it differs from the reading of English. Both of these objectives are oriented towards the future with an overarching goal of making some small contribution to the advancement of reading science.

6.1 English vs. Chinese: A Summary

Tables 6.1, 6.2, and 6.3 provide summaries of the main experimental findings related to the two languages and writing systems that have been

Table 6.1 *Key findings related to the orthographic processing of English vs. Chinese words**

Writing system properties	Category	Common findings	Findings specific to writing systems
English words consist of linear arrays of letters. Chinese words consist of 2-dimensional characters constituted by a hierarchy of radicals and strokes.	*Visual perception*	Longer words are acquired later and identified more slowly.	Visual-spatial skill is important for learning to read Chinese (especially early in learning). Visually complex characters are acquired later and are identified more slowly in Chinese.
	Orthographic similarity	Density and frequency of neighbors facilitates/inhibits lexical processing (i.e., is task dependent).	Orthographic neighbors in Chinese can be defined using strokes, radicals, or characters; different definitions result in different effects.
	Spatial coding	Detection of letter/character transposition/substitution varies by within-word position.	Chinese children develop an awareness of the radicals and their positions from an early age; this knowledge is critical to their subsequent reading development. Chinese skilled readers are sensitive to radical position in characters.
	Top-down influences	There is better identification of letters/characters in words than in isolation. There is better identification of characters/words than pseudo-characters/pseudo-words.	There are mixed findings on identification superiority of radicals in characters vs. isolation in Chinese.

*The table is organized by broad category and whether those findings are common to both writing systems or specific to one.

Table 6.2 *Key findings related to the phonological processing of English vs. Chinese words**

Writing system properties	Category	Common findings	Findings specific to writing systems
English word pronunciations are based on grapheme-phoneme correspondences that vary in regularity/consistency.	*Phonological structure*	English words/Chinese characters have internal phonological structure; awareness of this structure is critical for learning to read.	Knowledge and the use of phonetic radicals facilitate Chinese character acquisition.
Chinese characters are tonal syllables that can be segmented into onset and rime, resulting in many homophones; in phonogram characters, phonetic radicals provide some clues about pronunciation; word pronunciations are assembled from their characters.	*Orthographic-phonological regularity/consistency* *Phonological priming*	Identification of English words and Chinese characters varies by regularity/consistency. Access to phonology is rapid and obligatory during skilled reading.	Regularity and consistency are defined differently in English vs. Chinese. English words can be pronounced using assembled or addressed phonology; Chinese characters are pronounced using addressed phonology, but Chinese words can be pronounced using assembled phonology.

*The table is organized by broad category and whether those findings are common to both writing systems or specific to one.

Table 6.3 *Key findings related to the semantic processing of English vs. Chinese words**

Writing system properties	Category	Common findings	Findings specific to writing systems
English word meanings can be generated via derivation, inflection, compounding, etc. In Chinese phonogram characters, semantic radicals provide clues about meaning; most Chinese word meanings are generated by compounding characters.	*Morphological structure*	English and Chinese words have internal morphological structure. Knowledge of morphological structure is important for reading development.	Knowledge of semantic radicals in phonogram characters is important for learning to read Chinese. Children's morphological knowledge (e.g., the skills of lexical compounding and homophone production) appears to develop relatively early in Chinese and is particularly important for early learning development in Chinese.
	Categorical structure	Word meanings have categorical structure (e.g., typicality). Categorical structure can affect word meaning retrieval.	
	Semantic priming	Access to semantics can be cascaded.	Semantic priming effects may be more rapid in Chinese because of a more direct link between orthography and semantics.

*The table is organized by broad category and whether those findings are common to both writing systems or specific to one.

Table 6.4 *Key findings related to the skilled reading of English vs. Chinese**

Writing system properties	Category	Common findings	Findings specific to writing systems
English words are demarcated by clear word boundaries. Chinese text lacks clear word boundaries, often causing word-segmentation ambiguity.	*Reading rate*	Equating content, the eyes move through English and Chinese at a similar rate. Equating content, reading rates are similar in English and Chinese.	Eye-movement patterns are modulated by visual/linguistic density. Skilled Chinese readers make fewer, longer fixations reading sentences equated for content.
	Where the eyes move	Where the eyes move is jointly determined by visual (e.g., clear word boundaries) and lexical (e.g., frequency) properties of foveal and parafoveal characters/words.	Eyes are directed towards a few well-specified default targets, establishing a default-targeting strategy in English skilled reading. Uniformed fixation landing-site distribution without clear preferred viewing locations, and saccade lengths are sensitive to foveal and parafoveal word properties, dynamic-adjustment saccade targeting strategy in Chinese.
	When the eyes move	When the eyes move is determined by lexical (e.g., frequency) and linguistic (e.g., predictability) properties of text.	Chinese word segmentation remains a critical research question. Chinese reading models assume parallel character processing within the perceptual span but serial word identification.
	Perceptual span	Perceptual span is asymmetric, extends roughly one word to the left and two words to the right of fixations in both scripts, varying by reading direction, global text characteristics and reading skill. Skilled readers can extract orthographic and phonological information from parafovea (i.e., word $N+1$).	Perceptual span varies by script, being smaller in Chinese due to its visual and linguistic density. Depth (e.g., semantic) and extent (e.g., word $N+2$) of parafoveal information extraction may be more extensive in Chinese. There is mixed evidence of parafoveal-on-foveal effect in Chinese.

*The table is organized by broad category and whether those findings are common to both writing systems or specific to one.

discussed throughout this book – English, which has largely informed our understanding of the psychology of reading, and Chinese, which provides an important contrast. The tables are organized by type of lexical processing that the findings pertain to (i.e., orthographic vs. phonological vs. semantic), with the findings also being organized into broad categories and by whether they are common to English and Chinese or specific to one of the two writing systems. Table 6.4 provides a similar summary of the main findings related to the skilled reading of English versus Chinese text. These tables are intended to provide a "bird's eye view" of the topics that have been discussed at length in Chapters 3–5; for discussions of the findings listed, please see those chapters.

Close inspection of Tables 6.1–6.4 will hopefully convince you that there are many more points of correspondence between English and Chinese than there are differences. This is not unexpected; as discussed in Chapter 5, what has already been learned from cognitive neuroscience about reading shows quite convincingly that a single network of cortical regions is coordinated to support skilled reading, and that this network is largely the same across languages and writing systems as different as English and Chinese. However, as we indicated both there and elsewhere throughout this book, there are also some differences, and the ones listed above are interesting because they provide clues about how the mind might, across years of formal education and practice, adapt to one's native language and writing system. A better understanding of how this happens will obviously advance our basic understanding of reading and how it differs across languages and writing systems. We suspect that this, in turn, will inform a host of issues related to reading education and maybe even lead to the development of new methods for identifying and treating reading impairment. We also believe that a better understanding of the psychology of reading and the neural systems that support this remarkable skill will advance our more basic understanding of the mind and brain. In this spirit, we start this chapter by offering our predictions about how the study of Chinese reading might shape the future science of reading.

6.2   Our Predictions

In Chapter 2 we mentioned how the earliest evidence for Chinese writing comes from animal bones and turtle shells dating from the Shang dynasty (sixteenth to eleventh centuries BCE) and inscribed with Chinese characters for the purpose of divining the future. Millennia later these ancient artifacts were being sold as "dragon bone" curiosities and for traditional medicine before their true value was appreciated – as evidence for one of the earliest known writing systems. Although the expected success rate of oracles is chance, we could not help but speculate about the future of reading research, and how the study of Chinese and other neglected writing systems might inform our understanding of how people read English and other alphabetic writing systems (e.g., Arabic, which is read from right to left, does not mark its vowels, and uses ligatures to connect letters within words; for a review, see Hermena & Reichle, 2020). This section will therefore focus on a few questions that we believe have recently or soon will be the focus of new research by virtue of the fact that the study of Chinese reading has – at least for us – provided a new way of framing the questions. We do so cautiously, however, fully aware that our opinions are just that, and that many of our conjectures may well be proven wrong.

That being said, we will organize this discussion around the contents of Chapters 3–5, respectively. So to start, one of the notable conclusions of Chapter 3 was that the principles of the most influential model of word identification, McClelland and Rumelhart's (1981) interactive-activation model, were fairly easily adapted to explain how Chinese characters (Perfetti & Liu, 2006; Perfetti et al., 2005) and words (Taft et al., 1999; Taft & Zhu, 1997) are identified, and in one adaptation, how continuous strings of characters are segmented into words and identified (X. Li et al., 2009). And as discussed in Chapter 4, variants of the interactive-activation model have also been used as the word-identification "engine" in two models that simulate word identification and eye-movement control during Chinese reading (Fan & Reilly, 2022; X. Li & Pollatsek, 2020). The fact that the basic principles of the interactive-activation model are so broadly applicable is remarkable if for no other reason than that it demonstrates that, despite the marked differences between English and Chinese, the computational principles that allow configurations of orthographic features to be mapped onto the phonological or semantic representations of words are similar across the two writing systems. However, we would also argue that these demonstrations, although useful, have highlighted two sets of theoretical issues that will most likely be problematic for any model based on the interactive-activation framework – issues that would likely remain unappreciated had it not been for consideration of the model's application to Chinese.

The first issues are related to the learning of new vocabulary and the question of whether models based on the interactive-activation framework can in principle explain how beginning readers acquire a lexicon.

6.2 Our Predictions

We believe that the models cannot. Our reasons for this opinion are best explained through careful consideration of one specific model. For this purpose, we will focus on Perfetti et al.'s (2005) lexical constituency model because its exposition is extremely clear. However, we want to emphasize that our criticism is not against this particular model per se, but rather the entire class of models that are based on the interactive-activation framework.

As Perfetti and colleagues (2005) have indicated and as discussed in Chapter 3, the lexical constituency model consists of an interconnected network of nodes that map the patterns of activation across input nodes representing up to 623 distinct radicals onto 204 nodes representing individual characters, another set of 204 nodes representing the meanings of those characters, and 63 nodes representing the pronunciations of characters in a distributed manner. Although the model accurately simulates character naming (e.g., the experimental results reported by Perfetti & Tan, 1998) and provides novel insights into the nature of word identification (see our discussions of the model in Chapters 3 and 5), the model is a static description of the Chinese lexicon that provides no account of how new words might be learned. Furthermore, we would argue that the model is both "brittle" in that its performance is critically dependent upon the "hand-adjusted weighted connections" (Perfetti et al., 2005: 49) that propagate activation among nodes, and computationally "expensive" in that the number of connections required increases exponentially with the number of characters being represented. Both of these limitations will be discussed in turn.

The first limitation can be illustrated by noting that the model's accuracy in identifying any given character will depend upon several variables, including the similarity between the pattern of visual input and the character, the amount of between-character inhibition that the character receives from orthographically similar characters (which will be partially activated by the input), and the resting thresholds of the character and the orthographically similar characters. The capacity to identify a character accurately thus depends upon having just the right balance between these factors. To identify one of two orthographically similar characters correctly, for example, the resting threshold of the character being identified has to be high enough to ensure that it becomes most active in response to the character, but not so high that it is also most active in the presence of the other character (which would then prevent its identification). This balance also has to be maintained across *all* of the words in the lexicon, despite potentially large differences in their frequency of occurrence so that, for example, an extremely low-frequency character will still be identified as such and not a more frequent orthographic neighbor. Although existing variants of the interactive-activation model are able to do this, the models do this by virtue of the fact that the values of their connection weights and thresholds are determined by the model designers. In other words, the models are not designed to learn.

The second limitation of the interactive-activation framework can likewise be illustrated by noting that the 204 character nodes in the lexical constituency model require a total of 41,616 mutually inhibitory connections because each node inhibits both itself and every other character node. Doubling the number of characters would therefore necessitate a total of 166,464 inhibitory connections. And of course, this is ignoring all of the inhibitory and excitatory connections between the input (radical) nodes and character nodes, as well as all of the excitatory connections linking character nodes, semantic nodes, and phonological nodes – all of which require precise weights to ensure that the orthographic input reliably maps onto its correct meaning and pronunciation. Again, it is not clear how existing variants of the interactive-activation model would learn all of this in an unsupervised manner (i.e., without being configured by the designers of the models).

This second limitation of the interactive-activation framework can also be illustrated by considering another model that was reviewed in Chapter 4, the *Chinese reading model (CRM)* of X. Li and Pollatsek (2020). Recall that this model also incorporates a variant of the interactive-activation model as its word-identification core to simulate how word segmentation and identification influence eye-movement control during reading. One limitation of this model that was identified by the authors (e.g., 2020: 9) is that it requires multiple redundant lexicons to support the identification of words that are viewed from different fixation locations. This requirement stems from the fact that the words inhibit each other but also share input from spatially overlapping characters. This effectively means that, although the model only identifies one word at a time, the time and accuracy in doing this is affected by whatever spatially adjacent characters happen to be within the focus of attention. As the authors acknowledge (2020: 21), this assumption is "unrealistic because words at different positions should use the same lexicon for processing." And to underscore a point that we made earlier, this limitation is not limited to the CRM because it is equally applicable to other models that use variants of the interactive-activation model to explain eye-movement control in the reading, irrespective of

6.2 Our Predictions

whether the language being read is English (Reilly & Radach, 2003, 2006), French (Snell et al., 2018), or Chinese (Fan & Reilly, 2022).[1]

Although the aforementioned limitations are not insurmountable,[2] we would hasten to add that the solutions are likely to be both too complex to be plausible (i.e., they require some degree of intelligent engineering rather than being "dumb" solutions that are likely to emerge by themselves) and also likely to be subject to a number of tight restrictions (e.g., the connection weights and resting activation values of nodes only allow the models to perform correctly within a limited range of parameter values). For those reasons, we predict that future models of Chinese character and word identification will shift away from their reliance upon the interactive-activation framework and instead move towards the two other general classes of word-identification models:

1. connectionist models that use distributed representations and learning algorithms to learn the statistical structure of writing systems and the mappings between orthography, phonology, and semantics (e.g., Plaut et al., 1996; Seidenberg & McClelland, 1989); and
2. instance-based memory models that encode information about word experiences in a more holistic, contextually rich manner (Ans et al., 1998; Kwantes & Mewhort, 1999; Reichle, 2021; Reichle & Perfetti, 2003).

An interesting side note here is that several examples of the former have been developed to explain Chinese character and word identification (Y. Chang et al., 2016; Hsiao & Schillcock, 2004, 2005; Xing et al., 2002, 2004; J. F. Yang et al., 2006, 2009, 2013). However, to date, we are not aware of any attempts to adapt instance-based models of word identification to Chinese. We predict that future efforts to explain and simulate Chinese reading will examine the explanatory adequacy of the instance-based models, particularly because there appears to be renewed interest in this general class of models (e.g., Collins et al., 2020; Jamieson & Mewhort, 2009; Kelly et al., 2017; Ozen et al., 2022;

---

[1] For additional discussion of the limitations of the interactive-activation framework and the broader theoretical implications for models of eye-movement control in reading, see Reichle and Schotter (2020).

[2] For example, Pritchard et al. (2018) have demonstrated how the dual-route cascaded (*DRC*) model of English word identification can be adapted to simulate the learning of new vocabulary. This demonstration, however, underscores the point we are making here – that the solutions are inelegant at best, and that they also demonstrate how fragile the models are with respect to small perturbation in parameter values, etc.

Reichle et al., 2022) and their application to word identification (e.g., Reichle, 2021; Reichle & Schotter, 2020; Veldre et al., 2020).

Turning now to the second set of issues that we believe are intrinsic to and problematic for models based on the interactive-activation framework – providing an adequate account of the *alignment problem*, or how letters or other orthographic features are perceived and represented in their correct spatial positions. Recall that the original interactive-activation model completely sidestepped the question of how letter order is represented by assuming that they are simply encoded in designated "slots" (McClelland & Rumelhart, 1981: 406; see Chapter 1). For example, according to the model, the first letter in the word "cats" is encoded in a slot representing the first spatial position, the second letter is encoded in the second slot, and so on, with no chance of the letters being perceived out of order and "cats" being confused with the orthographically similar word "cast." This account of word identification is therefore limited because it cannot explain the transposition effects that were discussed in Chapter 3, with evidence, for example, that a letter string viewed under impoverished viewing conditions (e.g., during parafoveal preview) and involving a transposed letter pair is more likely to be misidentified as another word (e.g., "jugde" mistaken for "judge") than will two letter strings involving letter substitutions ("e.g., "junpe" mistaken for "judge"; Johnson et al., 2007). According to the interactive-activation model, letter strings involving a single transposed pair of letters or two letter substitutions should be equally similar to their base word in that in both cases they differ from the base word by exactly two letters.

To date, there are two types of theories that have been proposed to explain the alignment problem (at least as applied to the identification of alphabetic words).[3] The first introduces signals to encode relative differences in the time course over which the individual letters within a word are processed (Davis, 2010; Whitney, 2001; Whitney & Cornelissen, 2008). By such accounts, the letters in a word are scanned one at a time from the beginning of the word, with a different signal being initiated with the processing of each letter. Returning to our example "cats," the letter "c"

---

[3] This claim is not strictly correct if at least two other proposals that have been made are considered: Taft and Krebs-Lazendic's (2013) account based on the syllabic structures of words, and Grainger and van Heuven's (2003) account based on open bigrams. These two accounts will not be considered here because it is not clear prima facie how either would explain the alignment problem in Chinese. For example, the first of these accounts requires knowledge of word boundaries, whereas the second account seemingly requires pairs of orthographic units (e.g., letters) to be represented along one spatial dimension.

would first be converted into a signal indicating its presence in the first position, followed shortly by a signal indicating the presence of "a" in the second, and so on. The relative arrival times of the signals to the lexicon would then indicate the relative spatial positions of the letter within the word. For example, by introducing a small delay in when the letter signals are received by the lexicon, the signals for the letters "c," "a," "t," and "s" will arrive at the same time and thereby match only a single lexical representation, the word "cats." However, by introducing small perturbances in the timing (due to inherent randomness in the signals), this account also explains transposition effects. It is noteworthy that one of these accounts (Davis, 2010) was specifically designed within the framework of the interactive-activation model, allowing the model to explain the alignment problem and thereby address one of its main limitations.

The second type of theory that has been proposed to explain the alignment problem maintains that there is uncertainty about the precise spatial positions of each of the individual letters within a word (Gomez et al., 2008; Norris & Kinoshita, 2012). By this account, the perceptual information that affords knowledge of the identities and positions of individual letters accumulates over time, with greater uncertainty about the two types of information early in processing and decreasing levels of uncertainty later in processing. Although this second account has not been explicitly applied to the interactive-activation model, its core assumption applies equally to letters and other visual "objects" and is thus parsimonious because it does not require, for instance, additional assumptions about timing signals or delays in the receptions of those signals.

Given these two broad accounts of the alignment problem, the difficulty is to determine which might better explain how the relative spatial positions of the strokes, radicals, and characters that constitute Chinese words are perceived and represented in memory? (Of course, it is logically possible that neither does, or that both accounts are necessary to explain how the order characters and their constituents are represented, but we will ignore these logical possibilities in the present discussion.) Both accounts would obviously need to explain how the positions of these different units are represented, and how the positions of the strokes and radicals are represented across two – not one – spatial dimensions. So let us in turn consider how each account might do so, beginning with the timing-based account. Such an account would have to convert the relative spatial positions of strokes, radicals, and characters into temporal codes. A radical located in the upper left quadrant of a character, for example, might be represented by two rapidly initiated signals: one encoding the radical's position in the *x*-dimension (i.e., from left to right) and another encoding the radical's position in the *y*-dimension (i.e., from top to bottom). Assuming the same encoding scheme, another radical located in the upper right quadrant of the character would be encoded by a slower signal in the *x*-dimension so that its position to the right of the first radical would be accurately represented, along with a rapidly initiated signal in the *y*-dimension to encode the character's position at the top of the character.

Although such an account poses no inherent difficulty, the challenge faced by such a scheme is that it forces one to commit to one of the two additional assumptions:

1. three sets of independent signals are used to encode the respective positions of strokes, radicals, and characters within words; or
2. only the positions of some of the aforementioned orthographic units (e.g., only strokes) are encoded and represented.

The second possibility is seemingly inconsistent with evidence that all three types of orthographic information play important roles in word identification (e.g., Y. P. Chen et al., 1996; Cui et al., 2021; Leong et al., 1987; *D. Peng & Wang, 1997; Xiong et al., 2023; B. Yu & Cao, 1992; L. Yu et al., 2021; W. Zhang & Feng, 1992). The first possibility – that different sets of signals are used to represent the positions of strokes, radicals, and characters – is also untenable because it would seemingly require that strokes, radicals, and characters be identified in that order. Why? Because the positions of the strokes within a given radical would presumably have to be known prior to estimating the position of the radical itself, with a similar dependency existing between the radicals and characters. This prediction of a strict dependency in the order in which the positions of strokes, radicals, and characters can be determined lacks parsimony but also seems contrary to the word-superiority effects that have been reported in Chinese, where radicals within characters and characters within words are identified more rapidly than either radicals in pseudo-characters or characters in pseudo-words (e.g., Y. P. Chen et al., 1996; X. Li & Pollatsek, 2011; Mattingly & Xu, 1994; Mok, 2009).

Next consider the spatial-uncertainty account. By this account, perceptual information corresponding to the identities and positions of the strokes, radicals, and characters accumulates over time, allowing increasing levels of certainty about both the identities and locations of those different lexical units. Such a scheme seemingly allows for the positions of the different units to be known "for free" in that the information is directly available from the perceptual input. In other words, the information about the relative spatial locations of the strokes, radicals, and characters within words is available in the same way that, for example, the identities of those orthographic units are available, or the relative spatial locations of different facial features are available within a face. And if this conjecture is correct, then it suggests that the spatial-uncertainty account provides a parsimonious solution to the alignment problem – one that is equally applicable to words and other visual "objects," and one that scales from the relatively simple alphabetic writing systems where letters are arranged along a single spatial dimension to the more complex Chinese writing system where strokes and radicals are arranged along two spatial dimensions. We therefore predict that, in the near future, more research on the reading of Chinese will be directed towards discriminating between the timing versus spatial-uncertainty accounts of the alignment problem, with the results of these efforts likely favoring theories that are based on the latter.

As discussed in Chapter 4, during this past decade research on the skilled reading of Chinese has shown that the accepted view of how readers make "decisions" about where to move their eyes is an oversimplification. That is, rather than simply moving their eyes to a small number of possible default locations (as is typically assumed by models that simulate eye-movement control in the reading of alphabetic languages; e.g., Engbert et al., 2005; Reichle et al., 2012), the lengths of the saccades that move the eyes from one word to the next also appear to be influenced by differences in the relative difficulty of ongoing lexical processing (Wei et al., 2013). This finding has motivated a number of efforts to show experimentally that, for example, in reading Chinese, the frequency of the fixated word (Y. P. Liu et al., 2015, 2017) as well as both the frequency (Y. P. Liu et al., 2016) and predictability (Y. P. Liu et al., 2018) of the upcoming word will modulate the length of the saccade exiting the fixated word. Such findings are not without precedent, however, because earlier eye-movement experiments had already provided clear evidence of similar effects during the reading of English (Rayner et al., 2004; White & Liversedge, 2006). Such findings collectively suggest that there is a tendency during reading to execute longer saccades to the degree that ongoing lexical processing is easier, irrespective of the writing system.

This conclusion, if correct, will have to be incorporated into existing and new models of reading. For example, the two most comprehensive of these models to date, E-Z Reader (Reichle et al., 2012; Veldre et al., 2023) and SWIFT (Engbert et al., 2005; Schad & Engbert, 2012), simply assume that readers' eyes are directed towards the center of the next unidentified word. Although this appears to be a reasonable approximation in that both models can accurately simulate a wide variety of "benchmark" findings related to eye-movement control in reading (e.g., fixation landing-site distributions, the influence of lexical variables on fixation durations, etc.), the models would presumably have difficulty explaining the results of experiments which show that, even in alphabetic writing systems, the saccades exiting high-frequency words tend to be longer than those exiting low-frequency words (Rayner et al., 2004; White & Liversedge, 2006). Indeed, this shortcoming has been recognized in recent attempts to adapt the E-Z Reader model to the reading of Chinese, where it was necessary to assume that saccade lengths are adjusted dynamically as a function of parafoveal processing difficulty rather than being directed towards default targets (Y. P. Liu et al., 2023; L. Yu et al., 2021). Unfortunately, these modeling efforts are also of limited value because they overlook the evidence suggesting that, rather than saccadic targeting being determined exclusively by the dynamic adjustment of saccade length *or* the use of default targets, it instead reflects some combination of the two, with the relative weighting given to each perhaps being a function of the writing system and its properties (e.g., the relative difficulty associated with accurately gauging lexical processing difficulty vs. accurately identifying word boundaries).

The best evidence supporting this conjecture comes from a pair of experiments reported by Y. P. Liu et al. (2019). In these experiments, a boundary paradigm was used to demarcate the boundaries of parafoveal two-character target words during their preview either by introducing a blank space after the target words or by rendering the target words in red font. The frequency of the target words was also manipulated and could either be high or low. The results of these experiments indicated clear effects of both manipulations. With all else being equal, the saccades into the target words were shorter if their boundaries had been indicated during the preview. And with all else being equal, the saccades into the target words were longer if they were of higher frequency. This pattern suggests that skilled readers of Chinese are sensitive to factors that might indicate the boundaries of upcoming words (e.g., punctuation), and that they then use this information in a manner that is consistent with the default-targeting view by directing their eyes towards specific targets – the center of an upcoming (segmented) word. This tendency is countermanded, however, by the tendency to also use information about parafoveal processing difficulty to modulate saccade length, moving the eyes further if processing is easier. As Y. P. Liu and colleagues (2019) indicate:

> [T]o explain saccade targeting in different writing systems, it will be necessary ... to specify how the two saccade-targeting mechanisms are integrated and weighted to accommodate the different writing systems. (Y. P. Liu et al., 2019: 1376)

Therefore, in making our predictions about the future, we believe that new empirical research will be needed to understand better precisely how this happens and what variables are likely to influence a reader's decisions about where they move their eyes. And going hand-in-hand with this empirical work, models of eye-movement control will need to be modified to instantiate the two saccade-targeting mechanisms and to provide a better account of how those systems are differentially engaged by the reading of different writing systems. Although one might easily dismiss this endeavor as being esoteric and of little practical importance to our understanding of reading, we contend that having a better understanding of saccadic targeting in Chinese will be critical if eye-tracking methods are to retain their usefulness for understanding the mental processes involved in reading. For example, as we discussed in Chapter 4, at least some of the current discrepancies between findings in English versus Chinese reading (e.g., the absence vs. presence of semantic-preview effects; see Schotter, 2013; Tsai et al., 2012; M. Yan et al., 2009; J. M. Yang et al., 2012) may reflect differences in saccadic targeting in the two languages. For example, in the reading of English, the fact that words are clearly demarcated by spaces allows one to infer that the duration of a fixation on a given word largely reflects its processing (assuming that the eye-tracker has been properly calibrated; see Reichle & Drieghe, 2015). But such inferences are more difficult to justify in Chinese because both the shorter words and the lack of inter-word spaces make it more likely that a fixation duration on word N reflects the processing difficulty of word N-1 or word N+1. For that reason, we predict that further progress in using eye-tracking to understand reading will be critically dependent upon the development of more realistic models of eye-movement control in reading – models that allow empirical researchers to interpret their findings more accurately.

A second issue that follows directly from this discussion is related to the nature of attention allocation during reading. The core question here remains: Is attention allocated in a serial manner, to support the processing and identification of only one word at a time, or is attention instead allocated as a gradient to support the concurrent processing and identification of up to three or four words? Models of eye-movement control in reading have been explicitly designed to answer this question (see Engbert &. Kliegl, 2011; Reichle, 2011). For example, E-Z

Reader (Reichle et al., 2012), the Attention-Shift model (Reilly, 1993), and EMMA (Salvucci, 2001) share the assumption that attention is allocated in a strictly serial manner, whereas SWIFT (Engbert et al., 2005), Glenmore (Reilly & Radach, 2006), and OB1-Reader (Snell et al., 2018) share the assumption that attention is allocated as a gradient.[4] Importantly, these models were designed to simulate eye movements in the reading of English, German, and French, which use alphabetic writing systems that separate words with blank spaces. Perhaps for that reason, the question about how attention is allocated has been framed in an either-or manner, with the two groups of models taking extreme stances on the issue. The framing of the question becomes more nuanced, however, if one considers the reading of Chinese.

To illustrate why this is true, consider the X. Li and Pollatsek (2020) CRM. As indicated in Chapter 4, the central component of this model is McClelland and Rumelhart's (1981) interactive-activation model of word identification that has been adapted to the reading of Chinese, and interfaces with a system that uses ongoing lexical processing to decide when and where to move the eyes. The key modification that allows the model to segment and identify Chinese words is that characters and words are represented redundantly across different spatial locations, and in the words of Li and Pollatsek:

> All of the characters in the perceptual span are processed in parallel, and all of the possible words (which are position specific) constituted by the activated characters are also activated, and these word units that overlap in space complete in a 'winner-take-all' manner to identify a given word. (X. Li & Pollatsek, 2020: 1145)

Thus, in the context of explaining how attention is allocated during the reading of Chinese, the "either-or" framing of the attention-allocation question fails to capture all of the complexity of what is probably happening when continuous strings of characters are segmented into words. If the CRM provides some approximation to what actually happens during Chinese reading, then attention is neither a fixed "spotlight" that is

---

[4] The designers of Glenmore (Reilly & Radach, 2006) and OB1-Reader (Snell et al., 2018) claim that their models instantiate the parallel processing of words. Although these claims are technically true, the mutually inhibitory connections among the word nodes within these models guarantee that only one word will be identified at any given time. This constraint is inherited from the interactive-activation model (McClelland & Rumelhart, 1981) which is the word-identification component of both models. This constraint is explicitly acknowledged by X. Li and Pollatsek (2020: 20), whose model (as discussed in Chapter 4) is also designed around principles of the interactive-activation model. For further discussion of this issue, see Reichle and Schotter (2020).

allocated to only one word at a time *nor* is it a diffuse gradient that is simultaneously distributed across three–four words. Rather, attention might be more accurately described as being rapidly constricted to support the identification of individual "objects" that are represented in memory. By this interpretation, although attention might initially be distributed across a small number of characters, the processing of those characters rapidly evolves over time, allowing attention to engage more deeply with or focus upon some number of those characters as information that becomes available from memory is used to segment the characters into a pattern that corresponds to a known word. The implication of this perspective is that neither the "serial" nor "parallel" interpretation of the attention-allocation is entirely correct. Saying this another way, although lexical processing in Chinese may be parallel in that attention is initially focused on several characters and the representations of those characters are at least partially active in memory, the focus of that processing rapidly converges onto only those characters that uniquely specify a word in memory, allowing that word – and *only* that word – to be identified in the sense that its pronunciation and meaning are made available for further linguistic processing.

It is important to note that this perspective offered by the CRM (X. Li & Pollatsek, 2020) is not unique to that model. The CEZR model (Y. P. Liu et al., 2023; L. Yu et al., 2021), for example, shares the assumption that, upon identifying word N, attention shifts to the next four characters, thereby allowing attention to engage more deeply with some portion of those characters as they are segmented into word $N+1$, allowing it to be identified. This convergence between the two models in terms of how their assumptions about attention allocation are used to explain the segmentation and identification of words lends additional support to the notion that traditional "serial versus parallel" framing of the attention-allocation question (cf. Reichle et al., 2009; Snell & Grainger, 2019) may be overly simplistic. And to us, this convergence also suggests that the answers to the question of how attention is allocated, like those that have been offered to answer the question of saccadic targeting during reading, may differ somewhat between different writing systems.

For example, in the reading of scripts where words are clearly demarcated, attention is probably allocated in a manner that is approximately serial. But even here, there are likely to be some important exceptions. Two examples might include idioms, on one hand, and long, polymorphemic words, on the other. In the case of idioms, for example, it might not be unreasonable to assume that, at least in some instances, the words of common idioms like "kick the bucket" or "looking a gift horse in the mouth" might come to be treated as a single unit, allowing them to be identified in a more parallel manner (e.g., see Cacciari & Tabossi, 1988; Swinney & Cutler, 1979). Conversely, long and unfamiliar polymorphemic words like "uncopyrightable" might be identified by first parsing and then identifying their constituent morphemes so that the overall meaning of the words can be constructed (e.g., see Jarvella & Meijers, 1983; MacKay, 1978). These two examples illustrate boundary conditions under which attention might *not* be allocated in a strictly serial manner, but might instead either be allocated in parallel to a group of words comprising an idiom, or allocated sub-lexically to the individual morphemes within a word. That being said, such examples lead us to predict that future research on Chinese reading and how continuous arrays of characters are segmented into words will help inform our understanding of the more general nature of attention allocation during reading and the precise conditions under which it approximates serial versus parallel lexical processing. This will in turn likely advance our understanding of the topics that were used as examples here – the processing of common multi-word phrases like idioms, and the processing of complex, polymorphemic words.

Finally, in closing this section, we want to share one last (even more speculative!) idea related to the reading of Chinese and how its study might inform the psychology of reading. This idea is related to the fact that, as we have indicated throughout this book, the Chinese script is more complex than alphabetic scripts in that it is visually denser and involves a four-level hierarchy of orthographic components with two of those components (strokes and radicals) being configured along two spatial dimensions. We suspect that these differences are important and that visual processing likely plays a more significant role than in the identification of alphabetic words, where there is evidence suggesting that the visual information corresponding to the letter features is rapidly converted into abstract orthographic codes (e.g., McConkie & Zola, 1979). Although the hierarchical processing of Chinese word components is undoubtedly highly interactive with feedback from higher to lower levels of processing (as suggested by radical- and character-superiority effects; Y. P. Chen et al., 1996; X. Li & Pollatsek, 2011; Mattingly & Xu, 1994; Mok, 2009), this processing might also be more temporally extended than the processing of letters in alphabetic scripts. If correct, then one might hope to observe neural or behavioral evidence indicative of radical- versus character- versus word-level processing stages. For example, if radical processing precedes character processing by a sufficient amount of time, then this might be detected using ERP, MEG, or eye-movement measures.

Such findings would suggest that orthographic processing in Chinese is more temporally extended than in alphabetic scripts, perhaps analogous to how phonological processing is more temporally extended in alphabetic writing systems (where graphemes are converted to phonemes "cascade style") than in Chinese (where characters are converted to their pronunciations "threshold style"; Perfetti et al., 2005; Perfetti & Tan, 1998). If this conjecture is correct, then this important difference between Chinese and alphabetic scripts would obviously provide another interesting point of contract between the two – one that highlights the flexibility with which the cognitive systems that support lexical processing can adapt to accommodate markedly different writing systems.

6.3 Conclusions

Our main intention in writing this book has been to make the research on Chinese reading accessible to a broader audience of reading scientists by first briefly describing the Chinese languages and writing system and then, across successive chapters, reviewing what has been learned about the processing and identification of Chinese characters and words, the skilled reading of Chinese text, and how this skill develops, the ways in which it sometimes fails to develop, and what has been learned about Chinese reading from cognitive neuroscience. We sincerely hope that we have achieved at least some of those goals, and that you, the reader, have found something of value from reading this book. At a minimum, we hope to have provided a compelling case for why the science of reading will benefit from the study of other languages and writing systems, especially those that – like Chinese – differ in significant ways from the European languages and alphabetic scripts that have been the focus of the most efforts to understand reading. We are of course not the first to make this claim (see e.g., Perfetti et al., 2005; Share, 2008), but instead only add to what has already been said by providing another important and interesting example – that of Chinese. Indeed, Share (2008) made exactly the same point and, because his eloquence surpasses ours, his plea is worth citing in full:

> [A] complete science of reading ultimately requires a deep understanding of the universal and script-specific nature of reading and writing across all writing systems. Reading science cannot be founded on a single, outlier orthography. (Share, 2008: 604)

Of course, the phrase "outlier orthography" refers to English, the language and writing system that, for a variety of scientific, cultural, and economic reasons, has largely determined the agenda of reading science.

We would, however, like to put a more positive spin on this fact by acknowledging that the science of reading had to start somewhere, and that although the reading of English might not be representative of the reading of most languages, what has been learned about the former has provided solid empirical and theoretical foundations for investigating the latter. And although we would like to be able to say that we predicted a rapid growth in reading research in languages like Chinese, we again have to acknowledge that we are too late because this "prediction" has already been happening, even prior to the writing of this book. We therefore remain content in knowing that we are contributing to these efforts in eager anticipation of what might be learned by broadening the science of reading, making it more inclusive of other writing systems, especially one of the most important but arguably most overlooked – that of Chinese.

References

Akmajian, A., Demers, R. A., Farmer, A. K., & Harnish, R. M. (2010). *Linguistics: An introduction to language and communication*. Sixth edition. Cambridge, MA: MIT Press.

Anderson, R. C., Li, W., Ku, Y. M., Shu, H., & Wu, N. (2003). Use of partial information in learning to read Chinese characters. *Journal of Educational Psychology*, 95, 52–7.

Andrews, S. (1989). Frequency and neighborhood effects on lexical access: Activation or search? *Journal of Experimental Psychology: Learning, Memory, and Cognition*, 15, 802–14.

Andrews, S. (1992). Frequency and neighborhood effects on lexical access: Lexical similarity or orthographic redundancy? *Journal of Experimental Psychology: Learning, Memory, and Cognition*, 18, 234–54.

Andrews, S. (1997). The effect of orthographic similarity on lexical retrieval: Resolving neighborhood conflicts. *Psychonomic Bulletin & Review*, 4, 439–61.

Ans, B., Carbonnel, S., & Valdois, S. (1998). A connectionist multiple-trace memory model for polysyllabic word reading. *Psychological Review*, 105, 678–723.

Antúnex, M., Milligan, S., Hernández-Cabrera, J. A., Barber, H. A., & Schotter, E. (2021). Semantic parafoveal processing in natural reading: Insight from fixation-related potentials & eye movements. *Psychophysiology*, e13986. https://doi.org/10.1111/psyp.13986.

Bai, X., Hu, X., & Yan, G. (2009). Parafoveal-on-foveal effects in Chinese reading: The influence of semantic transparencies of word N on word N-1 processing. *Acta Psychologica Sinica*, 41, 377–86. [白学军, 胡笑羽, & 闫国利. (2009). 中文阅读的副中央凹-中央凹效应：词n的语义透明度对词n-1加工的影响. 心理学报, 41, 377–86.]

Bai, X., Yan, G., Liversedge, S. P., Zang, C., & Rayner, K. (2008). Reading spaced and unspaced Chinese text: evidence from eye movements. *Journal of Experimental Psychology: Human Perception and Performance*, 34, 1277–87.

Baillet, S. (2017). Magnetoencephalography for brain electrophysiology and imaging. *Nature Neuroscience*, 20, 327–39.

Balota, D. A., & Chumbley, J. I. (1984). Are lexical decisions a good measure of lexical access? The role of word frequency in the neglected decision stage. *Journal of Experimental Psychology: Human Perception and Performance*, 10, 340–57.

References

Balota, D. A., Pollatsek, A., & Rayner, K. (1985). The interaction of contextual constraints and parafoveal visual information in reading. *Cognitive Psychology*, 17, 364–90.

Balota, D., Yap, M. J., Hutchinson, K. A., Cortese, M. J., Kessler, B., Loftis, B., et al. (2007). The English Lexicon Project. *Behavior Research Methods*, 39, 445–59.

Bi, H., Hu, W., & Weng, X. (2006). Orthographic neighborhood effects in the pronunciation of Chinese words. *Acta Psychologica Sinica*, 38, 791–7. [毕鸿燕, 胡伟, & 翁旭初. (2006). 汉语形声字声旁家族大小对整字发音的影响. 心理学报, 38, 791–7.]

Binder, J. R., Medler, D. A., Westbury, C. F., Liebenthal, E., & Buchanan, L. (2006). Tuning of the human fusiform gyrus to sublexical orthographic structure. *NeuroImage*, 33, 739–78.

Bishop, D. V., & Snowling, M. J. (2004). Developmental dyslexia and specific language impairment: Same or different? *Psychological Bulletin*, 130, 858–86.

Bolger, D. J., Perfetti, C. A., & Schneider, W. (2005). Cross-cultural effect on the brain revisited: Universal structure plus writing system variation. *Human Brain Mapping*, 25, 92–104.

Bouma, H. (1973). Visual interference in the parafoveal recognition of initial and final letters of words. *Vision Research*, 13, 767–82.

Brysbaert, M. (2019). How many words do we read per minute? A review and meta-analysis of reading rate. *Journal of Memory and Language*, 109, 104047.

Brysbaert, M., Mandera, P., & Keuleers, E. (2018). The word frequency effect in word processing: An updated review. *Current Directions in Psychological Science*, 27, 45–50.

Brysbaert, M., & New, B. (2009). Moving beyond Kucera and Francis: A critical evaluation of current word frequency norms and the introduction of a new and improved word frequency measure for American English. *Behavior Research Methods*, 41, 977–90.

Cacciari, C., & Tabossi, P. (1988). The comprehension of idioms. *Journal of Memory and Language*, 27, 668–83.

Cai, H., Qi, X., Chen, Q., & Zhong, Y. (2012). Effects of phonetic radical position on the regularity effect for naming pictophonetic characters. *Acta Psychologica Sinica*, 44, 868–81. [蔡厚德, 齐星亮, 陈庆荣, & 钟元. (2012). 声旁位置对形声字命名规则性效应的影响. 心理学报, 44, 868–81.]

Cao, F., Peng, D., Liu, L., Jin, Z., Fan, N., Deng, Y., Booth, J. L. (2009). Developmental differences of neurocognitive networks for phonological and semantic processing in Chinese word reading. *Human Brain Mapping*, 30, 797–809.

Cao, F., & Perfetti, C. A. (2016). Neural signatures of the reading-writing connection: Greater involvement of writing in Chinese reading than English reading. *PloS One*, 11, e0168414.

Cao, F., Vu, M., Chan, D. H. L., Lawrence, J. M., Harris, L., Guan, Q. Xu, Y., & Perfetti, C. A. (2013). Writing affects the brain network of reading in Chinese: A functional magnetic resonance imaging study. *Human Brain Mapping*, 34, 1670–84.

References

Cao, H., Lan, Z., Gao, F., Yu, H., Li, P., & Wang, J. (2023). The role of character positional frequency on word recognition during Chinese reading: Lexical decision and eye movements studies. *Acta Psychologica Sinica*, 55, 159–76. [曹海波, 兰泽波, 高峰, 于海涛, 李鹏, & 王敬欣. (2023). 词素位置概率在中文阅读中的作用: 词汇判断和眼动研究. 心理学报, 55, 159–76.]

Caravolas, M., Lervag, A., Defior, S., Malkova, G. S., & Hulme, C. (2013). Different patterns, but equivalent predictors, of growth in reading in consistent and inconsistent orthographies. *Psychological Science*, 24, 1398–407

Carlisle, J. F. (2000). Awareness of the structure and mean- ing of morphologically complex words: Impact on reading. *Reading and Writing*, 12, 169–90.

Caroll, J. B., & White, M. N. (1973a). Age-of-acquisition norms for 220 picturable nouns. *Journal of Verbal Learning and Verbal Behavior*, 12, 563–76.

Caroll, J. B., & White, M. N. (1973b). Word frequency and age of acquisition as determiners of picture-naming latency. *Quarterly Journal of Experimental Psychology*, 25, 85–95.

Castles, A., & Coltheart, M. (1993). Varieties of developmental dyslexia. *Cognition*, 47, 149–80.

Castles, A., Rastle, K., & Nation, K. (2018). Ending the reading wars: Reading acquisition from novice to expert. *Psychological Science in the Public Interest*, 19, 5–51.

Chang, L. Y., Chen, Y. C., & Perfetti, C. A. (2018). GraphCom: A multidimensional measure of graphic complexity applied to 131 written languages. *Behavior Research Methods*, 50, 427–49.

Chang, R. & Chang, M. S. (1978). *Speaking of Chinese*. New York: Norton.

Chang, Y. N., & Lee, C. Y. (2020). Age of acquisition effects on traditional Chinese character naming and lexical decision. *Psychonomic Bulletin & Review*, 27, 1317–24.

Chang, Y. N., Welbourne, S., & Lee, C. Y. (2016). Exploring orthographic neighborhood size effects in a computational model of Chinese character naming. *Cognitive Psychology*, 91, 1–23.

Chen, B. (1993). An experimental study of Collin's semantic hierarchical network model. *Acta Psychologica Sinica*, 25, 359–65. [陈宝国. (1993). 柯林斯语义层次网络模型的实验研究. 心理学报, 25, 359–65.]

Chen, B., & Ning, A. (2005). Homophone effects in the recognition of Chinese character：The evidence of phonology influencing the graphic processing of Chinese character. *Psychological Exploration*, 25, 35–9. [陈宝国, & 宁爱华. (2005). 汉字识别中的同音字效应: 语音影响字形加工的证据. 心理学探新, 25, 35–9.]

Chen, B., & Peng, D. (2001). The time course of graphic, phonological and semantic information processing in Chinese character recognition (I). *Acta Psychologica Sinica*, 33, 1–6. [陈宝国, & 彭聃龄. (2001). 汉字识别中形音义激活时间进程的研究(Ⅰ). 心理学报, 33, 1–6.]

Chen, B., Wang, L., & Peng, D. (2003). The time course of graphic, phonological and semantic information processing in Chinese character recognition (II). *Acta Psychologica Sinica*, 35, 576–81. [陈宝国, 王立新, & 彭聃龄. (2003). 汉字识别中形音义激活时间进程的研究 (Ⅱ). 心理学报, 35, 576–81.]

Chen, B., Wang, L., Wang, L., & Peng, D. (2004). The effect of age of word acquisition and frequency on the identification of Chinese double-character words. *Journal of Psychological Science*, 27, 1060–4. [陈宝国, 王立新, 王璐璐, & 彭聃龄. (2004). 词汇习得年龄和频率对词汇识别的影响. 心理科学, 27, 1060–4.]

Chen, B., You, W., & Zhou, H. (2007). Age of acquisition effects in reading Chinese: Evidence in favor of the semantic hypothesis. *Acta Psychologica Sinica*, 39, 9–17. [陈宝国, 尤文平, & 周会霞. (2007). 汉语词汇习得的年龄效应: 语义假设的证据. 心理学报, 39, 9–17.]

Chen, B., Zhou, H., Dunlap, S., & Perfetti, C. A. (2007). Age of acquisition effects in reading Chinese: Evidence in favour of the arbitrary mapping hypothesis. *British Journal of Psychology*, 98, 499–516.

Chen, H. C., Vaid, J., & Wu, J. T. (2009). Homophone density and phonological frequency in Chinese word recognition. *Language and Cognitive Processes*, 24, 967–82.

Chen, H. C., Song, H., Lau, W. Y., Wong, K. F. E., & Tang, S. L. (2003). Developmental characteristics of eye movements in reading Chinese. In C. McBride-Chang & H. C. Chen (eds.), *Reading Development in Chinese Children*. Westport, CT: Praeger, 157–69.

Chen, H. C. & Tang, C. K. (1998). The effective visual field in reading Chinese. In C. K. Leong & K. Tamaoka (eds.), *Cognitive Processing of the Chinese and the Japanese Languages*. Dordrecht and Boston, MA: Kluwer Academic, 91–100.

Chen, J., & Zhang, J. (2005). The phonological activation of unfamiliar pictophonetic characters of lower-grade pupils. *Journal of Psychological Science*, 28, 901–05. [陈俊 & 张积家. (2005). 小学低年级学生对陌生形声字的语音提取. 心理科学, 28, 901–05.]

Chen, M., Wang, Y., Zhao, B., Li, X., & Bai, X. (2022). The role of text familiarity in Chinese word segmentation and Chinese vocabulary recognition. *Acta Psychologica Sinica*, 54, 1151–66. [陈茗静, 王永胜, 赵冰洁, 李馨, & 白学军. (2022). 中文文本熟悉性在词切分和词汇识别中的作用. 心理学报, 54, 1151–66.]

Chen, M. J. & Weekes, B. S. (2004). Effects of semantic radicals on Chinese character categorization and character decision. *Chinese Journal of Psychology*, 46, 181–96.

Chen, X., Shu, H., Wu, N., & Anderson, R. C. (2003). Stages in learning to pronounce Chinese characters. *Psychology in the Schools*, 40, 115–24.

Chen, Y. P., Allport, D., & Marshall, J. (1996). What are the functional orthographic units in Chinese word recognition: The stroke or the stroke pattern? *The Quarterly Journal of Experimental Psychology*, 49A, 1024–43.

Chen, Y. M., & Peng, R. (1985). Preliminary study of semantic retrieval for Chinese language. *Acta Psychologica Sinica*, 2, 162–9. [陈永明, & 彭瑞祥. (1985). 汉语语义记忆提取的初步研究. 心理学报, 2, 162–9.]

Cheng, C. M. (1981). The process of recognition of Chinese characters and words. *Chinese Journal of Psychology*, 70, 137–53. [郑昭明. (1981). 漢字認知的歷程. 中華心理學刊, 70, 137–53.]

References

Chomsky, N. (1959). A review of Skinner's Verbal Behavior. *Language*, 35, 26–58.

Christianson, K. (2017). Psycholinguistics. In M. Aronoff & J. Rees-Miller (eds.), *The Handbook of Linguistics*. Hoboken, NJ: Wiley-Blackwell, 345–69.

Clifton, C., Jr., Staub, A., & Rayner, K. (2007). Eye movements in reading words and sentences. In R. P. G. van Gompel, M. H. Fischer, W. S. Murray, & R. L. Hill (eds.), *Eye Movements: A Window on Mind and Brain*. Oxford: Elsevier, 341–72.

Cohen, L., Dehaene, S., Naccache, L., Lehericy, S., Dehaene-Lambertz, G., Henaff, M.-A., & Michel, F. (2000). The visual word form area: Spatial and temporal characterization of an initial stage of reading in normal subjects and posterior split-brain patients. *Brain*, 123, 291–307.

Cohen, L., Lehericy, S., Chochon, F., Lemer, C., Rivaud, S., & Dehaene, S. (2002). Language-specific tuning of visual cortex? Functional properties of the Visual Word Form Area. *Brain*, 125, 1054–69.

Cohen, L., & Dehaene, S. (2009). Ventral and dorsal contributions to word reading. In M. Gazzaniga (ed.), *The Cognitive Neurosciences*. Fourth edition. Cambridge, MA: MIT Press, 789–804.

Collins, A. M., & Loftus, E. F. (1975). A spreading-activation theory of semantic processing. *Psychological Review*, 82, 407–28.

Collins, R. N., Milliken, B., & Jamieson, R. K. (2020). MINERVA-DE: An instance model of the deficient processing theory. *Journal of Memory and Language*, 115, 104151.

Coltheart, M. (1987). *Attention and Performance XII: The Psychology of Reading*. Plymouth: Lawrence Erlbaum.

Coltheart, M., Curtis, B., Atkins, P., & Haller, M. (1993). Models of reading aloud: Dual-route and parallel-distributed-processing approaches. *Psychological Review*, 100, 589–608.

Coltheart, M., Curtis, B., Atkins, P., & Haller, M. (2013). Models of reading aloud: Dual-route and parallel-distributed-processing approaches. In G. Cohen, R. A. Johnstone, K. Plunkett (eds.), *Exploring Cognition: Damaged Brains and Neural Networks*. London: Psychology Press, 381–422.

Coltheart, M., Davelaar, E., Jonasson, J. T., & Besner, D. (1977). Access to the internal lexicon. In S. Dornic (ed.), *Attention and Performance VI*. Hillsdale, NJ: Erlbaum, 535–55.

Coltheart, M., Rastle, K., Perry, C. Langdon, R., & Ziegler, J. (2001). DRC: A dual route cascaded model of visual word recognition and reading aloud. *Psychological Review*, 108, 204–56.

Courtney, S. M., Petit, L., Maisog, J. M., Ungerleider, L. G., & Haxby, J. V. (1998). An area specialized for spatial working memory in human front cortex. *Science*, 279, 1347–52.

Crowder, R. G., & Wagner, R. K. (1992). *The Psychology of Reading: An Introduction*. Oxford: Oxford University Press.

Cui, L., Wang, J., Zhang, Y., Cong, F., Zhang, W., & Hyönä, J. (2021). Compound word frequency modifies the effect of character frequency in reading Chinese. *Quarterly Journal of Experimental Psychology*, 74, 610–33.

Cui, L., Wang, S., Yan, G., & Bai, X. (2010). Parafoveal-on-foveal interactions in normal Chinese reading. *Acta Psychologica Sinica*, 42, 547–58. [崔磊, 王穗苹, 闫国利, & 白学军. (2010). 中文阅读中副中央凹与中央凹相互影响的眼动实验. 心理学报, 42, 547–58.]

Cui, L., Yan, G., Bai, X., Hyönä, J., Wang, S., & Liversedge, S. P. (2013). Processing of compound-word characters in reading Chinese: An eye-movement-contingent display change study. *Quarterly Journal of Experimental Psychology: Human Experimental Psychology*, 66, 527–47.

Cutter, M. G., Drieghe, D., & Liversedge, S. P. (2014). Preview benefit in English spaced compounds. *Journal of Experimental Psychology: Learning, Memory, and Cognition*, 40, 1778–86.

Davis, C. J. (2010). The spatial coding model of visual word identification. *Psychological Review*, 117, 713–58.

de Wit, B., & Kinoshita, S. (2014). Relatedness proportion effects in semantic categorization: Reconsidering the automatic spreading activation process. *Journal of Experimental Psychology: Learning, Memory, and Cognition*, 40, 1733–44.

de Wit, B., & Kinoshita, S. (2015). An RT distribution analysis of relatedness proportion effects in lexical decision and semantic categorization reveals different mechanisms. *Memory & Cognition*, 43, 99–110.

Deacon, T. W. (1997). *The Symbolic Species: The Co-evolution of Language and the Brain*. New York: Norton.

Dehaene, S. (2009). *Reading in the Brain*. New York: Penguin.

Dehaene, S., & Cohen, L. (2007). Cultural recycling of cortical maps. *Neuron*, 57, 384–98.

Ding, G., Peng, D., & Taft, M. (2004). The nature of the mental representation of radicals in Chinese: A priming study. *Journal of Experimental Psychology: Learning, Memory, and Cognition*, 30, 530–9.

Dong, Y., Nakamura, K., Okada, T., Hanakawa, T., Fukuyama, H., Mazziotta, J. C., & Shibasaki, H. (2005). Neural mechanisms underlying the processing of Chinese words. *Neuroscience Research*, 52, 139–45.

Durso, F. T., & Johnston, M. K. (1979). Facilitation in naming and categorizing repeated pictures and words. *Journal of Experimental Psychology: Human Learning and Memory*, 5, 449–59.

Ehri, L. C. (2005). Learning to read words: theory, findings, and issues. *Scientific Studies of Reading*, 9, 167–88

Ehrlich, S. F., & Rayner, K. (1981). Contextual effects on word perception and eye movements during reading. *Journal of Verbal Learning and Verbal Behavior*, 20, 641–55.

Ellis, A. W., & Morrison, C. M. (1998). Real age-of-acquisition effects in lexical retrieval. *Journal of Experimental Psychology: Learning, Memory, and Cognition*, 24, 515–23.

Engbert, R., & Kliegl, R. (2011). Parallel graded attention models of reading. In S. P. Liversedge, I. D. Gilchrist, & S. Everling (eds.), *Oxford Handbook on Eye Movements*. Oxford: Oxford University Press, 787–800.

Engbert, R., Nuthmann, A., Richter, E., & Kliegl, R. (2005). SWIFT: A dynamical model of saccade generation during reading. *Psychological Review*, 112, 777–813.

References

Eysenck, M. W., & Keane, M. T. (2015). *Cognitive Psychology: A Student's Handbook.* New York: Psychology Press.

Fan, X., & Reilly, R. G. (2022). Eye movement control in reading Chinese: A matter of strength of character? *Acta Psychologica*, 230, 103711.

Farrell, S., & Lewandowsky, S. (2018). *Computational Modeling of Cognition and Behavior.* Cambridge: Cambridge University Press.

Feldman, L. B., & Siok, W. W. (1997). The role of component function in visual recognition of Chinese characters. *Journal of Experimental Psychology: Learning, Memory, and Cognition*, 23, 776–81.

Feldman, L. B., & Siok, W. W. (1999). Semantic radicals contribute to the visual identification of Chinese characters. *Journal of Memory and Language*, 40, 559–76.

Ferreira, F., & Clifton, C., Jr. (1986). The independence of syntactic processing. *Journal of Memory and Language*, 25, 348–68.

Feustel, T. C., Shiffrin, R. M., & Salasoo, A. (1983). Episodic and lexical contributions to the repetition effect in word identification. *Journal of Experimental Psychology: General*, 112, 309–46.

Forster, K. I., & Chambers, S. M. (1973). Lexical access and naming time. *Journal of Verbal Learning and Verbal Behavior*, 12, 627–35.

Forster, K. I., & Davis, C. (1984). Repetition priming and frequency attenuation in lexical access. *Journal of Experimental Psychology: Learning, Memory, and Cognition*, 10, 680–98.

Forster, K. I., & Hector, J. (2002). Cascaded versus noncascaded models of lexical and semantic processing: The *turple* effect. *Memory & Cognition*, 30, 1106–17.

Fowler, C. A., Napps, S. E., & Feldman, L. (1985). Relations among regular and irregular morphologically related words in the lexicon as revealed by repetition priming. *Memory & Cognition*, 13, 241–55.

Francis, W., & Kucera, H. (1982). *Frequency Analysis of English Usage: Lexicon and grammar.* Boston: Houghton Mifflin.

Frazier, L., & Rayner, K. (1982). Making and correcting errors during sentence comprehension: Eye movements in the analysis of structurally ambiguous sentences. *Cognitive Psychology*, 14, 178–210.

Frazier, L., & Rayner, K. (1987). Resolution of synactic category ambiguities: Eye movements in parsing lexical ambiguous sentences. *Journal of Memory and Language*, 26, 505–26.

Frey, A., & Bosse, M. L. (2018). Perceptual span, visual span, and visual attention span: Three potential ways to quantify limits on visual processing during reading. *Visual Cognition*, 26, 412–29.

Gao, B., & Gao, F. (2005). The interaction between word frequency and semantic transparency in the recognition of Chinese words. *Journal of Psychological Science*, 28, 1358–60. [高兵, & 高峰强. (2005). 汉语字词识别中词频和语义透明度的交互作用. 心理科学, 28, 1358–60.]

Gao, L., & Peng, D. (2005). The pre-lexical route in the phonological processing of Chinese phonograms. *Journal of Psychological Science*, 28, 885–8. [高立群, & 彭聃龄. (2005). 汉语形声字语音加工的前词汇通路. 心理科学, 28, 885–8.]

Geng, S., Guo, W., Rolls, E. T., Xu, K., Jia, T., Zhou, W., et al. (2023). Intersecting distributed networks support convergent linguistic functioning across different languages in bilinguals. *Communications Biology*, 6, 99.

Gerhand, S., & Barry, C. (1998). Word frequency effects in oral reading are not merely age-of-acquisition effects in disguise. *Journal of Experimental Psychology: Learning, Memory, and Cognition*, 24, 267–83.

Gerhand, S., & Barry, C. (1999a). Age-of-acquisition and frequency effects in speeded word naming. *Cognition*, 73, B27–B36.

Gerhand, S., & Barry, C. (1999b). Age of acquisition, word frequency, and the role of phonology in the lexical decision task. *Memory & Cognition*, 27, 592–602.

Gomez, P., Ratcliff, R., & Perea, M. (2008). The overlap model: A model of letter position coding. *Psychological Review*, 115, 577–601.

Gough, P. B., & Tumner, W. E. (1986). Decoding, reading, and reading disability. *Remedial and Special Education*, 7, 6–10.

Grainger, J. (1990). Word frequency and neighborhood frequency effects in lexical decision and naming. *Journal of Memory and Language*, 29, 228–40.

Grainger, J., & Jacobs, A. M. (1996). Orthographic processing in visual word recognition: A multiple read-out model. *Psychological Review*, 103, 518–65.

Grainger, J., O'Regan, J. K., Jacobs, A. M., & Segui, J. (1989). On the role of competing word units in visual word recognition: The neighborhood frequency effect. *Perception & Psychophysics*, 45, 189–95.

Grainger, J. & van Heuven, W. (2003). Modeling letter position coding in printed word perception. In P. Bonin (ed.), *The Mental Lexicon*. New York: Nova Science, 1–23.

Gu, J., & Li, X. (2015). The effects of character transposition within and across words in Chinese reading. *Attention, Perception, & Psychophysics*, 77, 272–81.

Gu, J., Li, X., & Liversedge, S. P. (2015). Character order processing in Chinese reading. *Journal of Experimental Psychology: Human Perception and Performance*, 41, 127–37.

Guo, W., Geng, S. Cao, M., & Feng, J. (2022). The brain connectome for Chinese reading. *Neuroscience Bulletin*, 1–17.

Guo, Y., Wang, Q., & Wang, T. (2021). Interaction between semantic priming and stimulus quality in Chinese words of single character. *Journal of Psychological Science*, 44, 282–9. [郭艺璇, 王权红, & 王彤彤. (2021). 汉字刺激质量与语义启动间的交互作用. 心理科学, 44, 282–9.]

Han, B. (1994). Development of database of Chinese constituents information – Statistical analysis of the frequency of the constituents and their combination. *Acta Psychologica Sinica*, 26, 147–52. [韩布新. (1994). 汉字部件信息数据库的建立——部件和部件组合频率的统计分析. 心理学报, 26, 147–52.]

Handy, T. (2005). *Event-Related Potentials: A Methods Handbook*. Cambridge, MA: MIT Press.

Harm, M. W., & Seidenberg, M. S. (1999). Phonology, reading acquisition, and dyslexia: Insights from connectionist models. *Psychological Review*, 106, 491–528.

References

Harm, M. W., & Seidenberg, M. S. (2004). Computing the meanings of words in reading: Cooperative division of labor between visual and phonological processes. *Psychological Review*, 111, 662–720.

Henderson, J. M., & Ferreira, F. (1990). Effects of foveal processing difficulty on the perceptual span in reading: Implications for attention and eye movement control. *Journal of Experimental Psychology: Learning, Memory, and Cognition*, 16, 417–29.

Hermena, E. W., & Reichle, E. D. (2020). Insights from the study of Arabic reading. *Language and Linguistic Compass*, 14, 1–26.

Hintzman, D. L. (1991). Why are formal models useful in psychology? In W. E. Hockley & S. Lewandowsky (eds.), *Relating Theory and Data: Essay on Human Memory in Honor of Bennet B. Murdock*. Hillsdale, NJ: Erlbaum, 39–56.

Hoosain, R. (1992). Psychological reality of the word in Chinese. *Advances in Psychology*, 90, 111–30.

Hsiao, J. H. W. & Shillcock, R. (2004). Connectionist modelling of Chinese character pronunciation based on foveal splitting. *Proceedings of the Annual Meeting of the Cognitive Science Society*, 26, 601–06.

Hsiao, J. H. W. & Shillcock, R. (2005). Differences of split and non-split architectures emerged from modelling Chinese character pronunciation. *Proceedings of the Annual Meeting of the Cognitive Science Society*, 27, 989–94.

Hsu, S. H., & Huang, K. C. (2000). Interword spacing in Chinese text layout. *Perceptual and Motor Skills*, 91, 355–65.

Ho, C. S. H., & Bryant, P. (1997a). Learning to read Chinese beyond the logographic phase. *Reading Research Quarterly*, 32, 276–89.

Ho, C. S. H., & Bryant, P. (1997b). Phonological skills are important in learning to read Chinese. *Developmental Psychology*, 33, 946–51.

Ho, C. S. H., Chan, D. W., Chung, K. K., Lee, S. H., & Tsang, S. M. (2007). In search of subtypes of Chinese developmental dyslexia. *Journal of Experimental Child Psychology*, 97, 61–83.

Ho, C. S. H., Wong, W. L., & Chan, W. S. (1999). The use of orthographic analogies in learning to read Chinese. *The Journal of Child Psychology and Psychiatry and Allied Disciplines*, 40, 393–403.

Ho, F. C., & Siegel, L. (2012). Identification of sub-types of students with learning disabilities in reading and its implications for Chinese word recognition and instructional methods in Hong Kong primary schools. *Reading and Writing*, 25, 1547–71.

Howes, D. H., & Solomon, R. S. (1951). Word frequency, personal values, and visual duration thresholds. *Psychological Review*, 58, 256–70.

Hu, C. F., & Catts, H. W. (1998). The role of phonological processing in early reading ability: What we can learn from Chinese. *Scientific Studies of Reading*, 2, 55–79.

Hu, Y. (1981). *Modern Chinese*. Expanded edition. Shanghai: Shanghai Educational Publishing House. [胡裕树. (1981). 现代汉语 (增订本). 上海: 上海教育出版社.]

Huang, H. S., & Hanley, J. R. (1997). A longitudinal study of phonological awareness, visual skills, and Chinese reading acquisition among first-graders in Taiwan. *International Journal of Behavioral Development*, 20, 249–68.

Huang, H. W., Lee, C. Y., Tsai, J. L., Lee, C. L., Hung, D. L., & Tzeng, O. J. L. (2006). Orthographic neighborhood effects in reading Chinese two-character words. *Neuroreport*, 17, 1061–5.

Huang, L., & Li, X. (2020). Early, but not overwhelming: The effect of prior context on segmenting overlapping ambiguous strings when reading Chinese. *Quarterly Journal of Experimental Psychology*, 73, 1382–95.

Huang, L., Staub, A., & Li, X. (2021). Prior context influences lexical competition when segmenting Chinese overlapping ambiguous strings. *Journal of Memory and Language*, 118, 104218.

Hue, C. (1992). Recognition processes in character naming. In H. C. Chen & O. J. L. Tzeng (eds.), *Language Processing in Chinese*. Amsterdam: North-Holland, 93–107.

Huey, E. B. (1908). *The Psychology and Pedagogy of Reading*. New York: Macmillan.

Hutchinson, K. A., Balota, D. A., Neely, J. H., Cortese, M. J., Cohen-Shikora, E. R., Tse, C.-S., et al. (2013). The semantic priming project. *Behavior Research Methods*, 45, 1099–114.

Inhoff, A. W., Eiter, B. M., & Radach, R. (2005). Time course of linguistic information extraction from consecutive words during eye fixations in reading. *Journal of Experimental Psychology: Human Perception and Performance*, 31, 979–95.

Inhoff, A. W., & Liu, W. (1998). The perceptual span and oculomotor activity during the reading of Chinese sentences. *Journal of Experimental Psychology: Human Perception and Performance*, 24, 20–34.

Inhoff, A. W., & Rayner, K. (1986). Parafoveal word processing during eye fixations in reading: Effects of word frequency. *Perception & Psychophysics*, 40, 431–9.

Inhoff, A. W., & Wu, C. (2005). Eye movements and the identification of spatially ambiguous words during Chinese sentence reading. *Memory & Cognition*, 33, 1345–56.

Irwin, D. E. (1998). Lexical processing continues during saccadic eye movements. *Cognitive Psychology*, 36, 1–27.

Jamieson, R. K., & Mewhort, D. J. K. (2009). Applying an exemplar model to the artificial-grammar task: Inferring grammaticality from similarity. *The Quarterly Journal of Experimental Psychology*, 62, 550–75.

Jarvella, R., & Meijers, G. (1983). Recognizing morphemes in spoken words: Some evidence for a stem-organized mental lexicon. In G. B. Flores d'Arcaos & R. Jarvella (eds.), *The Process of Language Understanding*. New York: Wiley, 81–112.

Jacoby, L. L. (1983). Perceptual enhancement: Persistent effects of an experience. *Journal of Experimental Psychology: Learning, Memory, and Cognition*, 9, 21–38.

Jatoi, M. A., Kamel, N., Malik, A. S., Faye, I., & Begum, T. (2014). A survey of methods used for source localization using EEG signals. *Biomedical Signal Processing and Control*, 11, 42–52.

References

Johnson, R. L., Perea, M., & Rayner, K. (2007). Transposed-letter effects in reading: Evidence from eye movements and parafoveal preview. *Journal of Experimental Psychology: Human Perception and Performance*, 33, 209–29.

Jordan, T. R., Almabruk, A. A. A., Gadalla, E. A., McGowan, V. A., White, S. J., Paterson, K. B., et al. (2014). Reading direction and the central perceptual span: Evidence from Arabic and English. *Psychonomic Bulletin & Review*, 21, 505–11.

Just, M. A., & Carpenter, P. A. (1980). A theory of reading: From eye fixations to comprehension. *Psychological Review*, 87, 329–54.

Kanwisher, N., & Yovel, G. (2006). The fusiform face area: A cortical region specialized for the perception of faces. *Philosophical Transactions of the Royal Society B*, 361, 2109–28.

Keay, J. (2009). *China: A history*. London: Harper Press.

Kelly, M. A., Mewhort, D. J. K., & West, R. L. (2017). The memory tesseract: Mathematical equivalence between composite and separate storage memory models. *Journal of Mathematical Psychology*, 77, 142–55.

Kennison, S. M., & Clifton, C., Jr. (1995). Determinants of parafoveal preview benefit in high and low working memory capacity readers: Implications for eye movement control. *Journal of Experimental Psychology: Learning, Memory, and Cognition*, 21, 68–81.

Kintsch, W. (1998). *Comprehension: A Paradigm for Cognition*. Cambridge: Cambridge University Press.

Klein, R. M., & McMullen, P. A. (2001). *Converging Methods for Understanding Reading and Dyslexia*. Cambridge, MA: MIT Press.

Kliegl, R., Nuthmann, A., & Engbert, R. (2006). Tracking the mind during reading: The influence of past, present, and future words on fixation durations. *Journal of Experimental Psychology: General*, 135, 12–35.

Kohonen, T. (1995). *Self-Organizing Maps*. Heidelberg: Springer.

Ku, Y. M., & Anderson, R. C. (2003). Development of morphological awareness in Chinese and English. *Reading and Writing*, 16, 399–422.

Kuo, W. J., Yeh, T. C., Lee, C. Y., Wu, Y. T., Chou, C. C., Ho, L. T., Hung, D. L., Tzeng, O. J. L., & Hsieh, J. C. (2003). Frequency effects of Chinese character processing in the brain: An event-related fMRI study. *NeuroImage*, 18, 720–30.

Kwantes, P. J., & Mewhort, J. K. (1999). Modeling lexical decision and word naming as a retrieval process. *Canadian Journal of Experimental Psychology*, 53, 306–15.

Lam, S. S. Y., & McBride-Chang, C. (2013). Parent-child joint writing in Chinese kindergarteners: Explicit instruction in radical knowledge and stroke writing skills. *Writing Systems Research*, 5, 88–109.

Landerl, K., Castles, A., & Parrila, R. (2022). Cognitive precursors of reading: A cross-linguistic perspective. *Scientific Studies of Reading*, 26, 111–24.

Lee, C. Y., Tsai, J. L., Kuo, W. J., Yeh, T. C., Wu, Y. T., Ho, L. T., Hung, D. L., Tzeng, O. J. L., & Hsieh, J. C. (2004). Neuronal correlates of consistency and frequency effects on Chinese character naming: An event-related fMRI study. *NeuroImage*, 23, 1235–45.

Lee, C. Y., Tsai, J. L., Su, E. C. I., Tzeng, O. J., & Hung, D. L. (2005). Consistency, regularity, and frequency effects in naming Chinese characters. *Language and Linguistics*, 6, 75–107.

Leong, C. K., Cheng, P. W., & Mulcahy, R. (1987). Automatic processing of morphemic orthography by mature readers. *Language and Speech*, 30, 181–96.

Lewellen, M. J. Goldinger, S. D., Pisoni, D. B., & Greene, B. G. (1993). Lexical familiarity and processing efficiency: Individual differences in naming, lexical decision, and semantic categorization. *Journal of Experimental Psychology: General*, 122, 316–30.

Lexicon of Common Words in Contemporary Chinese Research Team. (2008). *Lexicon of Common Words in Contemporary Chinese*. Beijing: Commercial Press.

Li, H., Peng, H., & Shu, H. (2006). A study on the emergence and development of Chinese orthographic awareness in preschool and school children. *Psychological Development and Education*, 22, 35–8. [李虹, 彭虹, & 舒华. (2006). 汉语儿童正字法意识的萌芽与发展. 心理发展与教育, 22, 35–8.]

Li, H., Shu, H., McBride-Chang, C., Liu, H., & Peng, H. (2012). Chinese children's character recognition: Visuo-orthographic, phonological processing and morphological skills. *Journal of Research in Reading*, 35, 287–307.

Li, L., Wang, H. C., Castles, A., Hsieh, M. L., & Marinus, E. (2018). Phonetic radicals, not phonological coding systems, support orthographic learning via self-teaching in Chinese. *Cognition*, 176, 184–94.

Li, J., Fu, X., & Lin, Z. (2000). Study on the development of Chinese orthographic regularity in school children. *Acta Psychologica Sinica*, 32, 121–6. [李娟, 傅小兰, & 林仲贤. (2000). 学龄儿童汉语正字法意识发展的研究. 心理学报, 32, 121–6.]

Li, M. F., Gao, X. Y., Chou, T. L., & Wu, J. T. (2017). Neighborhood frequency effect in Chinese word recognition: Evidence from naming and lexical decision. *Journal of Psycholinguistic Research*, 46, 227–45.

Li, M. F., Lin, W. C., Chou, T. L., Yang, F. L., & Wu, J. T. (2015). The role of orthographic neighborhood size effects in Chinese word recognition. *Journal of Psycholinguistic Research*, 44, 219–36.

Li, Q., Bi, H., Wei, T., & Chen, B. (2011). Orthographic neighborhood size effect in Chinese character naming: Orthographic and phonological activations. *Acta Psychologica*, 136, 35–41.

Li, W., Anderson, R. C., Nagy, W., & Zhang, H. (2002). Facets of metalinguistic awareness that contribute to Chinese literacy. In L. Wenling, J. S. Gaffney, & J. L. Packard (eds.) *Chinese Children's Reading Acquisition*. Boston, MA: Springer, 87–106.

Li, X., Bicknell, K., Liu, P., Wei, W., & Rayner, K. (2014). Reading is fundamentally similar across disparate writing systems: A systematic characterization of how words and characters influence eye movements in Chinese reading. *Journal of Experimental Psychology: General*, 143, 895–913.

Li, X., Gu, J., Liu, P., & Rayner, K. (2013). The advantage of word-based processing in Chinese reading: Evidence from eye movements. *Journal of Experimental Psychology: Learning, Memory, and Cognition*, 39, 879–89.

References

Li, X., Liu, P., & Rayner, K. (2011). Eye movement guidance in Chinese reading: Is there a preferred viewing location? *Vision Research, 51,* 1146–56.

Li, X., & Pollatsek, A. (2011). Word knowledge influences character perception. *Psychonomic Bulletin & Review, 18,* 833–9.

Li, X. & Pollatsek, A. (2020). An integrated model of word processing and eye-movement control during Chinese reading. *Psychological Review, 127* (6), 1139–62.

Li, X., Rayner, K., & Cave, K. R. (2009). On the segmentation of Chinese words during reading. *Cognitive Psychology, 58,* 525–52.

Li, Y., & Bi, H. Y. (2022). Comparative research on neural dysfunction in children with dyslexia under different writing systems: A meta-analysis study. *Neuroscience & Biobehavioral Reviews, 137,* 104650.

Liao, S., Yu, L., Reichle, E. D., & Kruger, J. L. (2021). Using eye movements to study the reading of subtitles in video. *Scientific Studies of Reading, 25,* 417–35.

Lin, D., McBride-Chang, C., Shu, H., Zhang, Y., Li, H., Zhang, J., et al. (2010). Small wins big: Analytic Pinyin skills promote Chinese word reading. *Psychological Science, 21,* 1117–22.

Liu, I. M., Wu, J. T., & Chou, T. L. (1996). Encoding operation and transcoding as the major loci of the frequency effect. *Cognition, 59,* 149–68.

Liu, P., Li, W, Lin, N. & Li, X. (2013). Do Chinese readers follow the national standard rules for word segmentation during reading? *PLOS ONE, 8,* e55440.

Liu, Y., Dunlap, S., Fiez, J., & Perfetti, C. (2007). Evidence for neural accommodation to a writing system following learning. *Human Brain Mapping, 28,* 1223–34.

Liu, Y. P., Guo, S., Yu, L., & Reichle, E. D. (2018). Word predictability affects saccade length in Chinese reading: An evaluation of the dynamic-adjustment model. *Psychonomic Bulletin & Review, 25,* 1891–9.

Liu, Y. P., Huang, R., Gao, D., & Reichle, E. D. (2017). Further tests of a dynamic-adjustment account of saccade targeting during the reading of Chinese. *Cognitive Science, 41,* 1264–87.

Liu, Y. P., Reichle, E. D., & Li, X. (2015). Parafoveal processing affects outgoing saccade length during the reading of Chinese. *Journal of Experimental Psychology: Learning, Memory, and Cognition, 41,* 1229–36.

Liu, Y. P., Reichle, E. D., & Li, X. (2016). The effect of word frequency and parafoveal preview on saccade length during the reading of Chinese. *Journal of Experimental Psychology: Human Perception and Performance, 42,* 1008–25.

Liu, Y. P., Yu, L., Fu, L., Li, W., Duan, Z., & Reichle, E. D. (2019). The effects of parafoveal word frequency and segmentation on saccade targeting during Chinese reading. *Psychonomic Bulletin & Review, 26,* 1367–76.

Liu, Y. P., Yu, L., & Reichle, E. D. (2019). The influence of parafoveal preview, character transposition, and word frequency on saccadic targeting in Chinese reading. *Journal of Experimental Psychology: Human Perception and Performance, 45,* 537–52.

Liu, Y. P., Yu, L., & Reichle, E. D. (2023). *Towards a model of eye-movement control in Chinese reading.* Unpublished manuscript.

Liu, Y. Y., Shu, H., & Li, P. (2007). Word naming and psycholinguistic norms: Chinese. *Behavior Research Methods*, 39, 192–8.

Liu, Z., Tong, W., Zhang, Z., & Zhao, Y. (2020). Predictability impacts word and character processing in Chinese reading: Evidence from eye movements. *Acta Psychologica Sinica*, 52, 1031–47. [刘志方, 仝文, 张智君, & 赵亚军. (2020). 语境预测性对阅读中字词加工过程的影响: 眼动证据. 心理学报, 52, 1031–47.]

Liversedge, S. P., Drieghe, D., Li, X., Yan, G., Bai, X., & Hyönä, J. (2016). Universality in eye movements and reading: A trilingual investigation. *Cognition*, 147, 1–20.

Lo, L. Y., Yeung, P. S., Ho, C. S. H., Chan, D. W. O., & Chung, K. (2016). The role of stroke knowledge in reading and spelling in Chinese. *Journal of Research in Reading*, 39, 367–88.

Logothetis, N. K. (2003). The underpinnings of the BOLD functional Magnetic Resonance Imaging signal. *The Journal of Neuroscience*, 23, 3963–71.

Luo, Y., Wang, P., Li, X., Shi, Y., Chen, M., Wang, P., Hu, S., & Luo, Y. (2010). The effect of character's whole recognition on the processing of components in the processes of Chinese characters. *Acta Psychologica Sinica*, 42, 683–94. [罗艳琳, 王鹏, 李秀军, 石雅琪, 陈墨, 王培培, 胡斯秀, & 罗跃嘉. (2010). 汉字认知过程中整字对部件的影响. 心理学报, 42, 683–94.]

Ma, G., Li, X., & Rayner, K. (2014). Word segmentation of overlapping ambiguous strings during Chinese reading. *Journal of Experimental Psychology: Human Perception and Performance*, 40, 1046–59.

Ma, G., Li, X., & Rayner, K. (2015). Readers extract character frequency information from nonfixated-target word at long pretarget fixations during Chinese reading. *Journal of Experimental Psychology: Human Perception and Performance*, 41, 1409–19.

MacDonald, M. C., Just, M. A., & Carpenter, P. A. (1992). Working memory constraints on the processing of syntactic ambiguity. *Cognitive Psychology*, 24, 56–98.

MacKay, D. G. (1978). Derivational rules and the internal lexicon. *Journal of Verbal Learning and Verbal Behavior*, 17, 61–71.

Makita, K. (1974). Reading disability and the writing system. In J. E. Merritt (eds.) *New Horizons in Reading: Proceedings of the Fifth International Reading Association World Congress on Reading, Vienna, Austria, August 12–14*. Newark, NJ: International Reading Association, 250–4.

Manis, F. R., Seidenberg, M. S., Doi, L. M., McBride-Chang, C., & Petersen, A. (1996). On the bases of two subtypes of development dyslexia. *Cognition*, 58, 157–95.

Marcel, A. J. (1983). Conscious and unconscious perception: Experiments on visual masking and word recognition. *Cognitive Psychology*, 15, 197–237.

Masson, M. E. J., & Freedman, L. (1990). Fluent identification of repeated words. *Journal of Experimental Psychology: Learning, Memory, and Cognition*, 16, 355–73.

Matin, E. (1974). Saccadic suppression: A review. *Psychological Bulletin*, 81, 899–917.

References

Mattingly, I. G., & Xu, Y. (1994). Word superiority in Chinese. *Advances in the Study of Chinese Language Processing*, 1, 101–11.

McBride, C. A. (2016). Is Chinese special? Four aspects of Chinese literacy acquisition that might distinguish learning Chinese from learning alphabetic orthographies. *Educational Psychology Review*, 28 (3), 523–49.

McBride, C., & Wang, Y. (2015). Learning to read Chinese: Universal and unique cognitive cores. *Child Development Perspectives*, 9, 196–200.

McBride, C., Wang, Y., & Cheang, L. M. L. (2018). Dyslexia in Chinese. *Current Developmental Disorders Reports*, 5, 217–25.

McBride-Chang, C. (2004). *Children's Literacy Development*. London: Arnold.

McBride-Chang, C., Bialystok, E., Chong, K. K., & Li, Y. (2004). Levels of phonological awareness in three cultures. *Journal of Experimental Child Psychology*, 89, 93–111.

McBride-Chang, C., Chung, K. K., & Tong, X. (2011). Copying skills in relation to word reading and writing in Chinese children with and without dyslexia. *Journal of Experimental Child Psychology*, 110, 422–33.

McBride-Chang, C., & Ho, C. S. H. (2000). Developmental issues in Chinese children's character acquisition. *Journal of Educational Psychology*, 92, 50–5.

McBride-Chang, C., Shu, H., Zhou, A., Wat, C. P., & Wagner, R. K. (2003). Morphological awareness uniquely predicts young children's Chinese character recognition. *Journal of Educational Psychology*, 95, 743–51.

McBride-Chang, C., Tong, X., Shu, H., Wong, A. M. Y., Leung, K. W., & Tardif, T. (2008). Syllable, phoneme, and tone: Psycholinguistic units in early Chinese and English word recognition. *Scientific Studies of Reading*, 12, 171–94.

McCandliss, B. D., Cohen, L., & Dehaene, S. (2003). The visual word form area: Expertise for reading in the fusiform gyrus. *Trends in Cognitive Sciences*, 7, 293–9.

McClelland, J. L. & Rumelhart, D. E. (1981). An interactive activation model of context effects in letter perception: Part 1. An account of basic findings. *Psychological Review*, 88, 375–407.

McConkie, G. W., Kerr, P. W., Reddix, M. D., & Zola, D. (1988). Eye movement control during reading: I. The location of initial eye fixations in words. *Vision Research*, 28, 1107–18.

McConkie, G. W., Kerr, P. W., Reddix, M. D., Zola, D., Jacobs, A. M. (1989). Eye movement control during reading: II. Frequency of refixating a word. *Perception & Psychophysics*, 46, 245–53.

McConkie, G. W., & Rayner, K. (1975). The span of the effective stimulus during a fixation in reading. *Perception & Psychophysics*, 17, 578–86.

McConkie, G. W., & Rayner, K. (1976). What guides a reader's eye movements? *Vision Research*, 16, 829–37.

McConkie, G. W., & Zola, D. (1979). Is visual information integrated across successive fixations in reading? *Perception & Psychophysics*, 25, 221–4.

McNamara, T. P. (2005). *Semantic Priming: Perspectives from Memory and Word Recognition*. New York: Psychology Press.

McCormack, M. (2016). *Solar Bones*. Dublin: Tramp Press.

McDonald, S. A., Carpenter, R. H. S., & Shillcock, R. C. (2005). An anatomically constrained, stochastic model of eye movement control in reading. *Psychological Review*, 112, 814–40.

Meyer, D. E., & Schvaneveldt, R. W. (1971). Facilitation in recognizing pairs of words: Evidence of a dependence between retrieval operations. *Journal of Experimental Psychology*, 90, 227–34.

Miao, X., & Sang, B. (1991). A further study of the semantic memory of Chinese words. *Journal of Psychological Science*, 1, 8–11. [缪小春, & 桑标. (1991). 汉语词汇语义记忆的再研究. 心理科学, 1, 8–11.]

Miellet, S., O'Donnell, P. J., & Sereno, S. C. (2009). Parafoveal magnification: Visual acuity does not modulate the perceptual span in reading. *Psychological Science*, 20, 721–8.

Miikkulainen, R. (1997). Dyslexic and category-specific aphasic impairments in a self-organizing feature map model of the lexicon. *Brain and Language*, 59, 334–66.

Modern Chinese Frequency Dictionary. (1986). Beijing: Beijing Language and Culture University Press. [现代汉语频率词典. (1986). 北京:北京语言大学出版社.]

Mok, L. W. (2009). Word-superiority effect as a function of semantic transparency of Chinese bimorphemic compound words. *Language and Cognitive Processes*, 24, 1039–81.

Morrison, C. M., & Ellis, A. W. (1995). Roles of word frequency and age of acquisition in word naming and lexical decision. *Journal of Experimental Psychology: Learning, Memory, and Cognition*, 21, 116–33.

Morrison, C. M., & Ellis, A. W. (2000). Real age of acquisition effects in word naming and lexical decision. *British Journal of Psychology*, 91, 167–80.

Morton, J. (1969). Interaction of information in word recognition. *Psychological Review*, 76, 165–78.

Nation, K. (2009). Form-meaning links in the development of visual word recognition. *Philosophical Transactions of the Royal Society B*, 364, 3665–74.

Nation, K. (2017). Nurturing a lexical legacy: Reading experience is critical for the development of word reading skill. *npj Science of Learning*, 2, 1–4.

Nation, K., Angell, P., & Castles, A. (2007). Orthographic learning via self-teaching in children learning to read English: Effects of exposure, durability, and context. *Journal of Experimental Child Psychology*, 96, 71–84.

Neely, J. H. (1976). Semantic priming and retrieval from lexical memory: Evidence for facilitatory and inhibitory processes. *Memory & Cognition*, 4, 648–54.

Neely, J. H. (1977). Semantic priming and retrieval from lexical memory: Roles if inhibitionless spreading activation and limited-capacity attention. *Journal of Experimental Psychology: General*, 106, 226–54.

Neely, J. H. (1991). Semantic priming effects in visual word recognition: A selective review of current findings and theories. In D. Besner & G. W. Humphreys (eds.), *Basic Processes in Reading: Visual Word Recognition*. Hillsdale, NJ: Erlbaum, 264–336.

Nelson, J., Liu, Y., Fiez, J., & Perfetti, C. A. (2009). Assimilation and accommodation patterns in ventral occipitotemporal context in learning a second writing system. *Human Brain Mapping*, 30, 810–20.

References

Norman, J. (1988). *Chinese*. Cambridge: Cambridge University Press.

Normann, R. A., & Guillory, K. S. (2002). Anatomy and physiology of the retina. In G. K. Hung & K. J. Ciuffreda (eds.), *Models of the Visual System*. Boston, MA: Springer, 109–45.

Norris, D. (1994). A quantitative multiple-levels model of reading aloud. *Journal of Experimental Psychology: Human Perception and Performance*, 20, 1212–32.

Norris, D., & Kinoshita, S. (2012). Reading through a noisy channel: Why there's nothing special about the perception of orthography. *Psychological Review*, 119, 517–45.

Nuthmann, A., Engbert, R., & Kliegl, R. (2005). Mislocated fixations during reading and the inverted optimal viewing position effect. *Vision Research*, 45, 2201–17.

O'Regan, J. K. (1981). The 'convenient viewing location' hypothesis. In D. F. Fisher, R. A. Monty, & J. W. Senders (eds.), *Eye Movements: Cognition and Visual Perception*. Hillsdale, NJ: Erlbaum, 289–98.

O'Regan, J. K. (1992). Optimal view position in words and the strategy-tactics model of eye movements in reading. In K. Rayner (ed.), *Eye Movements and Visual Cognition: Scene Perception and Reading*. New York: Springer, 333–54.

O'Regan, J. K., & Jacobs, A. M. (1992). Optimal viewing position effect in word recognition: A challenge to current theory. *Journal of Experimental Psychology: Human Perception and Performance*, 18, 185–97.

O'Regan, J. K., & Lévy-Schoen, A. (1987). Eye-movement strategy and tactics in word recognition and reading. In M. Coltheart (ed.), *Attention and Performance, XII*. Hillsdale, NJ: Erlbaum, 363–84.

O'Regan, J. K., Lévy-Schoen, A., Pynte, J., & Brugaillere, B. (1984). Convenient fixation location within isolated words of different length and structure. *Journal of Experimental Psychology: Human Perception and Performance*, 10, 250–7.

Ozen, R., West, R. L., & Kelly, M. A. (2022). Minvera-Q: A multiple-trace memory system for reinforcement learning. *Proceedings of the 44th Annual Conference of the Cognitive Science Society*.

Packard, J. L. (2015). Morphology: Morphemes in Chinese. In Wang, W. S., & Sun, C. (eds.), *The Oxford Handbook of Chinese Linguistics*. Oxford: Oxford University Press, 262–73.

Packard, J. L., Chen, X., Li, W., Wu, X., Gaffney, J. S., Li, H., & Anderson, R. C. (2006). Explicit instruction in orthographic structure and word morphology helps Chinese children learn to write characters. *Reading and Writing*, 19, 457–87.

Palmer, K. (2009). What can MEG neuroimaging tell us about reading? *Journal of Neurolinguistics*, 22, 266–80.

Peng, D., Liu, Y., & Wang, C. (1999). How is access representation organized? The relation of polymorphemic words and their morphemes in Chinese. In J. Wang, A. W. Inhoff, & H. C. Chen (eds.), *Reading Chinese Script: A Cognitive Analysis*. Mahwah, NJ: Lawrence Erlbaum Associates, 65–89.

Peng, D., & Wang, C. (1997). Basic processing unit of Chinese character recognition: Evidence from stroke number effect and radical number effect. *Acta*

Psychologica Sinica, 29, 8–16. [彭聃龄, & 王春茂. (1997), 笔画数效应和部件数效应. 心理学报, 29, 8–16.]

Peng, P., Wang, C., Tao, S., & Sun, C. (2017). The deficit profiles of Chinese children with reading difficulties: A meta-analysis. *Educational Psychology Review*, 29, 513–64.

Perea, M., & Lupker, S. J. (2003). Does jugde activate COURT? Transposed-letter similarity effects in masked associative priming. *Memory & Cognition*, 31, 829–41.

Perea, M., & Lupker, S. J. (2004). Can CANISO activate CASINO? Transposed-letter similarity effects with nonadjacent letter positions. *Journal of Memory and Language*, 51, 231–46.

Perea, M., Rosa, E., & Gomez, C. (2005). The frequency effect for pseudo-words in the lexical decision task. *Perception & Psychophysics*, 67, 301–14.

Perfetti, C. A. (2005). Reading ability: Lexical quality to comprehension. *Scientific Studies of Reading*, 11, 357–83.

Perfetti, C. A., & Liu, Y. (2006). Reading Chinese characters: Orthography, phonology, meaning, and the Lexical Constituency Model. In P. Li, L. H. Tan, E. Bates, & O. J. L. Tzeng (eds.), *The Handbook of East Asian Psycholinguistics, Volume 1: Chinese*. New York: Cambridge University Press, 225–36.

Perfetti, C. A., Liu, Y., Fiez, J. Nelson, J., Bolger, D. J., & Tan, L. H. (2007). Reading in two writing systems: Accommodation and assimilation of the brain's reading network. *Bilingualism: Language and Cognition*, 10, 131–46.

Perfetti, C. A., Liu, Y., & Tan, L. H. (2005). The lexical constituency model: Some implications of research on Chinese for general theories of reading. *Psychological Review*, 112, 43–59.

Perfetti, C. A., & Tan, L. H. (1998). The time course of graphic, phonological, and semantic activation in Chinese character identification. *Journal of Experimental Psychology: Learning, Memory, and Cognition*, 24, 101–18.

Perfetti, C. A., & Tan, L. H. (1999). The constituency model of Chinese word identification. In J. Wang, A. W. Inhoff, & H. C. Chen (eds.), *Reading Chinese Script: A Cognitive Analysis*. Mahwah, NJ: Lawrence Erlbaum Associates, 115–34.

Perfetti, C. A., & Tan, L. H. (2013). Write to read: the brain's universal reading and writing network. *Trends in Cognitive Sciences*, 17, 56–7.

Perfetti, C. A., & Zhang, S. (1995). Very early phonological activation in Chinese reading. *Journal of Experimental Psychology: Learning, Memory, and Cognition*, 21, 24–33.

Perry, C., Ziegler, J. C., & Zorzi, M. (2007). Nested incremental modeling in the development of computational theories: The CDP+ model of reading aloud. *Psychological Review*, 114, 273–315.

Peterson, R. L., & Pennington, B. F. (2012). Developmental dyslexia. *The Lancet*, 379, 1997–2007.

Pinker, S. (2015). *The Language Instinct: How the Mind Creates Language*. London: Penguin.

Plaut, D. C. (2005). Connectionist approaches to reading. In M. Snowling, C. Hulme, & M. S. Seidenberg (eds.), *The Science of Reading: A Handbook*. Oxford: Oxford University Press, 24–38.

References

Plaut, D. C., McClelland, J. L., Seidenberg, M. S., & Patterson, K. (1996). Understanding normal and impaired word reading: Computational principles in quasi-regular domains. *Psychological Review*, 103, 56–115.

Pollatsek, A., Bolozky, S., Well, A. D., & Rayner, K. (1981). Asymmetries in the perceptual span for Israeli readers. *Brain and Language*, 14, 174–80.

Pollatsek, A., Reichle, E. D., & Rayner, K. (2006). Serial processing is consistent with the time course of linguistic information extraction from consecutive words during eye fixations in reading: A response to Inhoff, Eiter, and Radach (2005). *Journal of Experimental Psychology: Human Perception and Performance*, 32, 1485–9.

Pollatsek, A., & Treiman, R. (2015). *The Oxford Handbook of Reading*. Oxford: Oxford University Press.

Pritchard, S. C., Coltheart, M., Marinus, E., & Castles, A. (2018). A computational model of the self-teaching hypothesis based on the dual-route cascaded model of reading. *Cognitive Science*, 42, 722–70.

Pugh, K. R., Shaywitz, B. A., Shaywitz, S. E., Constable, R. T., Skudlarski, P., Fulbright, R. K., et al. (1996). Cerebral organization of component processes in reading. *Brain*, 119, 1221–38.

Qian, Y., Song, Y. W., Zhao, J., & Bi, H. Y. (2015). The developmental trend of orthographic awareness in Chinese preschoolers. *Reading and Writing*, 28, 571–86.

Raichle, M. E. (1983). Positron emission tomography. *Annual Review of Neuroscience*, 6, 249–67.

Rastle, K., & Davis, M. (2002). On the complexities of measuring naming. *Journal of Experimental Psychology: Human Perception and Performance*, 28, 307–14.

Rayner, K. (1975). The perceptual span and peripheral cues in reading. *Cognitive Psychology*, 7, 65–81.

Rayner, K. (1979). Eye movements and cognitive psychology: On-line computer approaches to studying visual information processing. *Behavior Research Methods & Instruments*, 11, 164–71.

Rayner, K. (1986). Eye movements and the perceptual span in beginning and skilled readers. *Journal of Experimental Child Psychology*, 41, 211–36.

Rayner, K. (1998). Eye movements in reading and information processing: 20 years of research. *Psychological Bulletin*, 124, 372–422.

Rayner, K. (2009). Eye movements and attention in reading, scene perception, and visual search. *The Quarterly Journal of Experimental Psychology*, 62, 1457–506.

Rayner, K. (2014). The gaze-contingent moving window in reading: Development and review. *Visual Cognition*, 22, 242–58.

Rayner, K., Ashby, J., Pollatsek, A., & Reichle, E. D. (2004). The effects of frequency and predictability on eye fixations in reading: Implications for the E-Z Reader model. *Journal of Experimental Psychology: Human Perception and Performance*, 30, 720–32.

Rayner, K., & Bertera, J. J. (1979). Reading without a fovea. *Science*, 206, 468–9.

Rayner, K., Carlson, M., & Frazier, L. (1983). The interaction of syntax and semantics during sentence processing: Eye movements in the analysis of semantically biased sentences. *Journal of Verbal Learning and Verbal Behavior*, 22, 358–74.

Rayner, K., & Duffy, S. A. (1986). Lexical complexity and fixation times in reading: Effects of word frequency, verb complexity, and lexical ambiguity. *Memory & Cognition*, 14, 191–201.

Rayner, K., Foorman, B. R., Perfetti, C. A., Pesetsky, D., & Seidenberg, M. S. (2001). How psychological science informs the teaching of reading. *Psychological Science in the Public Interest*, 2, 31–74.

Rayner, K., Li, X., Juhasz, B. J., & Yan, G. (2005). The effect of word predictability on eye movements on Chinese readers. *Psychonomic Bulletin & Review*, 12, 1089–93.

Rayner, K., Li, X., & Pollatsek, A. (2007). Extending the E-Z Reader model of eye movement control to Chinese readers. *Cognitive Science*, 31, 1021–33.

Rayner, K., McConkie, G. W., & Zola, D. (1980). Integrating information across eye movements. *Cognitive Psychology*, 12, 206–26.

Rayner, K., & Pollatsek, A. (1981). Eye movement control during reading: Evidence for direct control. *The Quarterly Journal of Experimental Psychology*, 33A, 351–73.

Rayner, K., & Pollatsek, A. (1989). *The Psychology of Reading*. Englewood Cliffs, NJ: Prentice Hall.

Rayner, K., Pollatsek, A., Ashby, J., & Clifton, C., Jr. (2012). *The Psychology of Reading*. Second edition. New York: Psychology Press.

Rayner, K., Sereno, S. C., & Raney, G. E. (1996). Eye movement control in reading: A comparison of two types of models. *Journal of Experimental Psychology: Human Perception and Performance*, 22, 1188–1200.

Rayner, K., Schotter, E. R., Masson, M. E. J., Potter, M. C., & Treiman, R. (2016). So much to read, so little time: How do we read, and can speed reading help? *Psychological Science in the Public Interest*, 17, 4–34.

Rayner, K., & Well, A. D. (1986). Effects of contextual constraint on eye movements in reading: A further examination. *Psychonomic Bulletin & Review*, 3, 504–09.

Rayner, K., Well, A. D., Pollatsek, A., & Bertera, J. H. (1982). The availability of useful information to the right of fixation in reading. *Perception & Psychophysics*, 31, 537–50.

Reicher, G. M. (1969). Perceptual recognition as a function of meaningfulness of stimulus material. *Journal of Experimental Psychology*, 81, 274–80.

Reichle, E. D. (2006). Computational models of eye-movement control during reading: Theories of the "eye-mind" link. *Cognitive Systems Research*, 7, 2–3.

Reichle, E. D. (2011). Serial attention models of reading. In S. P. Liversedge, I. D. Gilchrist, & S. Everling (eds.), *Oxford Handbook on Eye Movements*. Oxford: Oxford University Press, 767–86.

Reichle, E. D. (2021). *Computational Models of Reading: A handbook*. Oxford: Oxford University Press.

Reichle, E. D., & Drieghe, D. (2015). Using E-Z Reader to examine the consequences of fixation-location measurement error. *Journal of Experimental Psychology: Learning, Memory, and Cognition*, 41, 262–70.

Reichle, E. D., Liversedge, S. P., Pollatsek, A., & Rayner, K. (2009). Encoding multiple words simultaneously in reading is implausible. *Trends in Cognitive Sciences*, 13, 115–19.

Reichle, E. D., & Perfetti, C. A. (2003). Morphology in word identification: A word-experience model that accounts for morpheme frequency effects. *Scientific Studies of Reading*, 7, 219–37.

Reichle, E. D., Pollatsek, A., Fisher, D. L., & Rayner, K. (1998). Toward a model of eye-movement control in reading. *Psychological Review*, 105, 125–57.

Reichle, E. D., Pollatsek, A., & Rayner, K. (2006). E-Z Reader: A cognitive-control, serial-attention model of eye-movement control during reading. *Cognitive Systems Research*, 7, 4–22.

Reichle, E. D., Pollatsek, A., & Rayner, K. (2012). Using E-Z Reader to simulate eye movements in non-reading tasks: A unified framework for understanding the eye-mind link. *Psychological Review*, 119, 155–85.

Reichle, E. D., & Reingold, E. M. (2013). Neurophysiological constraints on the eye-mind link. *Frontiers in Human Neuroscience*, 7, 361. https://doi.org/10.3389/fnhum.2013.00361.

Reichle, E. D., & Schotter, E. R. (2020). A computational analysis of the constraints on parallel word identification. In *CogSci 2020: Proceedings of the 42nd Annual Conference of the Cognitive Science Society*. Austin, TX: Cognitive Science Society, 164–70.

Reichle, E. D., Veldre, A., Yu, L., & Andrews, S. (2022). A neural implementation of MINERVA 2. In *CogSci2022: Proceedings of the 44th Annual Conference of the Cognitive Science Society*. Austin, TX: Cognitive Science Society, 2278–84.

Reichle, E. D., & Yu, L. (2018). Models of Chinese reading: Review and analysis. *Cognitive Science*, 42, 1154–65.

Reilly, R. (1993). A connectionist framework for modeling eye-movement control in reading. In G d'Ydewalle & J. Van Rensbergen (eds.), *Perception and Cognition: Advances in Eye Movement Research*. Amsterdam: Elsevier, 193–212.

Reilly, R., Aranyanak, I., Yu, L., Yan, G., & Tang, S. (2011). Eye movement control in reading Thai and Chinese. *Studies of Psychology and Behavior*, 9, 35–44.

Reilly, R., & Radach, R. (2003). Foundations of an interactive activation model of eye movement control in reading. In J. Hyönä, R. Radach & H. Deubel (eds.), *The Mind's Eyes: Cognitive and Applied Aspects of Oculomotor Research*. Oxford: Elsevier, 429–56.

Reilly, R., & Radach, R. (2006). Some empirical tests of an interactive activation model of eye movement control in reading. *Cognitive Systems Research*, 7, 34–55.

Reingold, E. M., Reichle, E. D., Glaholt, M. G., & Sheridan, H. (2012). Direct lexical control of eye movements in reading: Evidence from survival analysis of fixation durations. *Cognitive Psychology*, 65, 177–206.

Ren, P., Xu, F., & Zhang, R. (2006). Effects of Pinyin in learning on development of phonological awareness. *Acta Psychologica Sinica*, 38, 41–6. [任萍, 徐芬, & 张瑞平. (2006). 拼音学习对幼儿语音意识发展的影响, 心理学报, 38, 41–6.]

Rips, L. J., Shoben, E. J., & Smith, E. E. (1973). Semantic distance and the verification of semantic relations. *Journal of Verbal Learning and Verbal Behavior*, 12, 1–20.

Robinson, A. (1995). *The Story of Writing: Alphabets, Hieroglyphs, & Pictograms*. London: Thames & Hudson.

Rosch, E. (1973). Natural categories. *Cognitive Psychology*, 4, 328–350.

Rosch, E., & Mervis, C. B. (1975). Family resemblances: Studies in the internal structure of categories. *Cognitive Psychology*, 7, 573–605.

Rossmeissl, P. G., & Theios, J. (1982). Identification and pronunciation effects in a verbal reaction time task for words, pseudo-words, and letters. *Memory & Cognition*, 10, 443–50.

Rueckl, J. G., Paz-Alonso, P. M., Molfese, P. J., Kuo, W.-J., Bick, A., Frost, S. J., et al. (2015). Universal brain signature of proficient reading: Evidence from four contrasting languages. *Proceedings of the National Academy of Sciences*, 112, 11510–15.

Rumelhart, D. E., & McClelland, J. L. (1982). An interactive activation model of context effects in letter perception: Part 2. The contextual enhancement effect and some tests and extensions of the model. *Psychological Review*, 89, 60–94.

Sagan, C. (1980). *Cosmos*. New York: Random House.

Salvucci, D. D. (2001). An integrated model of eye movements and visual encoding. *Cognitive Systems Research*, 1, 201–20.

Scarborough, D. L., Cortese, C., & Scarborough, H. S. (1977). Frequency and repetition effects in lexical memory. *Journal of Experimental Psychology: Human Perception and Performance*, 3, 1–17.

Schad, D. J., & Engbert, R. (2012). The zoom lens of attention: Simulating shuffled versus normal text reading using the SWIFT model. *Visual Cognition*, 20, 391–421.

Schilling, H. E. H., Rayner, K., & Chumbley, J. I. (1998). Comparing naming, lexical decision, and eye fixation times: Word frequency effects and individual differences. *Memory & Cognition*, 26, 1270–81.

Schoonbaert, S., & Grainger, J. (2004). Letter position coding in printed word perception: Effects of repeated and transposed letters. *Language and Cognitive Processes*, 19, 333–67.

Schotter, E. R. (2013). Synonyms provide semantic preview benefit in English. *Journal of Memory and Language*, 69, 619–33.

Sears, C. R., Hino, Y., & Lupker, S. J. (1995). Neighborhood size and neighborhood frequency effects in word recognition. *Journal of Experimental Psychology: Human Perception and Performance*, 21, 876–900.

Segbers, J., & Schroeder, S. (2017). How many words do children know? A corpus-based estimation of children's total vocabulary size. *Language Testing*, 34, 297–320.

Seidenberg, M. S. (2017). *Language at the Speed of Sight: How We Read, Why So Many Can't, and What Can Be Done about It*. New York: Basic Books.

Seidenberg, M. S., & McClelland, J. L. (1989). A distributed, developmental model of word recognition and naming. *Psychological Review*, 96, 523–68.

Seyfarth, R. M., Cheney, D. L., & Marler, P. (1980). Monkey responses to three different alarm calls: Evidence of predator classification and semantic communication. *Science*, 210, 801–3.

Share, D. L. (2008). On the Anglocentricities of current reding research and practice: The perils of overreliance on an "outlier" orthography. *Psychological Bulletin*, 134, 584–615.

References

Share, D. L. (2021). Is the science of reading just the science of reading English?. *Reading Research Quarterly*, 56, S391–S402.

Shen, D., & Forster, K. (1999). Masked phonological priming in reading Chinese words depends on the task. *Language and Cognitive Processes*, 14, 429–60.

Shen, M., Pan, S., & Li, Z. (1997). The effects of global perception of Chinese character morphology on recognition of its radical. *Chinese Journal or Applied Psychology*, 3, 47-51. [沈模卫, 潘善会, 李忠平. (1997). 整体字形对部件识别的影响. 应用心理学, 3, 47-51.]

Shen, W., & Li, X. (2012). The uniqueness of word superiority effect in Chinese reading. *Chinese Science Bulletin*, 57, 3414–20. [申薇, & 李兴珊. (2012). 中文阅读中词优效应的特异性. 科学通报, 57, 3414–20.]

Shillcock, R. C., & Monaghan, P. (2001). Connectionist model of surface dyslexia based on foveal splitting: Impaired pronunciation after only two half pints. In *Proceedings of the 23rd Annual Conference of the Cognitive Science Society*, Edinburgh: LEA, 916–21.

Shu, H., & Anderson, R. C. (1997). Role of radical awareness in the character and word acquisition of Chinese children. *Reading Research Quarterly*, 32, 78–89.

Shu, H., & Anderson, R. C. (1999). Learning to read Chinese: The development of metalinguistic awareness. In J. Wang, A. W. Inhoff, & H. C. Chen (eds.), *Reading Chinese Script: A Cognitive Analysis*. Mahwah, NJ: Lawrence Erlbaum Associates, 1–18.

Shu, H., & Liu, B. X. (1994). The role of pinyin in early reading for Chinese junior primary school children. *Psychological Development and Education*, 10, 11–15. [舒华, & 刘宝霞. (1994). 拼音在小学低年级儿童早期阅读中作用的研究. 心理发展与教育, 10, 11–15.]

Shu, H., McBride-Chang, C., Wu, S., & Liu, H. (2006). Understanding Chinese developmental dyslexia: Morphological awareness as a core cognitive construct. *Journal of Educational Psychology*, 98, 122–33.

Shu, H., Meng, X., Chen, X., Luan, H., & Cao, F. (2005). The subtypes of developmental dyslexia in Chinese: Evidence from three cases. *Dyslexia*, 11, 311–29.

Shu, H., Peng, H., & McBride-Chang, C. (2008). Phonological awareness in young Chinese children. *Developmental Science*, 11, 171–81.

Shu, H., & Zeng, H. (1996). Awareness of phonological cues in pronunciation of Chinese characters and its development. *Acta Psychologica Sinica*, 28, 160–5. [舒华, & 曾红梅. (1996). 儿童对汉字结构中语音线索的意识及其发展. 心理学报, 28, 160–5.]

Shu, H., & Zhang, H. (1987). The processing of pronouncing Chinese characters by proficient mature readers. *Acta Psychologica Sinica*, 3, 282–90. [舒华, & 张厚粲. (1987). 成年熟练读者的汉字读音加工过程. 心理学报, 3, 282–90.]

Shu, H., Zhou, X., & Wu, N. (2000). Utilizing phonological cues in Chinese characters: A developmental study. *Acta Psychologica Sinica*, 32, 164–9. [舒华, 周晓林, & 武宁宁. (2000). 儿童汉字读音声旁一致性意识的发展. 心理学报, 32, 164–9.]

Siok, W. T., & Fletcher, P. (2001). The role of phonological awareness and visual-orthographic skills in Chinese reading acquisition. *Developmental Psychology*, 37, 886–99.

Snell, J., & Grainger, J. (2019). Readers are parallel processors. *Trends in Cognitive Sciences*, 23, 537–46.

Snell, J., van Leipsig, S., Grainger, J., & Meeter, M. (2018). OB1-Reader: A model of word recognition and eye movements in text reading. *Psychological Review*, 125, 969–84.

Snowling, M. (1987). *Dyslexia: A Cognitive Developmental Perspective*. Oxford: Blackwell.

Snowling, M. J., & Hulme, C. (2005). *The Science of Reading: A Handbook*. Oxford: Blackwell.

Song, S., Georgiou, G. K., Su, M., & Hua, S. (2016). How well do phonological awareness and rapid automatized naming correlate with Chinese reading accuracy and fluency? A meta-analysis. *Scientific Studies of Reading*, 20, 99–123.

Song, S., Zhang, Y., Shu, H., Su, M., & McBride, C. (2020). Universal and specific predictors of Chinese children with dyslexia – Exploring the cognitive deficits and subtypes. *Frontiers in Psychology*, 10, 2904.

Song, X., Xu, X., Yang, X., Sun, G., & Cui, L. (2022). The influence of predictability, word frequency and stroke number on Chinese word recognition: An eye movement study. *Journal of Psychological Science*, 45, 1061–8. [宋悉妮, 徐晓晨, 杨秀莉, 孙桂苓, & 崔磊. (2022). 预期性、词频和笔画数对中文词汇识别影响的眼动研究. 心理科学, 45, 1061–8.]

Spencer, L. H., & Hanley, J. R. (2004). Learning a transparent orthography at five years old: Reading development of children during their first year of formal reading instruction in Wales. *Journal of Research in Reading*, 27, 1–14.

Spinks, J. A., Liu, Y., Perfetti, C. A., & Tan, L. H. (2000). Reading Chinese characters for meaning: The role of phonological information. *Cognition*, 76, B1–B11.

Spivey, M. J., & Tanenhaus, M. K. (1998). Syntactic ambiguity resolution in discourse: Modeling the effects of referential context and lexical frequency. *Journal of Experimental Psychology: Learning, Memory, & Cognition*, 24, 1521–43.

State Language Commission & Ministry of Education China. (2013). *Standardized Common Chinese Character List*.

Stevenson, H. W., Stigler, J. W., Lucker, G. W., Lee, S. Y., Hsu, C. C., & Kitamura, S. (1982). Reading disabilities: The case of Chinese, Japanese, and English. *Child Development*, 53 (5), 1164–81.

Stroop, J. R. (1935) Studies of interference in serial verbal reactions. *Journal of Experimental Psychology*, 18 (6), 643–62.

Sun, F., & Feng, D. (1999). Eye movements in reading Chinese and English text. In J. Wang, A. W. Inhoff, & H. C. Chen (eds.), *Reading Chinese Script: A Cognitive Analysis*. Mahwah, NJ: Lawrence Erlbaum Associates, 189–205.

Swinney, D. A., & Cutler, A. (1979). The access and processing of idiomatic expressions. *Journal of Verbal Learning and Verbal Behavior*, 18, 523–34.

Sze, W. P., Yap, M. J., & Rickard Liow, S. J. (2015). The role of lexical variables in the visual recognition of Chinese characters: A megastudy analysis. *The Quarterly Journal of Experimental Psychology*, 68, 1541–70.

Taft, M. (1991). *Reading and the Mental Lexicon*. Hillsdale, NJ: Erlbaum.

Taft, M., & Chen, H. C. (1992). Judging homophony in Chinese: The influence of tones. In In H. C. Chen & O. J. L. Tzeng (eds.), *Language Processing in Chinese*. Amsterdam: North-Holland, 151–72.

Taft, M., & Krebs-Lazendic, L. (2013). The role of orthographic syllable structure in assigning letters to their position in visual word recognition. *Journal of Memory and Language*, 68, 85–97.

Taft, M., & van Graan, F. (1998). Lack of phonological medication in a semantic categorization task. *Journal of Memory and Language*, 38, 203–24.

Taft, M., & Zhu, X. (1997). Submorphemic processing in reading Chinese. *Journal of Experimental Psychology: Learning, Memory, and Cognition*, 23, 761–75.

Taft, M., Zhu, X., & Peng, D. (1999). Positional specificity of radicals in Chinese character recognition. *Journal of Memory and Language*, 40, 498–519.

Tan, L. H., Hoosain, R., & Peng, D. L. (1995). Role of early presemantic phonological code in Chinese character identification. *Journal of Experimental Psychology: Learning, Memory, and Cognition*, 21, 43–54.

Tan, L. H., Laird, A. R., Li, K., & Fox, P. T. (2005). Neuroanatomical correlates of phonological processing of Chinese characters and alphabetic words: A meta-analysis. *Human Brain Mapping*, 25, 83–91.

Tan, L. H., Liu, H. L., Perfetti, C. A., Spinks, J. A., Fox, P. T., & Gao, J. H. (2001). The neural system underlying Chinese logographic reading. *NeuroImage*, 13, 836–46.

Tan, L. H., & Perfetti, C. A. (1998a). Phonological codes as early sources of constraint in Chinese word identification: A review of current discoveries and theoretical accounts. *Reading and Writing*, 10, 165–200.

Tan, L. H., & Perfetti, C. A. (1998b). Phonological activation in visual identification of Chinese two-character words. *Journal of Experimental Psychology: Learning, Memory, and Cognition*, 25, 382–93.

Tan, L. H., Spinks, J. A., Eden, G. F., Perfetti, C. A., & Siok, W. T. (2005). Reading depends on writing, in Chinese. *Proceedings of the National Academy of Sciences*, 102, 8781–5.

Tan, L. H., Spinks, J. A., Gao, J. H., Liu, H. L., Perfetti, C. A., Xiong, J., Stofer, K. A., Pu, Y., Liu, Y., & Fox, P. T. (2000). Brain activation in the processing of Chinese characters and words. *Human Brain Mapping*, 10, 16–27.

Tang, S., & Wu, X. (2009). The early development of young children's Chinese phonological awareness. *Journal of Psychological Science*, 32, 312–15. [唐珊, & 伍新春. (2009). 汉语儿童早期语音意识的发展. 心理科学, 32, 312–15.]

Taylor, J. S. H., Plunkett, K., & Nation, K. (2010). The influence of consistency, frequency, and semantics on learning to read: An artificial orthography paradigm. *Journal of Experimental Psychology: Learning, Memory, and Cognition*, 37, 60–76.

Taylor, W. L. (1953). Cloze procedure: A new tool for measuring readability. *Journalism Quarterly*, 30, 415–33.

Tong, W., Liu, N., Fu, G., & Yan, G. (2014). The perceptual span in Chinese when reading sentence constructed by one-character words. *Studies of Psychology and Behavior*, 12, 298–303. [仝文, 刘妮娜, 伏干, & 闫国利. (2014). 中文单字词句的阅读知觉广度. 心理与行为研究, 12, 298–303.]

Tong, W., Yu, X., Liu, Z., Zhu, X., & Qi, Q. (2022). Differences in contextual information utilization between fast and slow readers: The role of processing depth. *Studies of Psychology and Behavior*, 20, 450–6. [仝文, 余雪, 刘志方, 朱星宇, & 齐琦. (2022). 快慢读者利用语境信息的差异：加工深度的作用. 心理与行为研究, 20, 450–6.]

Tong, X., & McBride-Chang, C. (2010). Developmental models of learning to read Chinese words. *Developmental Psychology*, 46, 1662–76.

Tong, X., McBride-Chang, C., Shu, H., & Wong, A. M. (2009). Morphological awareness, orthographic knowledge, and spelling errors: Keys to understanding early Chinese literacy acquisition. *Scientific Studies of Reading*, 13, 426–52.

Tong, X., Tong, X., & McBride-Chang, C. (2015). Tune in to the tone: Lexical tone identification is associated with vocabulary and word recognition abilities in young Chinese children. *Language and Speech*, 58, 441–58.

Treiman, R., & Cassar, M. (1996). Effects of morphology on children's spelling of final consonant clusters. *Journal of Experimental Child Psychology*, 63, 141–70.

Tsai, J. L., Kliegl, R., & Yan, M. (2012). Parafoveal semantic information extraction in traditional Chinese reading. *Acta Psychologica*, 141, 17–23.

Tsai, J. L., Lee, C. Y., Lin, Y. C., Tzeng, O. J., & Hung, D. L. (2006). Neighborhood size effects of Chinese words in lexical decision and reading. *Language and Linguistics (Taipei)*, 7, 659–75.

Tsai, J. L., & McConkie, G. W. (2003). Where do Chinese readers send their eyes? In J. Hyönä, R. Radach, H. Deubel (eds.), *The Mind's Eye: Cognitive and Applied Aspects of Eye Movement Research*. Amsterdam: North-Holland, 159–76.

Tsang, Y. K., Huang, J., Lui, M., Xue, M., Chan, Y. W. F., Wang, S., & Chen, H. C. (2018). MELD-SCH: A megastudy of lexical decision in simplified Chinese. *Behavior Research Methods*, 50, 1763–77.

Tse, C. S., & Yap, M. J. (2018). The role of lexical variables in the visual recognition of two-character Chinese compound words: A megastudy analysis. *Quarterly Journal of Experimental Psychology*, 71, 2022–38.

Tse, C. S., Yap, M. J., Chan, Y. L., Sze, W. P., Shaoul, C., & Lin, D. (2017). The Chinese Lexicon Project: A megastudy of lexical decision performance for 25,000+ traditional Chinese two-character compound words. *Behavior Research Methods*, 49, 1503–19.

Turner, J. E., Valentine, T., & Ellis, A. W. (1998). Contrasting effects of age of acquisition and word frequency on auditory and visual lexical decision. *Memory & Cognition*, 26, 1282–91.

Van Orden, G. C. (1987). A ROWS is a ROSE: Spelling, sound, and reading. *Memory & Cognition*, 15, 181–98.

Van Orden, G. O., Pennington, B. F., & Stone, G. O. (1990). Word identification in reading and the promise of subsymbolic psycholinguistics. *Psychological Review*, 97, 488–522.

Veldre, A., & Andrews, S. (2016). Is semantic preview benefit due to relatedness or plausibility? *Journal of Experimental Psychology: Human Perception and Performance*, 42, 939–52.

Veldre, A., Reichle, E. D., Yu, L., & Andrews, S. (2020). Towards a complete model of reading: Simulating lexical decision, word naming, and sentence reading with Über-Reader. In *CogSci 2020: Proceedings of the 42nd Annual Conference of the Cognitive Science Society*. Austin, TX: Cognitive Science Society, 151–7.

Veldre, A., Reichle, E. D., Yu, L., & Andrews, S. (2023). Understanding the visual constraints on lexical processing: New empirical and simulation results. *Journal of Experimental Psychology: General*, 152 (3), 693–722.

Vinckier, F., Dehaene, S., Jobert, A., Dubus, J. P., Sigman, M., & Cohen, L. (2007). Hierarchical coding of letter strings in the ventral stream: Dissecting the inner organization of the visual word-form system. *Neuron*, 55, 143–55.

Vitu, F., McConkie, G. W., Kerr, P., & O'Regan, J. K. (2001). Fixation location effects on fixation durations during reading: An inverted optimal viewing position effect. *Vision Research*, 41, 3513–33.

Wang, C., & Peng, D. (1999). Effects of semantic transparency and surface frequency on Chinese word processing. *Acta Psychologica Sinica*, 31, 266–73. [王春茂, & 彭聃龄. (1999). 合成词加工中的词频、词素频率及语义透明度. 心理学报, 31, 266–73.]

Wang, C., & Peng, D. (2000). The role of semantic transparencies in the processing of compound words. *Acta Psychologica Sinica*, 32, 127–32. [王春茂, & 彭聃龄. (2000). 重复启动作业中词的语义透明度的作用. 心理学报, 32, 127–32.]

Wang, J., Tian, J., Han, W., Liversedge, S. P., & Paterson, K. B. (2014). Inhibitory stroke neighbour priming in character recognition and reading in Chinese. *Quarterly Journal of Experimental Psychology*, 67, 2149–71.

Wang, L., & Yan, G. (2020). The interference effect of masking materials in Chinese reading: An eye movement study. *Psychological Exploration*, 40, 318–24. [王丽红, & 闫国利. (2020). 阅读知觉广度研究中掩蔽刺激干扰效应的眼动研究. 心理学探新, 40, 318–24.]

Wang, L., & Yan, G. (2021). The perceptual span for two-character compound-word sentence in Chinese: An eye movement study. *Psychological Exploration*, 41, 123–30. [王丽红, & 闫国利. (2021). 汉语双字词句知觉广度的眼动研究. 心理学探新, 41, 123–30.]

Wang, L. C., & Yang, H. M. (2014). Classifying Chinese children with dyslexia by dual-route and triangle models of Chinese reading. *Research in Developmental Disabilities*, 35, 2702–13.

Wang, W. S. Y. (1973). The Chinese language. *Scientific American*, 228, 50–63.

Warrington, K. L., Wu, S. H., Reichle, E. D., Sheridan, H., Peterson, K. B., & White, S. J. (2023). Eye movements during reading and skimming: Effects of word length and frequency. Unpublished manuscript.

Wegener, S., Wang, H. C., Beyersmann, E., Reichle, E. D., Nation, K., & Castles, A. (2023). The effect of spacing versus massing on orthographic learning. *Reading Research Quarterly*. PsyArXiv. https://doi.org/10.31234/osf.io/ey76v

Wei, W., Li, X., & Pollatsek, A. (2013). Word properties of a fixated region affect outgoing saccade length. *Vision Research*, 80, 1–6.

West, R. F., & Stanovich, K. E. (1982). Source of inhibition in experiments on the effect of sentence context on word recognition. *Journal of Experimental Psychology: Learning, Memory, and Cognition*, 8, 385–99.

Wheeler, D. D. (1970). Processes in word recognition. *Cognitive Psychology*, 1, 59–85.

White, S. J., & Liversedge, S. P. (2006). Foveal processing difficulty does not modulate non-foveal orthographic influences on fixation positions. *Vision Research*, 46, 426–37.

White, S. J., Rayner, K., & Liversedge, S. P. (2005). The influence of parafoveal word length and contextual constraint on fixation durations and word skipping in reading. *Psychonomic Bulletin & Review*, 12, 466–71.

Whitlow, J. W. (1990). Differential sensitivity of perceptual identification for words and pseudo-words to test expectations: Implications for the locus of word frequency effects. *Journal of Experimental Psychology: Learning, Memory, and Cognition*, 16, 837–51.

Whitney, C. (2001). How the brain encodes the order of letters in a printed word: The SERIOL model and selective literature review. *Psychonomic Bulletin & Review*, 8, 221–43.

Whitney, C., & Cornelissen, P. (2008). SERIOL reading. *Language and Cognitive Processes*, 23, 143–64.

Wolf, M. (2008). *Proust and the Squid: The Story and Science of the Reading Brain*. London: Icon.

Wu, J., Slattery, T. J., Pollatsek, A., & Rayner, K. (2008). Word segmentation in Chinese reading. In Rayner, K., Shen, D., Bai, X., & Yan, G. (eds.), *Cognitive and Cultural Influences on Eye Movements*. Tianjin: Tianjin People's Publishing House, 303–14.

Wu, J. T., Yang, F. L., & Lin, W. C. (2013). Beyond phonology matters in character recognition. *Chinese Journal of Psychology*, 55, 289–318. [吳瑞屯, 楊馥菱, & 林維駿. (2013). 跨越單字辨識歷程研究裡的語音處理議題. 中華心理學刊, 55, 289–318.]

Wu, X., Anderson, R. C., Li, W., Wu, X., Li, H., Zhang, J., et al. (2009). Morphological awareness and Chinese children's literacy development: An intervention study. *Scientific Studies of Reading*, 13, 26–52.

Wurtz, R. H., & Kandel, E. R. (1991). Central visual pathways. In E. R. Kandel, J. H. Schwartz, & T. M. Jessell (eds.), *Principles of Neural Science*. New York: McGraw-Hill, 523–47.

Xing, H., Shu, H., & Li, P. (2002). A self-organizing connectionist model of character acquisition in Chinese. *Proceedings of the Annual Meeting of the Cognitive Science Society*, 24, 950–5.

Xing, H., Shu, H., & Li, P. (2004). The acquisition of Chinese characters: Corpus analyses and connectionist simulations. *Journal of Cognitive Science*, 5, 1–49.

Xiong, J., Yu, L., Veldre, A., Reichle, E. D., & Andrews, S. (2023). A multi-task comparison of word- and character-frequency effects in Chinese reading. *Journal of Experimental Psychology: Learning, Memory, and Cognition*. 49, 793–811.

Xu, Y., Pollatsek, A., & Potter, M. C. (1999). The activation of phonology during silent Chinese word reading. *Journal of Experimental Psychology: Learning, Memory, and Cognition, 25,* 838–57.

Yan, G., Fu, G., & Bai, X. (2008). The perceptual span and eye movements in reading Chinese materials of different degrees of difficulty. *Journal of Psychological Science, 31,* 1287–90. [闫国利, 伏干, & 白学军. (2008). 不同难度阅读材料对阅读知觉广度影响的眼动研究. 心理科学, 31, 1287–90.]

Yan, G., Sun, S., Cui, L., & Bai, X. (2013). Homophone density effect in naming task and sentence reading. *Journal of Psychological Science, 36,* 776–80. [闫国利, 孙莎莎, 崔磊, & 白学军. (2013). 汉字命名与句子阅读中的同音字密度效应. 心理科学, 36, 776–80.]

Yan, G., Tian, H., Bai, X., & Rayner, K. (2006). The effect of word and character frequency on the eye movements of Chinese readers. *British Journal of Psychology, 97,* 259–68.

Yan, G., Zhang, Q., & Bai, X. (2013). Study on the influencing factors of perceptual span in Chinese reading. *Psychological Development and Education, 29,* 121–30. [闫国利, 张巧明, & 白学军. (2013). 中文阅读知觉广度的影响因素研究. 心理发展与教育, 29, 121–30.]

Yan, G., Zhang, Q., Zhang, L., & Bai, X. (2013). The effect of masking materials on perceptual span in Chinese reading. *Journal of Psychological Science, 36,* 1317–22. [闫国利, 张巧明, 张兰兰, & 白学军. (2013). 不同掩蔽材料对阅读知觉广度的影响. 心理科学, 36, 1317–22.]

Yan, M., & Kliegl, R. (2016). CarPrice versus CarpRice: Word boundary ambiguity influences saccade target selection during the reading of Chinese sentences. *Journal of Experimental Psychology: Learning, Memory, and Cognition, 42,* 1832–8.

Yan, M., Kliegl, R., Richter, E. M., Nuthmann, A., & Shu, H. (2010). Flexible saccade-target selection in Chinese reading. *The Quarterly Journal of Experimental Psychology, 63,* 705–25.

Yan, M., Richter, E. M., Shu, H., & Kliegl, R. (2009). Readers of Chinese extract semantic information from parafoveal words. *Psychonomic Bulletin & Review, 16,* 561–6.

Yan, X., Jiang, K., Li, H., Wang, Z., Perkins, K., & Cao, F. (2021). Convergent and divergent brain structural and functional abnormalities associated with developmental dyslexia. *elife, 10,* e69523.

Yang, H., Chen, J., Spinelli, G., & Lupker, S. J. (2019). The impact of text orientation on form priming effects in four-character Chinese words. *Journal of Experimental Psychology: Learning, Memory, and Cognition, 45,* 1511–26.

Yang, H., Hino, Y., Chen, J., Yoshihara, M., Nakayama, M., Xue, J., & Lupker, S. J. (2020). The origins of backward priming effects in logographic scripts for four-character words. *Journal of Memory and Language, 113,* 104107.

Yang, J. F., McCandliss, B. D., Shu, H., & Zevin, J. D. (2009). Simulating language-specific and language-general effects in a statistical learning model of Chinese reading. *Journal of Memory and Language, 61,* 238–57.

Yang, J. F., Shu, H., McCandliss, B. D., & Zevin, J. D. (2013). Orthographic influences on division of labor in learning to read Chinese and English:

Insights from computational modeling. *Bilingualism: Language and Cognition*, 16, 354–66.

Yang, J. F., Zevin, J. D., Shu, H., McCandliss, B. D., & Li, P. (2006). A "triangle model" of Chinese reading. In *Proceedings of the 28th Annual Conference of the Cognitive Science Society*. Mahwah, NJ: Cognitive Science Society, 912–17.

Yang, J. M, Staub, A., Li, N., Wang, S., & Rayner, K. (2012). Plausibility effects when reading one- and two-character words in Chinese: Evidence from eye movements. *Journal of Experimental Psychology: Learning, Memory, and Cognition*, 38, 1801–9.

Yang, J. M., Wang, S., Tong, X., & Rayner, K. (2012). Semantic and plausibility effects on preview benefit during eye fixations in Chinese reading. *Reading and Writing*, 25, 1031–52.

Yang, J. M., Wang, S., Xu, Y., & Rayner, K. (2009). Do Chinese readers obtain preview benefit from word *n* + 2? Evidence from eye movements. *Journal of Experimental Psychology: Human Perception and Performance*, 35, 1192–204.

Yang, L. P., Li, C., Li, X., Zhai, M., An, Q., Zhang, Y., et al. (2022). Prevalence of developmental dyslexia in primary school children: A systematic review and meta-analysis. *Brain Sciences*, 12, 240.

Yang, L. Y., Guo, J. P., Richman, L. C., Schmidt, F. L., Gerken, K. C., & Ding, Y. (2013). Visual skills and Chinese reading acquisition: A meta-analysis of correlation evidence. *Educational Psychology Review*, 25, 115–43.

Yao, P., Staub, A., & Li, X. (2022). Predictability eliminates neighborhood effects during Chinese sentence reading. *Psychonomic Bulletin & Review*, 29, 243–52.

Yen, M. H., Radach, R., Tzeng, O. J. L., & Tsai, J. L. (2012). Usage of statistical cues for word boundary in reading Chinese sentences. *Reading and Writing*, 25, 1007–29.

Yeung, P. S., Ho, C. S. H., Chan, D. W. O., & Chung, K. K. H. (2016). Orthographic skills important to Chinese literacy development: The role of radical representation and orthographic memory of radicals. *Reading and Writing*, 29, 1935–58.

Yeung, P. S., Ho, C. S. H., Wong, Y. K., Chan, D. W. O., Chung, K. K. H., & Lo, L. Y. (2013). Longitudinal predictors of Chinese word reading and spelling among elementary grade students. *Applied Psycholinguistics*, 34, 1245–77.

Yin, W. & Butterworth, B. (1992). Deep and surface dyslexia in Chinese. In H. C. Chen & O. J. L. Tzeng (eds.), *Language Processing in Chinese*. Amsterdam: North-Holland, 349–66).

Yonelinas, A. P. (2002). The nature of recollection and familiarity: A review of 30 years of research. *Journal of Memory and Language*, 46, 441–517.

Yu, B., & Cao, H. (1992). A new exploration on the effect of stroke-number in the identification of Chinese characters. *Acta Psychologica Sinica*, 24, 120–6. [喻柏林, & 曹河圻. (1992). 汉字识别中的笔画数效应新探——兼论字频效应. 心理学报, 24, 120–6.]

Yu, B., Li, C. & Zhang, S. (1995). Effects of complexities on recognition for tilted Chinese characters. *Acta Psychologica Sinica*, 27, 337–43. [喻柏林, 李朝晖, & 张蜀林. (1995). 复杂性对倾斜汉字识别的影响. 心理学报, 27, 337–43.]

Yu, L., Cutter, M. G., Yan, G., Bai, X., Fu, Y., Drieghe, D., & Liversedge, S. P. (2016). Word n+ 2 preview effects in three-character Chinese idioms and phrases. *Language, Cognition, and Neuroscience*, 31, 1130–49.

Yu, L., Liu, Y., & Reichle, E. D. (2021). A corpus-based vs. experimental examination of word- and character-frequency effects in Chinese reading: Theoretical implications for models of reading. *Journal of Experimental Psychology: General*, 150, 1612–41.

Yu, L., Zhang, Q., Ke, M., Han, Y., & Kinoshita, S. (2022). Some neighbors are more interfering: Asymmetric priming by stroke neighbors in Chinese character recognition. *Psychonomic Bulletin and Review*, 30, 1062–73.

Zang, C., Wang, Y., Bai, X., Yan, G., Drieghe, D., & Liversedge, S. P. (2016). The use of probabilistic lexicality cues for word segmentation in Chinese reading. *Quarterly Journal of Experimental Psychology*, 69, 548–60.

Zhang, J., & Jiang, M. (2008). The effects of the radical family size and high frequency phonetic radical family member on phonogram recognition. *Acta Psychologica Sinica*, 40, 947–60. [张积家, & 姜敏敏. (2008). 形旁家族、声旁家族和高频同声旁字对形声字识别的影响. 心理学报, 40, 947–60.]

Zhang, J., & Wang, H. (2001). The effects of phonological and tonal relations between phonetic radicals and whole characters on the processing of pictophonetic characters. *Acta Psychologica Sinica*, 33, 193–7. [张积家, & 王惠萍. (2001). 声旁与整字的音段、声调关系对形声字命名的影响. 心理学报, 33, 193–7.]

Zhang, L., Xia, Z., Zhao, Y., Shu, H., & Zhang, Y. (2023). Recent Advances in Chinese Developmental Dyslexia. *Annual Review of Linguistics*, 9. 439–61.

Zhang, Q., Zhou, Y., & Lou, H. (2022). The dissociation between age of acquisition and word frequency effects in Chinese spoken picture naming. *Psychological Research*, 86, 1918–29.

Zhang, W., & Feng, L. (1992). A study on the unit of processing in recognition of Chinese characters. *Acta Psychologica Sinica*, 24, 379–85. [张武田, & 冯玲. (1992). 关于汉字识别加工单位的研究. 心理学报, 24, 379–85.]

Zhang, Z., Han, B., & Chen, T. (2003). Frequency effect of phonetic component in naming Chinese character component in different target presenting speed. *Acta Psychologica Sinica*, 35, 178–82. [张喆, 韩布新, & 陈天勇. (2003). 两种呈现速度下整字及声旁命名. 心理学报, 35, 178–82.]

Zhao, J., & Li, S. (2014). Development of form recognition of visual word in Chinese children of 3 to 6 years old. *Journal of Psychological Science*, 37, 357–62. [赵静, & 李甦. (2014). 3~6 岁儿童汉字字形认知的发展. 心理科学, 37, 357–62.]

Zhou, J., & Li, X. (2021). On the segmentation of Chinese incremental words. *Journal of Experimental Psychology: Learning, Memory, and Cognition*, 47, 1353–68.

Zhou, J., Ma, G., Li, X., & Taft, M. (2018). The time course of incremental word processing during Chinese reading. *Reading and Writing*, 31, 607–25.

Zhou, Y. L., McBride-Chang, C., Fong, C. Y. C., Wong, T. T. Y., & Cheung, S. K. (2012). A comparison of phonological awareness, lexical compounding, and homophone training for Chinese word reading in Hong Kong kindergarteners. *Early Education and Development*, 23, 475–92.

Ziegler, J. C., Tan, L. H., Perry, C., & Montant, M. (2000). Phonology matters: The phonological frequency effect in written Chinese. *Psychological Science*, 11, 234–8.

Zorzi, M., Houghton, G., & Butterworth, B. (1998). Two routes or one in reading aloud? A connectionist dual-process model. *Journal of Experimental Psychology: Human Perception and Performance*, 24, 1131–61.

Index

accommodation hypothesis 161–2
addressed phonology 41–2
age-of-acquisition effect 56
alignment problem 43, 50, 178–81
Andrews, S. 49, 102
animal communication 3–5
assembled phonology 41–2, 144, 160
assimilation hypothesis 161–2
attention allocation 95, 184–6
Attention-Shift model 184

Bai, X. 101, 103–4
Balota, D. A. 8, 55, 98–9
Bolger, D. J. 157–9
boundary paradigm 93–4, 182
Brysbaert, M. 91, 98, 130

Cao, F. 159–60, 162–3
Cantonese 23
Castles, A. 130, 145–6
Chen, B. 67, 69–70
Chen, H. C. 67–8, 101, 103
Cheng, C. M. 60
Chinese characters 35–41
  clerical script 32–3
  complexity 38, 57–9, 103, 125–6
  compound radicals 74–5
  compound strokes 39
  consistency 40–1
  frequency effects 71, 103, 105
  history of 28–34
  modern 35–44
  pictographs 29–31
  phonetic radicals 40–1, 61–2, 66–8, 86, 130,
    133–46, 166, 170
  phonograms 39
  radicals 39–44, 59–64
  regularity 40–1
  seal script 32–3
  semantic radicals 39, 61, 88, 135–7, 145, 171
  simple radicals 44
  simplified 35

spelling reform 32–4
strokes 38–9
syllables 23–5
type frequency 36
types of 40
Chinese dynasties
  Han 32, 36, 38
  Qin 32
  Shang 29, 173
  Song 36
  Xia 30
Chinese E-Z Reader (CEZR) 120–4, 185
Chinese language
  dialects 21–3
  morphology 25–7, 69
  relation to other Asian languages 23, 27, 34
  tones 23–4
Chinese reading model (CRM) 114–20, 124,
    176, 184–5
Chinese words 25, 35
  boundaries 36–7
  compound words 40, 54, 69–71, 102,
    132–3, 137–8
  length 35–6
  segmentation of 36–7
Cohen, L. 155–8
Coltheart, M. 2, 6, 41–2, 49, 52, 56, 99, 142,
    144–7
corpus callosum 155, 165
Cui, L. 103, 105–6, 123, 180

default-targeting model 110–14, 123, 181
Dehaene, S. 2, 154–5, 157–8
dynamic-adjustment model 112–14,
    121–3, 181
dyslexia 47, 129, 143–53
  acquired 143
  deep 146
  developmental 143
  phonological 144–53
  surface 144–53, 166
dual-route model 144–7

Index

electroencephalogram (EEG) 10–11, 162
EMMA 184
Engbert, R. 18, 37, 124, 126, 181–4
event-related potentials (ERPs) 10
eye tracking 9, 92–3, 100–1
E-Z Reader 15–18, 109–10, 120, 124, 181

Fan, X. 124–6, 174, 177
Forster, K. I. 53, 61
fovea 95
frontal cortex 149, 155–63
functional magnetic resonance imaging (fMRI) 10–11, 156–8, 161–3
fusiform gyrus 156, 158, 161–3

gaze-contingent display change paradigms 93–6
Gerhand, S. 56
Glenmore 116, 124–6, 184
Grainger, J. 15, 43, 49–50, 56, 62, 99, 178, 185
graphemes 3–4, 41–2, 51
grapheme-phoneme correspondences (GPCs) 41–2, 46–52, 143

hangul 34
Ho, C. S. H. 131, 133–4, 136, 138–9
Hsiao, J. H. W. 84, 154, 163–6, 177
Hu, Y. 38
Huey, E. B. 6, 47

Inhoff, A. W. 18, 37, 98, 101, 107, 116
interactive-activation model 12–15, 48–9, 72, 74, 83, 89, 124, 126, 174–9, 184

Japanese 23, 27, 34, 143, 157

kanji 34, 157
Korean 23, 27, 34

language 1–6, 21–3, 27–8
learning
  characters/words 36, 54–6, 69, 71, 84, 87, 130–2, 134, 142–3, 151–3, 160
  to read 50, 56, 137–9, 143, 153, 161, 174–7
  to write 38–9, 136
letter-substitution effects 43, 50, 62–4, 178
letter-transposition effects, 43, 50, 62–4, 178–9
lexical access 7–8, 15–17
lexical-constituency model 75–80, 82, 84, 87, 162–3, 175–6
lexical-decision task 8, 50, 70–1, 96
Li, X. 80–4, 112–20, 176, 184–5
Liu, Y. P. 19, 101, 104, 111–16, 120–4, 181–3, 185

magnetoencephography (MEG) 11
Mandarin 22–4

McBride, C. 130–3, 135–8, 143, 160, 162
McBride-Chang, C., see McBride, C.
McClelland, J. 7, 12–15, 48–50, 56
McConkie, G. W. 17, 37, 44, 94–5, 97, 101, 110–11, 186
Min 23
models of reading 11–12, 18–19, 47, 71–2, 84, 109–11
morphology 56
moving-window paradigm 93–5

naming task 8, 49, 53, 55–71, 82–7, 134–9, 142, 144–53
Nation, K. 55, 130
Neely, J. H. 53
neighborhood density 48–9, 58, 60–2, 106
neighborhood frequency 48–9, 58, 60–2, 106
Nelson, J. 159–62
Norman, J. 21, 23, 25, 27–9, 32, 36–7

OB1-Reader 116, 184
occipital-temporal cortex 155–63
optimal-viewing position (OVP) 17, 96–7
O'Regan, J. K. 17, 37, 96
orthography 47

Packard, J. L. 25, 136
parafoveal-on-foveal (POF) effects 102–3
parafoveal preview 94–5, 102, 106, 118, 178, 182–3
Peng, D. 59, 66, 69–70, 180
perceptual-identification task 7, 50
perceptual span 95, 101–2, 116–17
Perea, M. 50
Perfetti, C. A. 42, 65, 67, 69, 75–80, 107–8, 158–63, 174–5
phonemes 3–4, 8, 24, 51
phonology 47
pinyin 33–4, 131–2, 136, 162–3
Pollatsek, A. 2, 18, 60, 92, 95–6, 98, 100, 114–20, 124, 126, 174, 176, 180, 184–6
positron emission tomography (PET) 10–11
preferred viewing location (PVL) 97
preview benefit, see parafoveal preview
priming 53–6, 77–80
pseudo-word-superiority effect 49

Rayner, K. 2, 9, 91–102, 104, 109–10, 114, 118, 120, 123, 130
Reichle, E. D. 2, 15–18, 109, 124, 126–7, 181–3
Reilly, R. 15, 18, 35, 110, 116, 124–6, 174, 177, 184
repetition priming, see priming
retinal eccentricity 110, 116, 118
Rueckl, J. G. 157–8

segmentation-identification model 80–4
semantic priming, see priming

Index

semantics 47
semantic-verification task 8–9
Shanghainese 23
Share, D. L. 130, 159, 187
Shillcock, R. C. 84, 154, 163–6
Shu, H. 66, 131–3, 135, 138, 146, 148
simple view of reading 90–1
split-fovea model 163–6
SWIFT 126, 181, 184

tachistoscope 7
Taft, M. 43, 50–1, 61, 63, 68, 70, 72–5,
77, 82, 84, 87
Taft's model 72–5
Tan, L. J. 65, 67, 69, 75–80, 107–8, 136,
157–60, 162–3, 175, 187
Thai, 27, 34–5, 110
Tong, X. 133, 135, 137–8
triangle model 84–8
Tsai, J. L. 102, 106, 111, 183
Tse, C. S. 69–71

Über-Reader 18, 124

Veldre, A. 17, 37, 81, 94, 102,
178, 181
visual word form area (VWFA) 158–60

Wang, C. 69–70
Wang, J. 61
Wang, W. 21, 24, 36
White, S. J. 114, 118, 181–2
word-frequency effect 15, 55–6, 103, 123
word-superiority effect 7, 12, 14
working memory 51, 147–8, 160
writing 5–6, 38–9
Wu, see Shanghainese

Xing, H. 84, 139–42, 152, 177
Xing et al.'s model 139–42

Yan, G. 67, 101, 104–5
Yan, M. 37, 107–8, 111–13, 181
Yang, H. 64
Yang, J. F. 84–7, 149–53, 163–6, 177, 183
Yang, J. M. 102–4, 119, 183
Yang et al.'s model 149–53
Yu, B. 59, 180
Yu, L. 61, 102–5, 110, 120–4, 180, 182, 185
Yue, see Cantonese

Zang, C. 106
Zhang, W. 59, 70, 180
Zhou, J. 104, 119
zhuyin 33, 132, 146–7

Printed by Printforce, United Kingdom